Philip M. Lloyd

December 2021

THE CHESTER AND HOLYHEAD RAILWAY

THE CHESTER AND HOLYHEAD RAILWAY

A NEW HISTORY

PHILIP M LLOYD

PEN & SWORD
TRANSPORT

AN IMPRINT OF PEN & SWORD BOOKS LTD.
YORKSHIRE – PHILADELPHIA

First published in Great Britain in 2021 by
Pen & Sword Transport
An imprint of
Pen & Sword Books Ltd
Yorkshire - Philadelphia

ISBN 978 1 52674 919 2

Typeset in Times New Roman 12/14.5 by
SJmagic DESIGN SERVICES, India.
Printed and bound in India by Replika Press Pvt. Ltd.

Pen & Sword Books Ltd incorporates the Imprints of Pen & Sword Books Archaeology, Atlas, Aviation, Battleground, Discovery, Family History, History, Maritime, Military, Naval, Politics, Railways, Select, Transport, True Crime, Fiction, Frontline Books, Leo Cooper, Praetorian Press, Seaforth Publishing, Wharncliffe and White Owl.

For a complete list of Pen & Sword titles please contact

PEN & SWORD BOOKS LIMITED
47 Church Street, Barnsley, South Yorkshire, S70 2AS, England
E-mail: enquiries@pen-and-sword.co.uk
Website: www.pen-and-sword.co.uk

Or
PEN AND SWORD BOOKS
1950 Lawrence Rd, Havertown, PA 19083, USA
E-mail: Uspen-and-sword@casematepublishers.com
Website: www.penandswordbooks.com

Contents

Preface and Acknowledgements   7

Abbreviations   10

1   The Race to Dublin   12

2   The Imperial Line   32

3   The Arrival of the Railway in North Wales   54

4   Accidents on the Railway   77

5   The Railway and the Crossing to Ireland   108

6   The Railway and Conflict   123

7   The Railway and Tourism   145

8   The Railway and the People of North Wales   174

9   Rapid Decline, Slow Recovery and New Threats   199

10   The Chester and Holyhead Railway: An Overview   231

Appendix 1: Stations on the CHR with Opening and Closing Dates   235

Appendix 2: Each Mile of the CHR Linked to Years, Incidents and
Photographs   237

Endnotes   242

Bibliography and Further Reading   264

Index   268

Preface and Acknowledgements

Writing this history of the Chester and Holyhead Railway (CHR) represents the culmination of a lifetime's interest in the line that began with family holidays at *Cae Col*, my grandparents' small farm near Conwy from 1955 to 1970. We travelled there by train from Manchester and I was fascinated by the whole experience as we left behind the blackened buildings of the city and moved through increasingly greener territory to Chester, followed by the industry of Deeside until the corner was turned beyond Mostyn and the sea appeared. Over time, I sensed that this railway was not like any other, but I could not quite identify what made it so. This book aims in part to answer that question.

My career was in criminal justice and social care rather than railways, although I acquired a taste for railway research during my history degree at York University in the 1970s. After retiring in 2011, I decided to pursue this interest and I am grateful for the support of Professor Colin Divall who agreed to supervise a return to York in 2013 to study for a doctorate in Railway Studies. My research concluded that the CHR was conceived as a political railway in relation to Ireland and, more unexpectedly, profoundly affected society and politics in north Wales. There are existing studies of the CHR such as that undertaken by Peter Baughan in 1972, covering the period from construction up to 1880. J.M. Dunn's slimmer and earlier volume was updated in the late 1960s and tends to focus on operational and technical issues consistent with his role on the railway. I provide details of other sources that I used at the end of the book.

My interests and career have led me to write a history that examines the impact of the CHR on every aspect of the area it served but particularly focused on the human experience. My PhD thesis concentrated on politics but there was abundant evidence that the CHR touched the lives of people in north Wales in so many ways and shaped the region for all time. This book does not provide a mass of technical information about engines, structures, operating practices and performance – though these are mentioned occasionally when relevant to the social, political, economic, military, environmental and cultural issues discussed in the chapters. I consider that the history of a railway should centre on the history of the people who designed it, built it, worked on it, used it or otherwise encountered it.

Perhaps the most significant point about this railway for at least its first 150 years is that it is an *English* railway that operated in a Welsh context. The tensions created by this formulation are apparent in all aspects of the history of the CHR. One obvious shortcoming of the book is that I have been unable to reflect the material written in Welsh as much as I would have liked. The Irish perspective is also important and was particularly so up to the achievement of independence for the Republic of Ireland in 1922. I have had to rely on quoting Irish and Welsh politicians and sources whenever possible to balance the analysis.

The chapters are organised by theme but arranged by date as far as possible to cover the different areas of engagement of the CHR with society. So, the political chapters are at the beginning and tourism and the environment towards the end to reflect the shift in importance of these issues over time. But I also cover time and geography by ensuring that each mile of the line, each station, and most years of its existence, are represented by an incident, anecdote, and in some cases a photograph. This is demonstrated by the table presented in Appendix 2. This interrelation of time, space, theme and incident creates greater potential for inaccuracy. I have checked dates, places and sources several times to eliminate these glitches but no doubt some remain. I am, of course, responsible for any errors that have occurred in any aspect of the book.

I have received support in this project from many people. I am grateful for the help of staff at the National Archives with access to material and for other advice. I have received similar assistance from British Library staff in relation to my extensive use of newspaper archives. My friend Paul Kelly read the manuscript and offered advice about wording and presentation, most of which I accepted. The photographs are a vital part of the project, especially in my endeavour to ensure that every station on the line has a photograph, even if it is only of its current location. For this I am particularly appreciative of the kindness of John Alsop in giving me access to his extensive collection. Peter Waller of the Online Transport Archive went the 'extra mile' to assist with photographs. David Plimmer and David Sallery supplied images and useful information from their websites, *Main Line Railways of North Wales* and *Penmorfa* respectively, especially about the period of change for the CHR during the 1980s and 1990s. Charlie Hulme of the North Wales Coast Railway website and Geoff Poole of the Llandudno Junction Steam Locomotive and Carriage Shed website were highly supportive in providing contacts. Those included Derek Williams, one of the few surviving employees from the Llandudno Junction shed and Richard Ellis-Hobbs, who was most helpful in providing photographs in honour of his parents Kathleen and John from his late father's excellent collection. Derek Williams gave his time to provide background on the working of the shed at Llandudno Junction. I also had useful conversations with Norman Lee of the London and North Western Railway Society and used the website of the Railway and Canal Historical Society. I am a member of both those societies. Details for many of those mentioned here are in the bibliography at the end of the book.

Finally, my family have been extremely supportive of the project, so that Ellen, Sarah and Nancy have heard more about railways in north Wales than they ever wanted to, or ever thought they would. My wife Ceri has supported and encouraged me throughout the project and travelled with me for many hundreds of miles on foot and by other means to help with photographs and other research.

I have made every effort to find the copyright holder of all the pictures and other material in the book and believe that I have done so. However, if I have missed anyone out please contact me through the publishers.

Personal Biography

Phil Lloyd was born in Stockport and has lived in the north-west of England all his life, apart from a first degree in history at York from 1971. He gained an MA (Econ) and social work qualification at Manchester University in 1978 and worked as a probation officer until 1998. He led Youth Offending Teams in Manchester and Cheshire before managing in social care in Cheshire. He retired from his post as a director in Cheshire East in 2011 and completed a doctorate in Railway Studies at York in 2017. He now lives in Merseyside with his wife Ceri and spends a lot of time in north Wales.

Author's Note

I use lower case for 'north' in 'north Wales', but it is often 'North' in most quoted text. I have chosen lower case because this is the convention when writing Welsh history for academic journals in Wales. I understand that the use of upper case tends to weaken the notion of Wales as a single nation. I use the current Welsh spelling of place names except in original titles or quotations where the old, anglicised format was employed.

I have given full/abbreviated forms chapter by chapter to save the reader from having always to refer to the abbreviation list. When monetary value is mentioned in the text it is calculated to 2019 prices.

Abbreviations

CHR	Chester and Holyhead Railway Company (also used generally to refer to the stretch of line from Chester to Holyhead)
DSP	City of Dublin Steam Packet Company
FR	Ffestiniog railway
GC	Gauge Commission
GHR	George's Harbour Railway
GJR	Grand Junction Railway
GWR	Great Western Railway
IRC	Irish Railway Commission
LBR	London and Birmingham Railway
LMR	Liverpool and Manchester Railway
LMS	London Midland and Scottish Railway
LNWR	London and North Western Railway
LSWR	London and South Western Railway
OWW	Oxford, Worcester and Wolverhampton Railway
PDR	Porth Dinllaen route (the two proposed routes to Porth Dinllaen)
RWF	Royal Welsh Fusiliers
TVR	Trent Valley Railway
UK	United Kingdom (Britain and all of Ireland until 1922; only the six counties of Northern Ireland included thereafter)
WMCQR	Wrexham, Mold and Connah's Quay Railway

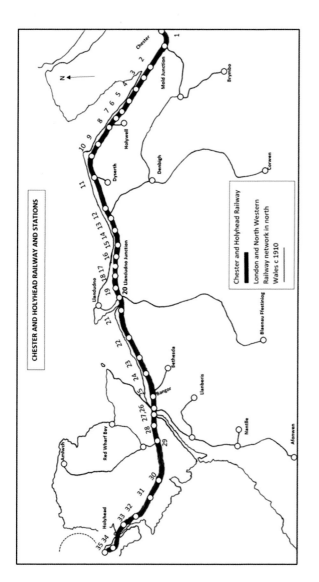

Number	Station	Distance
1	Chester	0
2	Sandycroft	5.75
3	Queensferry	7.25
4	Shotton	8.25
5	Connah's Quay	9.25
6	Flint	12.25
7	Bagillt	14.25
8	Holywell Junction	16.75
9	Mostyn	20

Number	Station	Distance
10	Talacre	23
11	Prestatyn	26.25
12	Rhyl	30
13	Foryd	31
14	Abergele and Pensarn	34.25
15	Llanddulas	36.75
16	Llysfaen	37.75
17	Old Colwyn	38.75
18	Colwyn Bay	40.25

Number	Station	Distance
19	Mochdre and Pabo	42.25
20	Llandudno Junction	44.75
21	Conwy	45.5
22	Penmaenmawr	50
23	Llanfairfechan	52.75
24	Aber	54.75
25	Bangor	60
26	Menai Bridge	61.25
27	Britannia Bridge	61.75

Number	Station	Distance
28	Llanfair PG	63.5
29	Gaerwen	66.25
30	Bodorgan	72.75
31	Ty Croes	75.25
32	Rhosneigr	77
33	Valley	81
34	Holyhead	84.5
35	Admiralty Pier	85

Map 1: The Chester and Holyhead Railway and its stations.

1

The Race to Dublin

No time should be lost in bringing forward a scheme more feasible and superior in every respect [than Porth Dinllaen] through Conway, Flint, and Chester, to join the Birmingham line [and an enlarged] Holyhead harbour.[1]

The prize of rapid communication between London and Dublin was a feature of British politics from the time of the Act of Union that brought Ireland within the United Kingdom (UK) in 1801. The priority was to make the journey as short as possible because the means of communication were limited by wind and horsepower. That phase ended with the completion of Thomas Telford's road from London to Holyhead via Shrewsbury in 1826. Ten years later the journey between

1. Admiralty Pier Holyhead – the terminus of Thomas Telford's brilliant road scheme that improved the speed of the mail and is marked by the arch. Between 1851 and 1925 there was a railway station on the pier. **(Photo: John Alsop Collection)**

London and Holyhead was possible in twenty-six hours and fifty-five minutes. By then the Liverpool and Manchester Railway (LMR) had been open for six years and its speed and capacity were already threatening the future of the stagecoach.

Access to the lucrative Irish market was important to the early railway promoters, just as it was important to the British government that wished to ensure that it kept the closest possible grip on its nearest colony. But those aims appeared secure when the LMR was extended to Birmingham via the Grand Junction Railway (GJR) in 1838 where it met the London and Birmingham Railway (LBR). The four most important cities in the UK during the Industrial Revolution were thus united by rapid travel – the financial centre of London, the engineering powerhouse in Birmingham, the cottonopolis of Manchester and the maritime gateway to empire, and portal for food and raw materials, at Liverpool – from where steamers could sail to Dublin.

The promoters of the LBR were explicit that the connection with Ireland was a major benefit of their scheme. James Marshall, secretary of the Provincial Bank noted advantages in rapid transport of gold bullion at times of financial or other crisis in Dublin; Henry Booth, treasurer of the LMR, emphasised the value of carrying troops to Ireland; while Augustus Godby, secretary to the Dublin Post Office, was sure the line would be useful if it was extended to Liverpool.[2] Clearly, the assumption at this early stage was that Liverpool would be the focus of improvements in contact between London and Dublin. Ideas of tackling the mountainous interior of north Wales, or its rocky and stormy north coast, were deemed impracticable and unnecessary by many railway promoters at that time.

But there were more optimistic railway promoters who were keen to suggest better connections between Britain and Ireland than the one via Liverpool, which had difficult sandbanks and involved a long voyage to Dublin. Henry Fairbairn proposed that a bridge be built across the narrowest point between Scotland and Ireland in 1832, noting a London to Dublin distance of 480 miles. He also saw profound political advantages to his scheme:

And it is better that Ireland should now continue to follow the fortunes of England, for a dissolution of the Union would soon lead to a democratical [*sic*] government, and the reign of revenge. Allowing our ancient rights of conquest to be no just claim, and that Ireland is a separate land, with sufficient territory, trade, and population, to form a right to an independent stand amongst the nations, still it is placed by nature too contiguous to England for a separate government, with different foreign alliances, and another religion. Perpetual collisions would ensue, each country sheltering the hostile fleets of foreigners, and a division of the Union would, at last, draw on the ruin of both nations. To divide is to destroy, and as we possess similar languages, natural productions, and channels of trade, so let us now overcome these few intervening miles of sea and make these islands one land.[3]

Wales was also prominent in the debate around the same time as Fairbairn's claims for a link through Scotland. The *Cambrian Quarterly* looked ahead in 1832 to the construction of the LBR and its role as a spine for the British railway system, and foresaw a branch through Wales to Aberystwyth so that:

A communication be opened up with England of so perfect a nature as that afforded by a Railway; and [prospects for Wales] will be changed as if by magic. [And] we do not forget that the Irish Mail now passes through Holyhead but we fear … the advantage for the Liverpool route when the Rail-road should be but partially brought on … would infallibly draw the mail and all passengers to it.[4]

Meanwhile, elsewhere in north Wales railways were being developed to improve the transport of slate: the first public railway there was opened in the form of the Nantlle Railway of 1829 that linked quarries with the port at Caernarfon. There was therefore much interest in rail technology in north Wales and an awareness of its value in linking quarries, towns and ports. But it was the Ffestiniog Railway (FR) that increased the scale and scope of such works – and in the process established a potential core for the development of a rail route from Dublin to London to rival Liverpool. Its plans had the approval of a visitor to Porthmadog whose influence and status its owners welcomed – but would later regret:

The far-famed [George] Stephenson, the Wellington of Railroad Engineers, passed through this place a few days ago on his way from Ffestiniog, where he has been for some days engaged in examining the line of railway [to] which … he gives his *unqualified* approbation. … The approving opinion of *such* a person [places] the 'hall mark' upon [the railway] the Railroad to fortune and to fame.[5]

It was Henry Archer, an Irish businessman with connections to the FR, who first considered making Porthmadog the centre of a much larger railway project. He put his proposals into a pamphlet that was advertised in the *North Wales Chronicle* in December 1835; probably the formal launch of the process to challenge the

Liverpool to Dublin connection. As he told the House of Commons Committee for Private Business in 1840:

> As director of the FR … I was reading some parliamentary documents … and I saw it was evidently an object with a party in the government at that time to throw Holyhead over and make the entire communication through Liverpool; it then struck me, that if that was the case, it was giving the go-bye to Wales.
>
> I saw clearly, that if the Railroad took place to Liverpool, communication must and ought to be made through Wales, that we had no chance unless there were a railway … I employed an engineer to report to me which was the best line; I felt, judging from myself, my interest would be to make it by Shrewsbury and Bala and the FR, and he reported to me that a line could be made from Port Dynllaen to Worcester, straight across; in consequence of that I wrote a pamphlet which was published and there were meetings in Wales and Dublin in consequence.[6]

2. *Porth Dinllaen came close to being the terminal port for a railway from London towards Dublin until the work of the Gauge Commission thwarted the Great Western Railway. This picture from 1915 shows the scope of the natural harbour which supporters claimed would avoid the expensive works at Holyhead and the need to cross the Menai Straits.* (Photo: Phil Lloyd Collection)

With this level and variety of support on both sides of the Irish Sea; with the prospect of government funding; and with a head start over the opposition, Archer and his consortium seemed very well placed to secure success in their bid for the lucrative mail contract between London and Dublin. However, there was a warning for the promoters of the Porth Dinllaen line from Irish nationalist leader Daniel O'Connell, who knew the political scene well and saw that:

> At Holyhead at present, a very considerable quantity of property belonging to individuals is vested in facilitating the conveyance from one country to the other, and that should not be lightly interfered with. The meeting should place themselves in the same situation as the men who vested in the property, and he [O'Connell] was sure, that if each individual considered himself standing in this position, he would not wish his interest to be meddled with lightly. ….
> Holyhead has natural defects which are incurable. It is a tide harbour, and the immense sums of money expended upon it, have facilitated the entrance at all times of vessels of a small class only.[7]

Even as he spoke, opposing forces were gathering; attracted no doubt by the prospect of government funding and perhaps equally motivated by the impact on their own interests of the proposed line. A meeting was soon called in Bangor with Sir Richard Bulkeley, an MP and major Anglesey landowner in the chair. Sir Richard was blunt in his assessment and determined about the response:

> No time should be lost in bringing forward a scheme more feasible and superior in every respect … through Conway, Flint, and Chester, to join the Birmingham line [and an enlarged] Holyhead harbour, which had been most unfairly underrated and ridiculously treated in a pamphlet that had been published in favour of Port Dinllaen harbour. … It was ridiculous to appeal to the gentry of North Wales in support of a project which would not be of the smallest advantage.[8]

The struggle for the right to Irish traffic through north Wales immediately became more complicated by the presence of the George's Harbour Railway (GHR) proposal by which the focus of Irish traffic in north Wales would switch from Holyhead to present day Llandudno, which it was intended to call Port Wrexham. The origins of this scheme show that the railway was not the primary consideration. There had been government concern about high shipping losses in the Irish Sea (especially ships to and from Liverpool) and the need for better harbour facilities, including a breakwater, for larger vessels than Holyhead could accommodate. It was a logical progression from this to connect any such harbour to the railway system. The GHR therefore announced in its prospectus an intention to:

> Convert [Llandudno] into an ASYLUM HARBOUR for St George's Channel, and to form a railway from thence along the coast of Denbighshire … to join the GJR at Crewe Hall … thus forming a shorter and more direct line of communication between Dublin and London … than any at present existing.[9]

The prospectus presented a confident argument from a consortium that appeared to have strong support for an affordable project. It noted that moves were afoot to secure government support for an enquiry into the best route between London and Dublin through the Select Committee on London and Dublin Roads, chaired by Irish leader Daniel O'Connell. This resolved on 8 July 1836:

> That an humble address be presented to His Majesty, requesting … an immediate survey be made of the harbours of Liverpool, Holyhead and Port Dynllaen, and such other points … as may appear suitable for a communication between London and Dublin.[10]

O'Connell's select committee eventually secured agreement by the House of Commons for their request for a survey of harbours at Liverpool, Porth Dinllaen and Holyhead via a Treasury Minute of 14 October 1836. The Chancellor, Thomas Spring Rice, was by then clear that there would be no government money forthcoming, even for a survey of railway lines; in contrast to his earlier position that even a price of £2m (£230m at 2019 prices) was not excessive:

> The Viscount Melbourne and the Chancellor of the Exchequer … are by no means prepared to recommend any survey of a line of railroad … any interposition on the part of the State, even if limited to the single object of a survey, would have a tendency of interfering with private enterprise.[11]

However, the survey of harbours was not just a matter of concern to mariners for the choice of harbour effectively decided the line of railway. When the answer came back to the Lords of the Treasury on 21 February 1837, it contained an unequivocal statement in favour of Porth Dinllaen; noting that the conclusion was reached without the need for further survey. The authority of the report could hardly have been higher, given that its author was Sir Francis Beaufort, the originator of the 'Beaufort Scale' of wind strengths.

> As long as the Dublin mails are carried by coaches on common roads, the best place of embarkation in every respect will be Holyhead which is only 62 statute miles from Kingstown Harbour, which only requires a little elongation of the pier in order to admit larger classes of steam vessels at low water.
> But if a railroad should be constructed for that purpose, it would be probably led to another port, because it is not likely that a steam carriage with a loaded train could be allowed to traverse the present chain Bridge at Bangor and the new bridge here, on arches, would add enormously to the expense of the undertaking; besides objection that would be raised to such a bridge from the obstruction it would give to the navigation of the straight [*sic*].

The judgement fulfilled the worst fears of the Holyhead lobby; that the crossing of the Menai Straits would be an insuperable obstacle, if not in engineering terms, then certainly because of its cost. The GHR was discounted because it did not deliver enough of an advantage over Liverpool to warrant additional investment in a packet station.

The government did not act immediately on these proposals but opted instead to subsume the decision under a wider issue of the railway system for Ireland. This new Treasury Minute did not specify that a route from London to a port with a direct route to Ireland would be part of the remit, although one section did give some grounds for pursuing this line of enquiry by suggesting that the commission should examine the means of, 'cheap, rapid and certain intercourse between Great Britain and Ireland'.[12]

The support of the Irish contingent was crucial to the survival of the government. O'Connell had pressed for repeal of the Union with Ireland between 1831 and 1834 but after the Lichfield House Compact of 1835, he consented to the Union of Great Britain and Ireland if steps were taken to equalise the treatment of Ireland with the rest of the UK. The task of delivering that outcome fell to Thomas Drummond as under-secretary to Lord Normanby at Dublin Castle. Drummond was an engineer by background and, though he supported and promoted administrative and political reforms, he also wanted pragmatic and practical measures to develop Ireland and tie it more closely to the Union. He particularly emphasised the lack of railway development in Ireland as he believed that it provided the key to the full integration of Ireland. According to Drummond's biographer, he wished to apply a more rational approach to railways in Ireland in the 1830s that avoided handing the task to what he considered to be the corrupt railway developers of mainland Britain. Drummond saw the creation of a railway system in Ireland as serving a number of purposes in the short, medium and longer term: temporary employment to the peasantry that in turn would bring a period of greater calm; while he anticipated that private capital would eventually be drawn into Ireland as its economy developed, which in turn would employ those released from railway building.

A key appointment to the Irish Railway Commission (IRC) was that of Charles Vignoles – the man chosen by Henry Archer for his earlier survey of the route to Porth Dinllaen. Vignoles had well-developed railway interests in Ireland, including the Dublin and Kingstown Railway and, as we have seen, the Porth Dinllaen project in north Wales. His appointment was therefore unlikely to be well received by those competing with him for the right to introduce Ireland to railways. One furious commentator remarked that:

The appointment of Mr Vignolles [*sic*] … has been a subject of frequent comment. I will not flinch from pronouncing it a daring indiscretion, which, more than any other circumstance, has raised suspicion of studied partiality, and cast distrust and odium from many quarters upon the whole enquiry.[13]

Thus, the commission began its work with a strong sense that it might not favour the CHR. The Treasury Minute of November 1836 had specified that the work of the IRC covered railways in Ireland rather than railways between Ireland and London. However, the Minute had arisen in part from the need to resolve the controversy over the best route towards Dublin from London. Chancellor Spring Rice had given some scope to extend that remit in his comments to the delegation in 1836 when he made a connection between the link with Dublin and a system of railways for the whole of Ireland.[14] The appointment of Charles Vignoles as an engineer to the IRC ensured that the if the issue was considered then it was most likely that its report would tend to favour the Porth Dinllaen line that Vignoles had surveyed in 1836, rather than rival routes, and particularly the CHR. Vignoles suggested that if public money was to be spent on the line then there was some requirement to give public advantage to areas such as the remote parts of north Wales that would not otherwise benefit from railways:

If the Government should be induced, as in the case of the Holyhead Road, to patronise or execute any portion of the Railway, should not such a line pass centrally through the country, affording the utmost general advantages, independent of being a route to the packet station; in fact be a Main Trunk Line, such as those now laying out by your commission in Ireland?[15]

Similarly, he adopted the approach of the IRC in limiting expense by accepting steeper gradients for the line from Porth Dinllaen, suggested a single line with passing points initially and thereby reckoned to save £5,000 per mile (£558,000).[16] He was, however, clear that the main purpose of the line was to enable rapid communication between London and Dublin; and he calculated that his line was shorter and would save an hour in the overall time of the journey compared to the Holyhead route. According to Vignoles, that hour was crucial to answering letters on the same day they were received. If that could not be accomplished any investment would was wasted in his view. Although the IRC attempted to be even-handed in its comments, the fact that its report included extensive details of the Porth Dinllaen route (PDR), but relatively little on the CHR, showed a marked tendency to support the former. The logic of the report was clear: Ireland needed its own comprehensive railway system with the best possible connection to the UK and its capital. A London to Dublin rail and sea link was clearly a vital part of the IRC proposals.

Lord Morpeth, the Irish Secretary, eventually committed the government to support Drummond and the IRC and to develop the Dublin to Cork line, with branches to Limerick and Clonmel, with a state investment of £2,556,000 (£267m). In contrast to this government support for the IRC, Sir Robert Peel, the Leader of the Opposition, delivered an understated but destructive speech that reflected a clear ideology in respect of railway development – an entirely laissez-faire approach to railway building in Ireland – the same as he had advocated in the rest of Britain. Eventually the House of Commons divided, and the measure was agreed by 144 votes to 100 – a result that apparently satisfied Drummond.[17] By contrast, Daniel O'Connell was in no doubt that Peel's opposition to the measure would prove fatal to it and: 'the Government scheme will be abandoned as hopeless'.[18]

Even before the debate on the IRC proposals, advocates of the CHR endeavoured to strengthen their position by attacking the PDR for its demand for state funding. The initiative to revive the rival CHR came from the Chester and Crewe Railway (CCR) which formed a link to Chester from the GJR and paved the way for a railway along the north Wales coast. The CCR board met the engineer Francis Giles in November 1838 and he outlined his scheme for a route from Chester to Holyhead. Despite earlier doubts about its feasibility Giles planned to tackle the crossing to Anglesey by use of a stationary engine to haul carriages over the existing Menai Suspension Bridge.[19] Given the controversial nature of this proposal, the CCR decided that it needed somebody with more political weight than Giles and so commissioned a report from George Stephenson on the relative merits of Vignoles' PDR and the CHR.[20]

George Stephenson was the most prominent railway engineer in 1838, and it was his status rather than his judgement that was needed, given the problems faced by the advocates of the CHR. Beaufort's report was against the CHR because it had to cross a wide river at Conwy and negotiate the large rocks at Penmaenmawr before crossing the Menai Straits. The promoters needed a report from a convincing source that made light of such problems and restored confidence in the CHR to galvanise supporters, financiers and the political powers in London. Stephenson provided exactly what was needed in December 1838, even as the IRC report was being considered. He made the CHR appear easy and inexpensive. He proposed to cross the Dee at Chester with a wooden bridge, regarded the threat from the sea along the coast as insignificant, considered the

3. *Chester was already a substantial rail centre when it was chosen as a key point on the route between London and Dublin. This picture is from 1965 and the importance of the route to Holyhead is still impressed on passengers by the ageing sign opposite Platform 3 in 2020.* (Main photo: David Sallery, Penmorfa.com; Inset photo: Phil Lloyd Collection)

crossing of the rivers at Rhyl and Conwy as minor matters – needing a 'common road bridge' and an 'embankment and wooden bridge' respectively. He dismissed the idea that a tunnel was needed to take the line beyond the rocky headland at Penmaenmawr, declaring the line from Conwy to Penmaenmawr as pursuing 'very favourable ground'.[21] He thought the tunnel at Llandegai near Bangor would prove the hardest part of the route and resolved fears about the cost of crossing the Menai Straits by asserting that the suspension bridge built by Telford was adequate for the purpose. Finally, he dismissed the rival PDR as utterly impracticable.[22]

The value of Stephenson's report in engineering terms may be evaluated by subsequent events. The bridge at Chester collapsed a few weeks after opening in 1847, killing five occupants of a train. The line between Chester and Abergele was breached by the sea. Extensive works, including a tunnel, were needed at Penmaenmawr – and these were breached before opening as Samuel Smiles – an early biographer of the Stephenson family – reported:

4. According to George Stephenson's rather complacent 1838 report on the CHR, the heaviest work on the line would be the tunnel at Llandegai near Bangor. In the event it proved rather easier than several other locations, though not for Michael Kelly who died after falling from a train in the tunnel in 1905. **(Photo: John Alsop Collection)**

While the sea wall [near Penmaenmawr] was still in progress, its strength was severely tried by a strong north-westerly gale which blew in October 1846, accompanied with a spring tide of 17 feet. On the following morning it was found that a large portion of the rubble was irreparably injured, and 200 yards of the wall were then replaced by an open viaduct, with the piers placed edgeways to the sea, the openings between them being spanned by ten cast-iron girders 42 feet long. ...

But the sea repeated its assaults, and made further havoc with the work, entailing heavy expenses and a complete reorganisation of the contract. ... The work was at length finished after about three years' anxious labour; but Mr Stephenson confessed that if a long tunnel had been made in the first instance through the solid rock of Penmaenmawr, a saving of from £25,000 to £30,000 [£3–£3.5m] would have been effected. He also said he had arrived at the conclusion that in railway works engineers should endeavour as far as possible to avoid the necessity of contending with the sea.[23]

5. *George Stephenson's optimistic estimate of the engineering difficulties of the CHR unravelled in October 1846 when a stretch of embankment near Penmaenmawr was washed away and his son Robert replaced it with a complex viaduct. To his credit it was still in place as 37417* **Highland Region** *crosses Pen-y-Clip viaduct on a Bangor–Crewe working in June 1996.* **(Photo: David Sallery, Penmorfa.com)**

The last observation would surely have brought a smile to the face of Charles Vignoles who had based his case against the CHR precisely on its proximity to the sea.

Above all, massive works at the River Conwy and the Menai Straits required costly tubular bridges. Those difficulties were fully understood in 1839. The *Railway Magazine*, for example, described the plan to use Telford's existing road suspension bridge for trains as 'perfectly absurd; in fact, it is monstrous'.[24] The political impact of Stephenson's report was, however, impressive. The *Chester Chronicle* had advocated the GHR to Llandudno, but that line had failed to gain substantial financial or political support. The *Chronicle* then switched support to the CHR and argued for the wider importance of 'the great imperial line'.[25] In January 1839 key supporters of the CHR met in Chester. These included the Marquis of Westminster, head of one of the richest families in England and most influential in Chester. The meeting was adamant that Stephenson's judgement on the utility of the Menai Suspension Bridge was entirely credible.[26]

Irish views were also important to the CHR lobby, especially the influential merchants and bankers of Dublin who had previously backed the PDR. Stephenson's report provided the catalyst for a meeting of those interests in January 1839 (two weeks after the Chester meeting) that was attended by lobbyists from Chester, Shrewsbury and north Wales. It was as tense as expected, given the conflicting views of those present and the imminent debate on the proposals of the IRC. The meeting refused to give outright support for any route but agreed to urge the government to institute a further enquiry to resolve the matter once and for all. As the *Chester Chronicle* pointed out, the failure to get Irish endorsement for the PDR in 1839 changed the issue of the favoured route from: 'one prejudged to one open … the game is safe for Chester'.[27] Vignoles had not helped the PDR supporters by failing to attend the Dublin meeting. The prospect of challenging George Stephenson (who did attend) had intimidated him as he noted: 'it is almost "bearding the lion in his den" to enter into a professional contest with such a high authority'.[28] There was optimism in Chester that, whatever decision was made about the harbour, the route of the railway along the coast from their city was secure.

The CHR gained ground with support from Anglesey landowners. Sir Richard Bulkeley assured the Holyhead meeting that he had the chancellor of the exchequer's word that there was no public funding for the PDR. As for the CHR, he reported that he had solid information that major railway companies in England were ready to fund it. It seemed likely that Bulkeley had the LBR in mind when he spoke, thus confirming that the CHR was the scheme that was backed by the most powerful English railway company.[29] The *Chester Chronicle* was jubilant. 'No longer is it a matter admitting of further controversy, as to either the principle or the details. Those are settled in favour of [the CHR]. One thing is certain; the [PDR] is *gone-gone.*'[30] The CHR supporters were thus well placed to go to Westminster with the Irish business community and key Anglesey landowners as allies.

It was O'Connell who picked up the issue in London where he successfully requested a fresh report.[31] That report overturned Beaufort's previous opinion and established the CHR as the first choice. The proposed line from Chester that terminated at Llandudno was discounted because it did not provide any clear advantage over the Liverpool route or the other two proposals. The authors also referred to the report of the Naval Committee, prepared by Rear-Admiral Sir J.A. Gordon and Captain Beechey, which clearly favoured Holyhead. That concluded the issue and Holyhead was identified as the best location for both the harbour and the railway at the terminus of the line from London towards Dublin.

A meeting in London in May 1840, attended by key CHR personnel and chaired by the Marquis of Westminster, then endorsed a proposal to proceed with the CHR before Captain Dundas, a Flintshire landowner, rather dampened enthusiasm when he identified a procedural problem. Parliamentary standing orders required a period of notification for railway schemes and the deposit of 10 per cent of the cost of the project. CHR supporters also had to contend with the lack of any commitment from government to fund a line from London towards Dublin. They had criticised the IRC for requesting state funding for railways but were forced to conclude in 1840 that public money was needed for their own scheme in lieu of the 10 per cent deposit requirement. They argued that it was available from saving £77,953 (£8m) through the concentration of all Irish mail traffic into Holyhead rather than using Liverpool and Milford Haven as well. That gave an effective monopoly to the CHR.[32] They supported those arguments for money and a monopoly of traffic with a claim that completion of the CHR was 'an imperial question' because of Ireland's rather strained political connection with the UK which it was perceived the railway would correct.[33]

When the debate opened in June 1840 Grosvenor (Marquis of Westminster) put those arguments and Daniel O'Connell reported on the support of the Dublin Chamber of Commerce and argued that Irish interests should not be frustrated by a procedural technicality. Government was unmoved. Henry Labouchere, the president of the Board of Trade, acknowledged that the railway had a national status, but he was unwilling to support a departure from standing orders.[34] Sir Robert Peel, Leader of the Opposition, reluctantly supported government, but signalled his future support for the CHR. He told Parliament that his studies of the subject had shown clearly:

> That the shortest line was that which they pointed out [to Holyhead], and that it should decidedly be preferred to others… He should be exceedingly sorry if the standing orders were enforced … as they posed an obstacle to the commencement of the work next year. He must at the same time say that he had the highest interest in coming to that conclusion.[35]

However, the motion to suspend standing orders was narrowly lost and Peel's intervention was critical.[36]

The *Chester Chronicle* expressed its fury at the outcome but later noted that: 'scarcely a day passes but produces some additional fact in favour of the Great Holyhead railway project'.[37] In truth, there was little to support their optimism. The main frustration for their opponents was the lack of a rail connection between Worcester or Shrewsbury and a main line to London.[38] By December 1840 even the bullish *Chester Chronicle* had to admit that there was: 'apathy in the public mind' but also reason to believe that a change was imminent because of discussions between the GJR and the government.[39]

The difficulty for both factions was that they could get no national support for their proposals, though Irish interests reaffirmed the importance of railway communication with London.[40] Thus, the rail and sea link to Ireland remained a stubbornly local dispute and the national election began to overshadow all else politically in London until August 1841 when Peel, the man who had frustrated both schemes for railway communication between London and Dublin, became prime minister.[41] However, despite his vote against the CHR in June 1840, the arrival of Peel's government clearly favoured the scheme. He had made positive references to it in 1840, even as he voted against. Interested parties began to anticipate the opportunity to restart the scheme in 1842; and in the last week of 1841 there was a meeting at Bangor with engineer Francis Giles present. Public support was apparently still weak and included some very strange alternatives to fund the railway in the absence of government backing – such as diverting the money spent on drink to the scheme.[42] There is no evidence that the suggestion was taken up.

The first sign of change was in March 1842, when Peel was in Caernarfon and the mayor of that town met Home Secretary James Graham. The *North Wales Chronicle* noted that at the same time Irish and Welsh MPs had asked for government support for a railway through Bangor to a suitable packet station.[43] Those representations produced the desired result. In June 1842, a further committee was appointed to re-investigate the whole issue and the period of national inactivity on the rail link that had endured since June 1840 was over. The CHR interest again suggested the scheme should be funded by concentrating all Dublin mail onto one route, and they wanted the railway to manage ships to carry the mail on the route to Dublin.[44] The approach was confirmed when the committee reported, although it could not reach a conclusion on the best harbour and urged government to appoint a further committee to advise it on that issue.[45]

The situation in Ireland was less problematic for government than domestic issues such as Chartism in 1842. But the security situation in Ireland began to worsen in 1843 and Unionist opinion was therefore more active. The Earl of Wicklow reported on a meeting in March 1843 at which Peel told him that the government would not undertake the scheme for a railway and steamer scheme between London and Dublin itself but was:

> … ready to listen to the terms on which any responsible company might be disposed to carry out a railway communication through North Wales [and provided] he was satisfied with the parties, and their proposition, [he would] carry out the report of the select committee.[46]

That report was greeted with cheers, perhaps reflecting growing concern with the state of Ireland that was shared by leading members of government. On 9 May 1843 Viscount Jocelyn posed a question to Peel in Parliament that highlighted increasing concerns with security in Ireland. Peel was clear that his government was:

> Fully alive to the evils which arise from the existing agitation [and] that there is no influence, no power, no authority … which shall not be exercised for the purpose of maintaining the Union – the dissolution of which would involve, not merely the repeal of an act of Parliament, but the dismemberment of this great empire.[47]

The next day Peel was asked about forming railways in Ireland but was clear in his response that his priority was to use railways for *English*, rather than Irish, interests. That marked a clear contrast with the work of the IRC which had taken a decidedly Irish perspective in its work. Peel told Parliament that:

> Inquiries had been directed and were still in progress, the object of which, however, was rather to facilitate the communication between England and Ireland than to aid in the construction of railways in the latter country.

How far an improved communication with Ireland from this country may tend to facilitate the introduction of railroads in the former, I am not prepared to say. I have only to repeat, that the subject of communication between this country and Ireland with a view to its improvement is under the consideration of Government.[48]

Two days later he made his own position on that communication clear. He was asked about his plans for speeding up the mail through Wales to Ireland, and whether the government had enough evidence on which to decide. Peel thought that the evidence favoured the line from Chester along the north Wales coast – but whether that line should end at Holyhead or go on from Bangor to Porth Dinllaen was less clear. He agreed that government should resolve doubts over the harbour by means of a 'Naval Survey', but he would not commit himself to the expenditure of any of the public money.[49]

In the promised naval survey, Captains Back and Fair were unequivocal in their support for Holyhead. They tried to allay any further controversy by saying that their report was: 'without bias of any kind … having regard solely to the quickest transit consistent with safety'. The Admiralty commissioned a report from the civil engineer James Walker in June 1843 to address its concerns that the bridges proposed by the CHR would interfere with shipping. By October 1843, the matter was urgent as the Repeal movement in Ireland reached its peak with the arrest of O'Connell after his public demonstration at Clontarf was banned on Peel's orders.[50]

If the government had hoped for a simple endorsement for the CHR (as implied in Peel's comments) they were frustrated. Walker's report noted a new consideration that had not been a part of previous plans – the needs of the Welsh population. He thought that if the: 'thinly populated and mountainous part of the country' did not get the railway as part of the line towards Dublin, it would be a long time before they benefited from any railway communication.[51] However, like Back and Fair, he favoured Holyhead, subject to improvements in the harbour and the provision of a breakwater at a cost of £400,000 (£51m).

The momentum was firmly with the CHR because it seemed to be part of the answer to the growing Irish rebellion. The *Morning Post* noted it as an example of the use of steam technology to support government policy in Ireland: 'The steam-boat and the railway are great marplots [means of defeating a plan or plot] – and, indeed, have afforded practical proof that an Irish insurrection is, in this our day, almost a hopeless thing.'[52] The paper (and government) got a practical demonstration of the need to improve the speed of communication in the announcement of the verdict in Dublin against O'Connell. Its reporter arrived in London on Monday, 12 February, 1844 at 2.00 a.m., having left Dublin at midnight on Saturday: 'by means of a steam-boat engaged for the purpose and a special train on the railway' – a journey of twenty-six hours.[53] Just five days later, Peel received a private letter on the notepaper of the LBR giving him the news that an improved link was finally in prospect as that railway would support the CHR financially with a contribution of £1m (£128m).[54]

The timing of these negotiations is significant. In February 1844 Peel began to articulate his more positive approach to governing Ireland, with less reliance on force and more concessions to the emerging Irish Roman Catholic middle class. Peel's negotiation with Robert Creed, the secretary of the LBR, took place *during* a debate about the repeal of the Union in February 1844. Peel put the CHR at the heart of his Irish policy:

> I trust and believe there is no foundation for that assertion [that Ireland can only be ruled by force]. I do not believe that it is impossible to govern Ireland by the ordinary rules by which a country should be governed – with a continuance of the principles which we have always professed. Sir, I see much cause for entertaining bright hopes for the future. By the wonderful applications of science, we are about, I trust, still further to shorten physical distance. I should not be surprised if, even during my own lifetime, we are able by its aid to bring Dublin nearer to London than many towns in England now are. I shall not be surprised … if the interval between London and Dublin shall be shortened to twelve hours. You have prospectuses before you, some drawn up by eminent engineers, which contemplate the shortening of that interval to fourteen hours; and my own belief is that with the progress of improvement the interval will be still further reduced.[55]

The CHR also had the advantage of serving Peel's more local interests. Thus, he was able to achieve both a national and a personal objective – and thereby answer the question as to why he was so adamant for the CHR. Expert opinion was clearly divided between Holyhead and Porth Dinllaen but at least one commentator thought: 'the great weight of opinion is in favour of Porth-Dynllaen as infinitely superior to Holyhead in its double capacity as a Packet Station and Harbour of Refuge'.[56] However, Peel had personal and political interests in securing the Trent Valley Railway (TVR) through his constituency of Tamworth. When the TVR eventually opened in 1847, a local newspaper was clear what had revived the scheme that had failed in 1844:

> To the memorable statement by [Peel] when Premier, that the line which would contribute most to lessen the distance between London and Dublin,

should receive the sanction and support of the Government, may be chiefly attributed the existence and progress of this important line of railway [because] the originators had almost abandoned their contemplated route in despair.[57]

The CHR was therefore an exceptional railway as it engaged the attention of the most senior figures in government. Thus, when there were further objections to Holyhead, yet another report was commissioned by the government from engineer James Rendel in May 1844. His report removed the remaining objections to Holyhead. He also quashed a final bid by the Shrewsbury lobby to cut across country via Mold (missing Chester) to reach the coast at Abergele as advocated by engineer Francis Giles. That route was unsuitable according to Rendel: 'for a line where great speed would have to be resorted to'.[58]

The PDR supporters were incensed because, according to them, Rendel was the engineer of the Birkenhead Dock Company which shared the same promoters, solicitor and agent as the CHR. They alleged that the company also held £70,000 (£8m) in CHR shares.[59] It was to no avail. In June, Lord Dalhousie confirmed Holyhead and the grant of money to improve the harbour – but only when the best line of railway was secured across the Menai Straits. The Duke of Wellington made clear in the House of Lords that unless the CHR built a new bridge the line would not be approved.[60] Once that was resolved, the measure cleared Parliament and received the Royal Assent on 4 July 1844. Thus, the status of the CHR was shown by the involvement of Peel, Dalhousie and Wellington, three of the most senior politicians in Victorian Britain, who ensured the passage of the measure through Parliament. It had been a long struggle for a controversial measure, but the direct engagement of the government in a matter that was at the heart of Irish policy ensured its success. There were further negotiations to conclude the route through – or rather around – Bangor that were complicated by the objections of the Bishop of Bangor. He considered that a route closer to the town centre would disturb his palace and so the CHR incurred an extra £100,000 (£13m) in constructing tunnels to ensure that the bishop was left in peace.[61]

With hindsight, the success of the CHR in securing an act and government funding might have seemed inevitable once the proposals of the IRC were defeated in 1839 and with them government's support for the line to Porth Dinllaen. But it was not so straightforward. Peel created the conditions that effectively revived the CHR and changed the nature of the project by overturning the policy of moderation towards Ireland and denying O'Connell any political influence. O'Connell then revived his ambition to repeal the Union and radicalised

6. *LMS Royal Scot class 6162* **Queen's Westminster Rifleman** – *bursts from the east end of Bangor tunnel in this 1930s photograph. The tunnel was constructed at great expense after objections in 1844 from the Bishop of Bangor who felt that a more direct route would disturb his palace near the city centre.* **(Photo: John Alsop Collection)**

Irish politics until he was arrested in October 1843. The CHR's fortunes grew in line with those changes in Irish politics. Peel's inclusion of rapid communication between London and Dublin in the outline of his Irish policy in February 1844 confirmed the status of the CHR as an important component in an approach that depended on constructive engagement in Ireland – with force as a last resort. The period from Peel's statements in May 1843 to the passage of the CHR Act in July 1844 confirmed the importance of the line in the policy of the government towards Ireland. The CHR moved from being a locally and regionally supported alternative to the PDR to securing a place in government policy towards Ireland.

2

The Imperial Line

The time has arrived for placing Ireland upon the same footing as Great Britain and removing an invidious distinction that was only justified by the difficulties of dilatory and doubtful communication.[1]

The passing of the Chester and Holyhead Railway Act in 1844 was not the end of the argument about the route to Ireland. Doubts remained about the viability of the railway, particularly that crossing the Menai Straits would prove too difficult thereby leaving the line stranded on the mainland. But the immediate threat to the Chester and Holyhead Railway (CHR) was the 1845 revival of the Porth Dinllaen route (PDR) supported by the Great Western Railway (GWR) which had significant financial weight behind it. It was not the same route as the original PDR. The route from London Paddington was to be via Oxford and Worcester before entering Wales, rather than the 1835 route via Birmingham and Shrewsbury. The diaries of engineer Charles Vignoles – who had surveyed the original PDR for Henry Archer – show that Vignoles met Isambard Kingdom Brunel, the GWR engineer, in May 1846. Clearly, they were in a hurry to proceed, and were willing to commit significant resources to the project, a necessary step given the scale of the proposed works. The new proposal was potentially more threatening to the CHR than a revised PDR as Vignoles and Brunel had a second crossing to Anglesey in mind, probably near Caernarfon.[2] That was confirmed in the evidence given at the Select Committee on the Oxford, Worcester and Wolverhampton Railway (OWW) in 1845 where a map 'with a line from Tremadoc [to] *Holyhead*' (my italics) was presented.[3] GWR chairman Charles Saunders made clear that intention – telling the select committee that he had, 'no doubt but that the Great Western would make the line to Port Dynllaen *or Holyhead*' (my italics) once the legislation for it was passed.[4] The seriousness of the GWR bid was reinforced by extensive commitments of cash, as reported at the OWW meeting in March 1846, which heard that the line was widely supported by landowners and had subscriptions that included '£1m (£117m) from the GWR, OWW £500,000 (£58.5m); Shrewsbury and Hereford Railway and other lines £2,750,000 (£323m)'.[5] Prime Minister Sir Robert Peel had emphasised the need for direct routes and a journey time that allowed mail to be

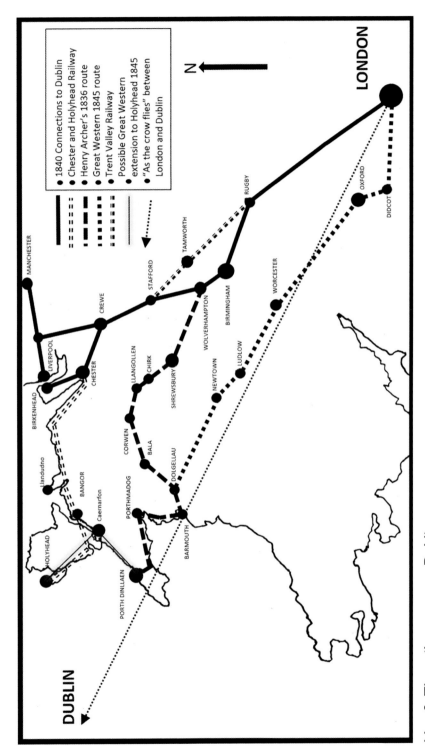

Map 2: The railway race to Dublin.

Legend:

1840 Connections to Dublin
Chester and Holyhead Railway
Henry Archer's 1836 route
Great Western 1845 route
Trent Valley Railway
Possible Great Western extension to Holyhead 1845
"As the crow flies" between London and Dublin

answered the day it was received in Dublin – so at this meeting Saunders tackled the prime minister's requirements head-on. He told the meeting that its route to Dublin was as direct: 'as if it were made by a ruler [and would] become the main through communication between the metropolis and our sister kingdom'.[6] Map 2 shows that he was correct in his assertion about the directness of the route.

But there was a note of caution in a report of the same meeting. The OWW and the PDR lines were to be built on the GWR's seven-foot gauge, as compared to the bulk of British railways in 1846 that were on the so-called 'narrow gauge' of four feet eight and a half inches. The issue was fiercely debated at that time: and the meeting heard that the Gauge Commission (GC) had concluded in 1845 that the narrow gauge should predominate north of a line roughly from Bristol to London – although some exceptions were allowed. Nonetheless, the GWR chairman remained optimistic that the branch to Porth Dinllaen would be allowed on broad gauge because in the summer of 1846 the powerful Grand Junction Railway (GJR) appeared to favour a route to London via Wolverhampton, Worcester and Oxford rather than via Birmingham. That would have effectively deprived the London and Birmingham Railway (LBR) of ready access to Manchester and Liverpool when the Corn Laws were to be abolished and international trade would boom from those major cities. Such an amalgamation would also frustrate Prime Minister Peel's plans for the Trent Valley Railway (TVR) in his own constituency, which he saw shortening the route to the north-west and Ireland and making Tamworth the heart of the postal network.

Peel's term as prime minister was coming to an end, amid the controversy of the abolition of the Corn Laws which was finally effected in May 1846. Other key decisions, such as that of the railway gauge, were taken as Peel's administration faded. Additionally, in July 1846 Parliament passed the London and North Western Railway (LNWR) Act that created the company of that name and bound together the GJR and the LBR. That put an end to GJR plans to collaborate with the GWR. The two decisions on the gauge and the creation of the LNWR thus left the GWR with no large allies north of Birmingham and no line towards Dublin, apart from the south Wales line to Milford Haven. That meant a sea crossing to south-east Ireland and a long and difficult coastal route north to Dublin that would not be built for many years. So, the GWR bid for a high-speed link to Dublin, the lucrative mail contract and the supremacy of Bristol over Manchester ended – and with it the hopes of Porth Dinllaen.

The Bill for the line to Porth Dinllaen, which had passed a second reading, was withdrawn because the effect of the decisions in Parliament was to prevent that line being made on the broad gauge. The whiff of parliamentary chicanery on behalf of the interests of Manchester and Liverpool hung heavily over the demise of the GWR scheme. It would have provided a shorter route, deployed more powerful locomotives, benefited the north Wales economy – and guaranteed a faster communication between London and Dublin – which had been the whole point of the race to Dublin. But it had been usurped by more parochial considerations. Government did at least recognise the huge benefit its decisions had bestowed on the CHR and required it to contribute £200,000 (£23.5m) towards the cost of the new harbour at Holyhead. In return, the CHR received exclusive use of the prime inner harbour site that included the right to run a railway onto it.[7] Even that demand on the CHR did not stick, as we shall see.

But the ever-demanding CHR wanted more, and in February 1847 requested that government permit it to run a complete service from London to Dublin, including the sea crossing. According to the CHR, Holyhead was only 'an intermediate station on a grand route' and it further argued that the only way to gain full advantage from it was to make 'the steamboat interest identical with that of the railway'.[8] That was a major step requiring a policy change by government, as the operation of steamships by railway companies was considered monopolistic in the 1840s.

The chairman of the Select Committee on Holyhead Harbour 'did not think that, under any circumstances, Parliament ought to sanction the avowed intention of [the CHR] to become steam-ship proprietors, either directly or indirectly'.[9] The issue was referred to the Railway Commissioners – established in 1846 partly to deal with such disputes – alongside a similar bid from the London and South Western Railway that wished to run steamships from the south coast to France.[10] The conclusions underline how different was the CHR from other railways. The commissioners considered that the sea passage to Dublin was: 'a portion of the railway enterprise' and that, although the route from the south coast to France was 'of considerable public importance [it] does not afford such strong grounds for exception … as the case of the [CHR]'.[11]

When the matter was referred to committee, the CHR opponents were doubtless dismayed that Sir Robert Peel was the chairman because there was surely no greater guarantee of the result. In committee, Peel did not disappoint the CHR supporters as he underlined the special nature of the railway and confessed that his government had:

> … always looked upon the railway as a great national undertaking the terminus of which was not, in fact, Holyhead, but Dublin [so that they] had departed from the ordinary rules and granted a sum of money to assist in carrying it out.[12]

Labouchere, as president of the Board of Trade: 'approached the consideration of the bill with a strong impression … against allowing railway companies to become steam-boat proprietors (hear, hear), he nonetheless assented to the company being given that power'.[13] The measure was agreed by 166 votes to 46, even though another company was willing and able to undertake the work.[14] Once again, the urgency of the situation in Ireland may have been a factor. In the same issue as the steamboat report, the *Freeman's Journal* referred to the situation in Ireland as the 'reign of Whiggery – the reign of famine, pestilence, and death, with the consummating perfection of military law, of summary tribunals [and] arbitrary hangings and burnings all over the country'.[15] In these circumstances, government perhaps preferred to have the whole route to Dublin under a single management to secure rapid and efficient communication.

Unsurprisingly, Irish opinion was not so favourable because the City of Dublin Steam Packet Company had acquired a wealthy and influential rival on the route between Holyhead and Dublin. No surprise too that the *Cork Examiner* accused Sir Robert Peel of favouritism. It described the decision as a 'job' and noted that Peel's performance as chairman has been subject to some:

> … animadversion [censure] in the accomplishment of a private agreement he made with the company, when in office, six or seven years since [that the CHR] shall have exclusive use of the most convenient part of the new Holyhead harbour [and] be allowed to become steamship owners [and have] a monopoly of traffic.[16]

But parliament ignored such opposition and duly granted the power to operate steamships to the CHR.

Another example of the special relationship between the CHR and the government was the electric telegraph. In this case, it was a requirement of government for its own benefit, although the telegraph was later a vital element in the management of railways. The use of the telegraph was proposed by government only two months after building the CHR began. The reason was summarised by the *Chester Chronicle:* 'closer connection between the metropolis and the sister isle, is of a nature not to be overlooked in a political or social point of view'.[17] By 1850, the Electric Telegraph Company was reported to be in the process of building the link.[18] In June 1852, the *Freeman's Journal* reported that a: 'final grand test was applied to the telegraphic cable by connecting the wire with one of the ships['] loaded guns and passing the word "Fire" to Holyhead. The answer was the immediate discharge of the gun'.[19]

The CHR began construction of its line amid all this political manoeuvring with little publicity and no ceremony on St David's Day 1845 at works for the tunnel just west of Conwy station. Two weeks later, there was praise for the directors' attempts to manage the behaviour of the navvies and some detail of the scale of operations:

We congratulate our readers on the actual commencement of the [CHR]. The determination on the part of the directors to incur no small pecuniary outlay in order to promote moral habits in the workmen, is as deserving of praise as their intention of utterly discountenancing the truck system [whereby workers received payment in kind or in the form of tokens redeemable only at company outlets]. Ten thousand tons of iron rails (half the quantity required for the entire line) are … already contracted for [and] several contracts have already been made for parts of the line at a much lower figure than the estimates; and the shares are obviously rising.[20]

7. *Work on the Chester and Holyhead railway began at the Conwy tunnel on St David's Day 1845. In January 2020, a rather grubby ten-coach Avanti West Coast train in Virgin Trains' colours passes the spot on its way to Holyhead.* (**Photo: Phil Lloyd Collection**)

There was activity at Chester too, with a tunnel under Upper Northgate Street, a breach in the town walls and various cuttings and embankments being formed. In one cutting there was a bed of blue clay that was used to make bricks, probably for the large viaduct adjacent to the racecourse. The city was thus a hive of activity with expectations that 'in a few days pile driving will commence for the bridge over the Dee'.[21] That optimistic description stands in stark contrast to the usual accounts of railway construction in the 1840s and could scarcely survive. Construction was soon accompanied by frequent death and injury, this account in a local newspaper being typical:

> On Thursday last, as Mr Farm, superintendent of the works … was proceeding along the beach under the cliff at Penmaenmawr, one of the men threw over a barrowful of stones from the road, which, falling upon Mr F, inflicted two severe wounds upon his head and face. … On the following day, a much more dreadful accident befell one of the men (named Henry Evans), by the sudden fall of a quantity of earth upon him. This poor fellow has received a fracture of the spine, and one of his thighs is broken in two places: he still survives, but there is little or no hope of his recovery as he is totally paralysed below the seat of injury in the spine. The sufferer is 31 years of age, unmarried, and is a native of Dwygyfylchi [near Conwy] where the accident happened. On the day after, another of the men had his head much injured in the tunnel at Penmaenmawr.[22]

By January 1846, it was reported that the 'truck system'– earlier claimed as absent from the works – was operating on the CHR as on many other railway construction sites: 'There was scarcely a sub-contractor who pays the men's wages in coin; and that the latter are compelled to take inferior necessaries of life from their employers, and at an enormous price'.[23] Within two months trouble erupted in Chester when workers struck for an advance of wages and marched along the line insisting that others joined the action. Those who refused were pelted with stones and order was only restored when the police took the ringleaders to court. Fearing a more widespread dispute, the company withdrew its complaint and work resumed.[24]

The issues were not just financial. These works were being undertaken in the 'Hungry Forties' when there was too little employment and fierce competition for jobs on the railway where pay was good. The contest for work took on a national character with a prominent Welsh literary figure called Iona Merion arguing in June 1845 that if 'a Welshman does anything, by word or deed, directly or indirectly, towards depriving Welsh labourers of the first chance of being employed on the CHR, [he] is a wretched traitor to his own country'.[25] A year later in the 'Battle of Penmaenmawr' Welsh and English navvies on the line took rather more direct action to reinforce his point when they attacked Irish labourers and drove them along the line towards Bangor, where one the leaders of the Welsh contingent was captured. A full-blown riot ensued that was only calmed by the escape of the prisoner and summoning troops by ship from Liverpool.[26]

The immense Victorian faith in the power of science to overcome all problems received a severe shock soon after the first trains began to operate from Chester over the new bridge across the Dee towards Wrexham. Milkman Thomas Jones paused to watch the novelty of a train going over the bridge and told the inquest what he saw in May 1847:

> When [the train] got to the nearest arch to Saltney, I perceived a crack open in the bottom of the girder. The engine and tender were then past the cracked girder. The engine went on, the tender gave a rise up, the carriages gave a jump, and fell back, and the last carriages went down first into the Dee.[27]

8. *Resentment of Irish workers by Welsh and English 'navvies' resulted in a serious and prolonged riot in May 1846 that began here at Penmaenmawr and spread along the works all the way to Bangor, where an urgent call for military help was issued. It was all a lot calmer in October 1978 as a diesel multiple unit trundles east in glorious sunshine.* **(Photo: John Hobbs)**

More troubling for the CHR was the account of Henry Robertson who was the engineer of the Shrewsbury and Chester Railway Company, and a prominent figure in Welsh railway construction for many years. It was not his business to inspect the bridge because it was not owned by his company, but he was concerned by the improper use of cast iron. He travelled over the bridge in a small train the day before the accident and he told the inquest that he did not approve of the way it had been built.

This severe blow to CHR chief engineer Robert Stephenson's reputation came as he was battling with the problem of crossing the Menai Straits at a level high enough to satisfy the Admiralty, but cheap enough to keep shareholders happy. The solution was the 'tunnel in the air' over the Menai Straits supported by chains, using the Britannia Rock as a base in the middle.[28] But before he reached the Menai Straits, he had to cross the River Clwyd at Rhyl and the Conwy at its estuary. Just four months after the Chester inquest, and with government still pondering the future of cast iron bridges such as the one that had failed at the Dee, it was his

9. *The collapse of the Dee Bridge in May 1847 was an early disaster for the CHR and its engineer Robert Stephenson. Here former GWR engine 6000* George V *is on a heritage trip as it passes the spot where the Shrewsbury and Chester Railway train fell into the river killing five people and imperilling Stephenson's reputation.* **(Photo: David Plimmer)**

father George Stephenson who took a party to examine the river crossing at Foryd near Rhyl, where he was described as the 'principal engineer'. Once again, his status was needed to deal with a political and technical problem:

> A special train arrived at the Rhyl station … conveying the directors, their friends, the principal engineer, George Stephenson, … and a numerous party of gentlemen … On their arrival, the train stopped to allow a few ladies to alight, the gentlemen immediately proceeding to the Foryd bridge [and] from thence by lorries with horsepower to Conway. … Every possible effort is being made to complete the works, and in a few weeks the public will be accommodated as far as Conway by this great national undertaking. The carriages were the property of the London and North Western Company, thousands of old and young thronged from all parts of the country to witness the event.[29]

10. *In 1839 George Stephenson claimed that the River Clwyd could be crossed by the railway equivalent of a 'common road bridge'. Eight years later he had to supervise a much more complex operation in the aftermath of the failure of his son Robert's efforts over the River Dee in 1847. In August 2020, under a leaden sky, a Transport for Wales class 158 crosses the substantial structure at high tide.* (**Photo: Phil Lloyd Collection**)

By March 1848 Robert Stephenson was facing a major engineering test in the form of the passage over the River Conwy and a dress rehearsal for the Menai Straits. In both cases he opted for the tubular bridge design but faced the problem of raising the tubes into position. At Conwy, the height of the bridge was much lower than for the crossing to Anglesey, but after the calamity at Chester Stephenson could take no risks. So:

> Certain experiments were made on the tube, under the immediate inspection of Mr [Robert] Stephenson, the engineer, when the interior of the tube was loaded with a weight to the extent of 100, 200, and 300 tons, by which its strength was properly tested, and proved to give the utmost satisfaction … Signals and telegraphs were properly stationed.
>
> There were two strong chains fixed at both ends … orders were given for the workmen at the cranes, fixed inside the pontoons, and the men stationed at the three crabs on shore, from which preventive ropes were fixed to the tube, to commence working, and instantly the immense island was observed to move majestically above the surface of the deep, and … amidst the shouts of the populace, the roars of cannon, and music of the band as the tide ran off, it was rested with ease on its proper foundation. … Three cheers for Mr Stephenson, who stood on the top of the tube, quite calm at the time, smoking a cigar, and also to Captain Claxton, rent the air, by some five or six thousand spectators. Thus, was one of the most stupendous works of human science brought to a successful issue, without the least accident, all the operations seeming to have the regularity of watch work movements.[30]

Stephenson's triumphant experience on top of the tube was rather different from that of 'a young English lad, about 14 years of age' during the previous November. The unnamed boy was:

> Engaged on the top of the railway tube at Conway: his foot tripped, and he fell over, down to the beach, striking against the platform, on which the tube rests, in his fall. The injuries he sustained were a dislocation of the hip and of the knee, and a severe fracture of the leg together with several cuts and bruises on the head and other parts of the body.[31]

He was not the first victim of Stephenson's bridge-building exploits and would not be the last: whether he was fit enough to witness the engineer's success is not known, but his experience was apparently insufficient to counter the view that the bridge had been completed 'without the least accident'.

11. *Robert Stephenson supervised operations from the roof of the first tube as it was placed at Conwy in 1848, all the while smoking a large cigar. In this picture trains are already running through that tube and the second will soon be in place.* (**Photo: Phil Lloyd Collection**)

By May 1848, the line had reached Bangor where there were elaborate celebrations. Some idea of the scale of the works may be seen from an advertisement for the sale of what was left at Talybont, on the outskirts of Bangor, in June 1848.

14 Boarded Cottages, with Brick Chimneys, Kitchen ranges and Grates, and 1 Boarded Shed. At Aber 8 Boarded and 3 Brick Cottages, with Brick Chimneys, Kitchen ranges and Grates; several Thousands of Bricks; a great number of Brick barrows; Moulding Tables, Screen Boards; and other necessaries suitable for extensive Brickfields. Also, 255 capital Oak Timbers, suitable for Ship and Boat builders, House Carpenters, Wheelwrights, Farmers etc.[32]

Meanwhile, Robert Stephenson maintained a consistent, nervous presence, but not always without mishap, including one at Conwy that nearly caused his death, and in which the behaviour of his employees was hardly reassuring. His famous father had died shortly before the incident in September 1848, so both these great engineers could have been lost in rapid succession. Stephenson was inspecting the works by train when:

> It appears that on the arrival of the express train [at Conwy] from Bangor it was deemed necessary to put on another first-class carriage. The porters were in the act of pushing the carriage across the down line, when the express train from Chester was observed coming along at full speed; and the men, to avoid the danger, left the carriage, and as it afterwards appeared, before it was quite clear of the line … In a few minutes, the Chester express train came up at a great speed; the engine caught the projecting corner of the carriage, throwing the whole about a yard from the rails, and smashing the wheels, glass door, and a portion of the framework in pieces. Immediately after the collision Mr Stephenson was seen descending the steps and was observed to fall on his back. He was instantly taken up and supported to the station house … It was found that he was much stunned and rendered almost unconscious by the shock and fall but we are happy to say that in a short time he was able to walk to the Castle Hotel. The next morning, he left for Chester.[33]

12. *Conway [sic] station opened in May 1848 and was constructed in keeping with the ancient surroundings. It was here that Robert Stephenson came close to a fatal accident in September 1848. This picture was taken in 1919 as the LNWR neared its end.* (Photo: John Alsop Collection)

The same process of bridge building used at Conwy was applied at the Menai Straits for the greater task of crossing that larger channel at a much greater height. Eight tubes were created close to the site with a total length of 2,760 feet, a total weight of 4,680 tons and using 2 million rivets. They were floated on pontoons to the correct position and then raised to the pillars that were created as the tubes were being constructed. It would have been a massive test of ingenuity in modern times: in the 1840s it was a venture into the unknown.

The process created a sense of excitement, as though this project represented a test of the stature of the nation itself, similar perhaps to the importance of the moon landing to the United States in the 1960s. The sense of anticipation was heightened in May 1849 when the engineers decided to hold a concert inside one of the completed tubes on the banks of the straits. No expense was spared as the son of the famous composer Haydn was engaged for the evening. Access to the tube was along a grove created by foliage and the lighting was by hundreds of candles. The engineers were careful to engage all levels of the local population and workforce, who attended in large numbers to hear a full programme of entertainment including a memorable solo – 'Thy smile dear maid' – by Master Haydn, set to music composed by his father.[34]

Once the lifting of the tubes began in June 1849 the sense of national drama was palpable. For example, in Manchester it was reported that:

On Monday evening the first experiment was made to test the buoyancy of the pontoons; and the tube was lowered about three feet by taking away the temporary packings in order that it might be floated off easier next day. Everything was perfectly satisfactory, and the greatest hopes were entertained that the giant fabric would be safely deposited in its resting place the next morning. Unfortunately, however, the day was ushered in with heavy driving showers, the barometer fell rapidly, and the wind rose to a hurricane, which entirely prevented anything being done at all until in the morning of Tuesday.[35]

By August, it was reported in Glasgow that the initial stage was passed, and the first tube was ready to be lifted amid the scientifically exact calculations that caused:

Considerable delay, inseparable from the stupendous character of the machinery, and the care required in adjusting it, and the calculations necessary to insure [*sic*] success in an experiment so vast and novel, have unavoidably taken place, so as to give time for the preparation of all appliances, and the bringing to bear all the engineering wisdom of the day upon a work that is watched with so much interest by the public and the scientific world … It is a grand sight to see the tube as it now hangs suspended in the chains swinging across the Straits during the present heavy gales in the Channel with a cradle-like motion.[36]

But in London three days later there was consternation:

All the fond and desired hopes of a successful realisation of raising the monster tube of this stupendous bridge to its final resting place are, for the next two months at least, suspended. A few minutes before noon of this day, the lower part of the cylinder of the huge hydraulic press on the Anglesea [*sic*] side burst with a tremendous explosion, and in its descent on to the tube, a height of about 84 feet, fell with a terrible crash. The press was at work at the time and had raised the tube about three feet during the lift this day; and had it not been for the very urgent and precautionary means adopted, by packing and bricking under with cement as the tube was being raised, the most dreadful consequences were inevitable.[37]

At least one man paid for the failure with his life, but that was passed over by the reports in a fairly desultory manner: as was the overall state of the works from a sanitary point of view although a local committee described the conditions for employees and their families as 'extremely filthy'.[38]

By October it was noted in Oxford that:

Active preparations are being made at the Menai Straits connected with the renewed attempt at raising the tube to its permanent level; a process looked forward to with considerable anxiety in consequence of the late misadventure. The new cylinder, intended to replace the one that sprung, is safely deposited at the works, and operations for hoisting it to its berth are being carried on incessantly.[39]

A week later an Ipswich newspaper noted that the: 'The process of raising the Britannia Bridge proceeds most successfully … There is now a clear height of 55 feet beneath the tube at high water, so that small vessels begin to pass under it.'[40] The sense of euphoria grew as the tube slowly moved to its elevated position. One man was so overwhelmed with the enormity of the achievement that he staged his own tribute in the form of a 'Curious Christening' for his new-born child:

> The [girl] was taken to the Britannia Rock in the middle of the straits, where the ceremony was performed by the Rev Mr Jackson. She was named Britannia Ann Stephenson Hodgkinson in compliment to the great work and the great engineer. At the conclusion of a powerful prayer, delivered by the Rev Gentleman, he shouted, 'May this rock stand as firm as the Word of God.'[41]

It was a further month before the first tube was reported as being in its final place and the equipment was moved to make ready for the second. Unfortunately for the poor little girl named after the project, the burial registers for Chorlton-on-Medlock in Manchester showed her reaching her own final resting place in April 1852.

Meanwhile, the drama was not over. On 3 December 1849:

> Precisely at ten o'clock, when all parties engaged in the great operation were at their posts, and the signals had been sent out to the various stations, one of the great 5-inch-thick cables, reaching from the pontoons to the opposite shoreline [was found to have been] maliciously cut by some miscreants.[42]

But the same report in Leeds maintained an optimistic tone about this major test of national strength. It pointed out that even though the opening date of the bridge was March 1850 – four years after it started and well behind schedule – it still compared favourably to the eight years it took Telford to cross the Menai Straits, and involved 10,000 tons of iron compared to a paltry 644 tons for Telford's effort. After all this national drama, the bridge and the line were duly opened in March 1850 with the aid of a 'deflectometer' to measure any bend in the bridge under the weight of 240 tons of train.

Although the attention of the public had been focused on issues such as the completion of the bridges, the priority for government was the practical use of the CHR to further its desire to cement Ireland into the domestic empire of the UK. That depended crucially on the ability to communicate more rapidly than ever before between London and Dublin. The early indications, even before the Britannia Bridge was in place, were encouraging. In February 1850, a senior

BRITANNIA TUBULAR BRIDGE. LOOKING N.W.

ROBERT STEPHENSON, ENGINEER.

13. The Britannia tubular bridge was a formidable achievement and was regarded as evidence of the power of science and industry to conquer all. It survived 120 years before its destruction by fire. (Photo: Phil Lloyd Collection)

official at Dublin Castle wrote to the CHR thanking it for help with an urgent government matter:

> Sir – I am directed by the Lord Lieutenant to acknowledge, with many thanks, the copy of the Queen's Speech which was delivered at the Castle on the night of the 31 January; and to convey to you his sense of the energy and enterprise displayed by the [CHR] in making such arrangements as enabled them to transmit that important document to Dublin by the electric telegraph, an express engine, and a special steamer with a rapidity hitherto unexampled.[43]

Perhaps encouraged by this example, the government decided to take an early opportunity to test the apparent efficacy of the improved London–Dublin communication that coincided with the opening of the Britannia Tubular Bridge a month later. *The Times* identified the political potential of the bridge as soon as it opened:

> The passage of the first railway train through the tubular bridge … would seem to suggest the propriety of at length disclosing a 'secret' which has been

long known to everybody – that the days of the Lord-Lieutenant in Ireland are numbered. The communication between London and Dublin for passengers is now reduced to an easy day's journey [and] we have the electric telegraph … to convey orders and intelligence at any rate as far as Holyhead – almost with the speed of thought … the little pageant in Dublin Castle has now become a mere burlesque – a ceremony without a meaning, an expense without a result … The time has arrived for placing Ireland upon the same footing as Great Britain and removing an invidious distinction that was only justified by the difficulties of dilatory and doubtful communication.[44]

This was a remarkable development; a proposal for a major constitutional change based directly on the creation of a railway line. The comments of *The Times* proved to be an accurate estimate of the government's intentions, as articulated in parliament by Prime Minister Lord John Russell the next day.[45] Russell brought his firm proposals to Parliament in May 1850 and noted that in former times it was necessary to have a person in authority in Dublin because of the problems of communication. That argument had vanished because of 'the facility and rapidity of the means of locomotion between the two countries'. If those listening were unsure of his meaning, he convinced them by producing a novel piece of evidence:

There is no document to which I could appeal – no papers I could lay before the House – which would be so convincing on that subject, as a work well known to the Members of this House, called *Bradshaw's Railway Guide.* [In it they would find] that a steamer arrives in Kingstown harbour at half-past 10 at night, conveying the intelligence which has left London the same morning.[46]

This was, he suggested, far better than the speed of communication with Edinburgh at the time of Scotland joining the Union in 1707 and provided the best reason to end the local government from Dublin Castle. Prime Minister Russell proposed replacing the lord lieutenant with a fourth secretary of state in his Cabinet.

His proposal was not well received by the Irish Members. For example, John Reynolds, the MP for Dublin City, was dismissive of the basis of Russell's argument:

First, it had been said that the office was to be abolished on principles of economy; and now it was to be abolished on scientific grounds, because Mr Stephenson the engineer had invented a tube to connect the two countries more closely together; but some fine morning the tube might break down; and

God help the country which depended for prosperity and for the maintenance of her institutions upon an iron tube![47]

The government won the vote, but it was unable to challenge the crushing authority of the Duke of Wellington, the victor of Waterloo and the 'greatest man in England', who pronounced on the issue ten days later.[48] He took no comfort from the improved technology available to government, but preferred a more old-fashioned version of battlefield command, conducted close to the action:

The civil and military power, at almost every moment during the last ten years, have been in constant communication with each other, and I tell your lordships that you cannot carry on any of these operations without the superintending direction and assistance of the Lord Lieutenant.[49]

The measure was dropped on 4 July 1850 because, as Russell later explained, the doubts 'of persons whose opinion was entitled to attention'.[50] The failure of the measure did not detract from the fact that this was a remarkable initiative by government: an imperial constitutional change that was proposed entirely because rapid transit by railway was available.

All this assumed that the CHR increased the speed of communication between London and Dublin. But did it? I conducted research for the period 1820–1859 which suggested that the CHR did not improve the time taken for postal communication between London and Dublin. The time lag data show that the completion of the London to Holyhead road in 1826 took about two days off the London to Dublin time compared to 1820 and 1821 when it took six days. There was little further change until the mail was switched to rail and concentrated at Liverpool in 1839, and then sent from Birkenhead in 1841 when a faster rail journey was established to that port. The latter change delivered a steady two-day time lag in summer and a two- to three-day time lag in winter – although in the last three years of this service, two days was a consistent performance in both summer and winter.

The most surprising conclusion is that there was no further improvement when the service switched to the CHR in 1848; and no improvement from that on the opening of the Britannia Bridge. That is a remarkable finding, given the immense effort and expense that had been incurred in completing this line. Stephenson's original estimate was £2.1m (£246.5m) but the CHR had authorised capital of £2.75m (£323m) and authorised loans of £926,000 (£109m), a total of £3.68m (£432m).[51] The bridge to Anglesey alone had cost £674,000 (£79m) although only estimated by Stephenson at £250,000 (£29m).[52] The evidence above suggests that this investment did not improve the time taken for communication from London to Dublin, even though that was the main – or only – justification for building the line.[53]

Although this failure of the CHR to deliver any benefit for the loss of lives and expense incurred in its construction has not been recorded by its historians, it was noticed at the time. Henry Herbert, MP for Kerry, addressed the House of Commons in April 1853:

> When [Russell] introduced his Bill for abolishing the office of Lord Lieutenant of Ireland, he had observed … that science had superseded the attributes of the gods, and had annihilated both time and space, so perfect had the communication become between the two countries. That communication, however, … did not in any way deserve the eulogium passed upon it.[54]

The subsequent select committee was extremely critical. The service was 'not only defective in speed and convenience, but inferior to what it was previous to the year 1850'.[55] The committee members picked out the slowness of the rail journey to Holyhead and the low calibre of the vessels from Holyhead to Dublin for particular mention. It concluded that with better management, the journey could be accomplished in eleven hours instead of the fourteen hours and twenty-five minutes it was found to take. Eleven hours was the exact time promised by the GWR in return for an agreement to its broad-gauge line from London to Porth Dinllaen via Worcester in 1846. One witness, for whom the 'abominations and nastiness' of the service were so bad that it was not 'polite to describe them in plain English', suggested that lack of competition on the route to Dublin was a cause of the slack performance and argued for a rival broad gauge route from London to Birkenhead.[56]

The subsequent detailed performance management by government finally provided the service it required by 1860 when the mail was only delayed on four occasions, and only one counted as an unreasonable delay.[57] This improvement was aided by innovations such as the troughs at Mochdre that allowed engines to collect water without stopping. These were relocated to Aber in 1871 because the water supply was better. By then the politics of Ireland had moved on and the moment for a decisive technological impact had passed, though in reality the complexities of the relationship between Ireland and Britain were always beyond resolution by the application of technology alone.

The political environment that emerged in Ireland after the Great Famine and O'Connell's death in 1847, including an abortive rebellion in 1848, was increasingly militant and nationalistic. The London government began to understand that

14. Non-stop running was an important feature of the CHR as it focused on the fast mail route between London and Dublin. The LNWR established the world's first water troughs at Mochdre in 1860 to support this, but the supply was better just east of Aber where the pictured troughs were located in 1871. (Photo: John Alsop Collection)

Irish nationalism was stronger and more deep-rooted than it had imagined and plans for direct rule were abandoned. The CHR continued to perform a valuable task by carrying the mail to Holyhead, though the government gave the contract for the sea passage of the mail to the City of Dublin Steam Packet Company in 1850 – a strange outcome given that the CHR was given special powers to operate steamships. That was probably the result of sustained Irish political pressure at Westminster. The CHR was routinely referred to as an 'imperial line' during the arguments for its establishment as the fast route between London and Dublin. The pace and direction of the decisions on the CHR followed the political pulse of Ireland in the period 1841–1850 and makes it difficult not to conclude that the CHR did serve an avowedly imperial purpose.

In 1843 Peel revived government interest in a rapid route to Ireland when its place in the UK was regarded as a pressing imperial question. The CHR was specified by Peel as part of government's Irish policy in 1843 and so the railway was effectively an imperial railway. But the presence of the Irish Sea meant that the link with Dublin was always about railway plus steamships and subsequently the electric telegraph as well. Thus, the most powerful combination of imperial technology available to government in the nineteenth century – railways, steamships and the electric telegraph – made its first appearance in the governance of Ireland and created the model for later rule in India and elsewhere around the globe. The fact that Westminster failed to create direct rule of Ireland based on the availability of the trilogy of technologies does not alter the fact that the CHR was commissioned for an imperial purpose – and therefore has a strong claim to be the world's first truly imperial railway.

3

The Arrival of the Railway in North Wales

The [LNWR] had only accomplished in commerce what [the landowners] had done in feudalism long ago. They had woven a girdle which now completed the circle round Wales, and they had done so in a manner that would neither disturb artists or tourists. Their object had been to bring coal into North Wales and take back slates.[1]

The struggle for control of north Wales in the mid-nineteenth century by the two major railway companies – the London and North Western (LNWR) and the Great Western (GWR) – was conducted as a strategic battle for a region that was important for the access that it gave to Ireland and especially Dublin. Wales was largely irrelevant within the spheres of government or commerce. If this was true of the whole country, it was especially true of north Wales. Here was an area with little manufacturing industry, small-scale extractive industries and no major towns of note. The contrast between the region and the company that operated the bulk of its railways could hardly have been greater. The LNWR was the largest industrial corporation in the world, was a national rather than regional railway and operated as such. Its interest in regions such as north Wales was initially for wider strategic purposes, rather than for any traffic that the region offered to them. The LNWR nonetheless dominated communication and transport *in* the region even while its focus was on *getting through* the region.

This lack of local interest was reinforced at a shareholders meeting in 1848 when one attendee pointed out, 'The commencement of the railway was at Chester, and it was desirable to know whether the directors contemplated any change in their plan, which was to result in the transfer of the offices to that town'[2] That received a vague reply that suggested that if it were cheaper to do so they might move to Chester. But Chester was not the start of the line as Peel's plans had made clear. The start was in London and the end was Dublin; what happened in between did not really concern the directors or government in 1848 – so long as delays did not occur in communication between the two capitals.

While Ireland may have been the greater political challenge to the London government, Wales was perhaps the more alien in terms of its language and customs; the least English of the countries that made up the UK, though for some it was not a country at all. Where Ireland had absentee landlords, Wales had a powerful, English, resident elite. In north Wales in particular, that elite was based on the ownership of land. The landowners were personally identifiable but the LNWR was a new brand of commerce, owned by shareholders and run by a professional elite. It was not, however, the *intention* of the LNWR to establish dominance of north Wales for itself, but rather for the strategic position that it held in relation to the lucrative Irish traffic. However, as an LNWR director pointed out, its presence in the region had repaid the company handsomely:

> It was true they were accused of a grasping policy in extending their lines in all directions [but] by subsidising, making and buying lines, the [LNWR] had opened up a series of branches to all parts of the country. … Every success had attended this enterprise [and north Wales had] amply compensated the company.[3]

The previous chapter showed that the Chester and Holyhead Railway (CHR) – and its parent company the LNWR – had unique advantages. Its line was authorised by Parliament and then built in the face of some technical advice to the contrary about the route and the harbour at Holyhead. It was given the power to operate steamers on a long-distance route ahead of any other major railway company – while its most serious opponent, the GWR, was prevented from competing by the decisions in favour of the narrower gauge and by the creation of the LNWR itself. While the CHR was not given the contract for the sea carriage of the mail, it was granted exclusive use of the best part of the harbour at Holyhead and allowed to extend its line right up to the packet harbour – giving it a distinct advantage over its rival shipping company.

The harbour was a massive investment of public money from which this private company benefited immensely. Nonetheless the CHR was not satisfied and wanted more money from government. Its complaints worked to the extent that the CHR was relieved in 1850 of its commitment to pay £200,000 (£27m) towards the harbour.[4] However, there was a continued sense of grievance into the 1850s against concessions to the CHR, especially from shipping interests in Liverpool who feared Holyhead as a rival for their own traffic, but there were no new substantial concessions for the CHR from government after 1850.[5] The failure of the government to secure the abolition of the lord lieutenancy noted in the previous chapter may have contributed, as may the knowledge that the CHR's partner and operating company – the LNWR – was an extremely wealthy concern, well able to sustain any short-term financial problems and exploit fully the opportunities in Irish and Welsh traffic.

The CHR weathered its 1850 crisis by securing the services of Samuel Morton Peto as chairman – a man with a long history of involvement with railway construction, and partner in the firm Peto and Betts that constructed part of the CHR. Peto gave the CHR some financial stability in the face of three problems encountered in 1850: the GWR's successful opposition to formal acquisition of the CHR by the LNWR; the government refusal of a loan for the CHR; and the death of Peel, a consistent and powerful supporter of the CHR.[6] Peto's energetic response to those challenges meant that the CHR finally engaged to some degree with the economy of north Wales as part of its recovery plan:

> Your directors are using all the means at their command so to increase their power of meeting the demand for accommodation for minerals [by the] construction by private parties, of several sidings and short branches for the purpose of bringing upon the line the produce of adjacent quarries.[7]

The greater exploitation of local trades was advocated in 1848 by Edward Parry, the first chronicler of the line, who argued that the CHR was missing a great opportunity of engaging with the local community and economy of north Wales by ignoring the language and culture of its people.[8] It was an important critique of the CHR's operational practice, demonstrating that it was unwilling to engage with the local economy, culture and language of the Welsh people and benefit from their local knowledge. His views were clearly unwelcome and, until Peto arrived, the CHR continued to insist that government should make up any shortfall in revenue because it had effectively commissioned the line. Peto addressed the potential for traffic from within north Wales, but the overall CHR attitude to the region, articulated by Parry, shows that it was essentially an English company operating in an unfamiliar environment in which the population spoke a different language, did not generally attend the established Church, and knew little of modernity in general and railways in particular.

There were some examples of innovative local working such as that given by Peto at the 1851 meeting. After referring to the creation of sidings at Conwy, he gave a local example of the wider liberal free trade vision of the new world created by railways – profit for the capitalist delivering a result for the poor. He also articulated the strict sense of status that existed within the railway hierarchy:

I would here just refer for a moment to a slight matter which, I think, reflects much credit on one of the officers of the company and although the person referred to is a subordinate officer, and simply occupies the position of stationmaster, yet I felt it right to state who he is, that this public notice of his services may stimulate others to a constant consideration of the company's interests.

[He] – observing the unemployed state of the fishing population of [Conwy] endeavoured to induce the fishermen to turn their attention to the matter, and with the approbation of the board he offered a small sum in furtherance of the object. The result is that you are at this moment carrying from that station to Manchester between 160 and 200 tons of shellfish monthly. The catching of those fish employs the fishermen themselves, while the sorting of the fish engages the services of a large number of the women and children of the district; so that in this instance we are not only contributing to the welfare of the community but securing a traffic which yields … something like £2,000 per annum [£280,000].[9]

In the same year, the Anglesey Coal Company was formed to exploit the three seams near the railway line at Malltraeth, for sale of coal in the region and for export to Ireland.[10] But it was the slate trade that held the greatest potential as north Wales became the centre of a worldwide demand. It is perhaps surprising that the CHR did not engage with this trade earlier but there had been problems. The Pennant family at Bangor had its own harbour and tramway to bring slate from its quarries and send it by sea, and they were initially reluctant to use the CHR. The Assheton Smith family near Caernarfon wanted a railway and harbour at Porth Dinllaen and so were initially hostile to the CHR. By 1851 reality had dawned on both families and Peto reported to the shareholders that traffic from both quarries would soon be carried by the railway.[11] By September 1852 Peto could report that: 'the slate depot at Saltney [Mold Junction] was progressing and would be finished in the course of two months. The cattle sheds, yard, and loading places at Holyhead, necessary for the full development of the Irish traffic, were completed and ready for use'.[12]

And the process continued at various places along the line in the succeeding decades, including the boom in coal mining in Flintshire that began in the late 1860s at places such as Mancot near Queensferry, where Lord Mostyn's Prestatyn Coal Company sank two pits close to the line.[13] The boom along the Flintshire coast attracted other railway developments, notably the Wrexham, Mold and Connah's Quay (WMCQR) railway that opened in 1862. Relations

15. In April 1978, 24035 is shunting at Mold Junction. Behind the train are the four main running lines and on the other side the remains of the yard that was once used to distribute slate from all the major north Wales quarries served by the LNWR. (Photo: David Plimmer)

between the companies were not always cordial, and although the LNWR built a station at Connah's Quay in April 1870 it did not appear in the LNWR timetable until September because of a dispute with the WMCQR over a siding.[14] In 1884 the LNWR opened another station in Flintshire at Sandycroft, largely to tap into traffic to and from the local engineering factory.[15] North Wales had not seen an English investment on the scale of the CHR since the chain of castles built by Edward 1 in the thirteenth century. The London to Holyhead Road, completed in the 1820s, was significant, but it did little more than enable horsepower to deliver a little extra speed.

The army of labourers building the line certainly made an impact on the senses of local people. According to the local paper, the CHR had provided:

16. *Transport for Wales 175107 takes advantage of the 75mph limit to speed past the site of Connah's Quay station on a hazy day in September 2020 on its way to Manchester Airport. The station closed in February 1966 – four years short of its centenary – and no trace remains.* (**Photo: Phil Lloyd Collection**)

Among other 'benefits', an inpouring of confessedly and notoriously the worst of our species, rough and ready for a strike, a shindy, or mischief of any sort. That was well beyond the district's capacity to manage for [apart from] a brace of constables and ten or a dozen specials in parishes … there were no other resources for keeping this large mass of combustible population from boiling over.[16]

SANDYCROFT RAILWAY STATION.

17. In October 1896 the body of Edward Benson, Archbishop of Canterbury, was sent from Sandycroft after he died in church during a visit to William Gladstone at Hawarden. This photograph of a Chester bound train was taken in 1904, fifteen years after the station opened. Sandycroft station closed in 1961 leaving little trace by 2020. (Photo: John Alsop Collection)

There was also the significant visual impact of the railway, for example with the arrival of the royal train for the first time in north Wales and particularly its emergence from the gigantic Britannia Tubular Bridge:

> Looking through the Tube you see the firebox of the engine gleaming as it advances from the other extremity. You hear the throb of the locomotive and the reverberation of the iron: the shriek of the steam whistle startles you with its almost demonical expression and as you listen and gaze, a mass of sound gradually accumulating to a perfect hurricane, swells upon the ear, while the brightening glow of the furnace and the majestic progress of the engine fill the eye and impress the imagination.[17]

The queen's visit to the famous bridge was an indication of the importance of the line and the scale of the architecture, even without the statue of Britannia, intended to adorn it but never built.[18] The Duke of Wellington made a private visit a month

18. *'The shriek of the steam whistle startles you with its almost demonical expression':* **45740** Munster *tries to recreate that 1852 impression of steam in north Wales as it bursts from the Britannia Tubular Bridge in 1960, past the site of the bridge station that closed in 1858.* **(Photo: Neville Stead Collection, Transport Library)**

after the station that served the bridge was opened in July 1851, when he, 'gazed on that stupendous pile with silent admiration ... wrapped up in his thoughts'.[19] Given his experience of bloody battlefields across the globe, the impression on local sensibilities was surely even greater.

That last point may be gauged by considering what may have been the first death of a bystander on the line:

Two ancient cockle-gatherers left their home ... in pursuit of their vocation. ... Having filled their baskets, the women bent their course homewards, passing through the gate on the line. One was short-sighted, the other deaf. At that instant, a train was rushing up at full speed. The deaf woman shouted to her companion, who, irresolute, hesitated for a moment and then pushed forward – fatal resolve. The engine caught her and crushed life out in an instant! Her name was Catherine Williams, aged 72 years, who might have calculated on dying in her bed at least, as the natural close of a long and laborious life.[20]

19. *Catherine Williams, a short-sighted cockle-gatherer aged seventy-two years, crossed the line between Aber and Bangor in July 1848 and was hit by an express train. She may have been the first bystander killed on the CHR. In September 2020, 158882 Birmingham to Holyhead strains to make up lost time at the same Wîg crossing now provided with safety gates.* **(Photo: Phil Lloyd Collection)**

Here was the clash between the old and new made real. The arrival of the railway first intruded on Catherine Williams' route to her work and then ended her life. It was a small example of what was happening on a larger scale in the region, if not always in death, then at least in a shock effect on many of the population.

Two more examples illustrate the failure of local people to appreciate the enormity of the new power. At Bangor, a man wandered onto the line and was removed just ahead of the emergence of a train from the tunnel.[21] A similar case at

Conwy station led the *North Wales Chronicle* to suggest a new proverb for the age; 'Tide, time and *train* wait for no man!'[22] (original italics) The railway also showed its power over nature in a manner that would have impressed itself forcibly upon the population and was important enough to warrant a newspaper report:

> [As] one of the trains on the [CHR] was passing down the line, at a rapid rate, a hare, startled at the noise, darted suddenly across the rails. Quick as [she was]; she was not rapid enough to escape her death; for in her spring, she was caught by the engine, and the head severed from the body. It was found in the engine on its stoppage at Bangor station.[23]

The hare – one of the fastest creatures – was no match for the power and speed of the railway. It seems likely that such a report could have startled the local population as much, if not more, than the death of the cockle gatherer.

Part of the loss of old ways was local time. The CHR adopted Greenwich Mean Time and even carried a clock throughout the *Irish Mail* journeys to ensure that timings were not confused with local time along the line. It was not an easy discipline for some to learn:

> We were sorry to observe a car with passengers come full tilt into the railway yard [at Bangor] just as the train had started for Chester. Here was a disappointment, the cause of which was the difference set in point of time, the railway clock being set to Greenwich time, the Town ditto as before. This will no doubt be set to right.[24]

But those with the means to use railways were more concerned to have more of them rather than concern themselves with their impact on the wider population. Thus, in November 1862 the local paper protested against the LNWR's reduced winter schedule and the difficulty in holding the company to account. From 1859, the line was no longer formally operated by the CHR, though its independent status had always been mostly a fiction. Three years later an influential gathering in Bangor attempted to influence the mighty LNWR. It included Lord Paget, Colonel Pennant and W.O. Stanley, who had all supported the CHR. The power of the LNWR was apparent in the meeting's reassurance that it was: 'got up in no hostile feeling for that company' and Lord Paget 'deprecated any spirit of hostility to [the LNWR]'.[25] However, reality was dawning that the interests of the LNWR were in getting *through* north Wales, rather than getting to or from the region. The meeting therefore complained that expresses no longer stopped at Bangor and that this was to the detriment of the town. These influential residents understood that the CHR was built 'not out of love for [Wales] but in order to get cheaply and quickly to that hotbed of loyalty and treason – Ireland'. But, according to the same correspondent in the local press, the results were:

> Something to astonish the Welsh nation … Look at the fine houses in those formerly deserted places – Aber, Llanfairfechan and Penmaenmawr [and] Bangor … its terraces which look like kings' palaces. … Now all this prosperity, and the increased trade, travelling accommodation … and the yearly rush of tens of thousands of rich visitors into every part of the country, are solely and entirely owing to railways. … As railways do so much good, we can scarcely have too many of them.[26]

A change of mood was apparent, nationally as well as locally, after the Abergele crash of August 1868 in which thirty-three people died, almost all of whom were from the more privileged sectors of society. It was the worst railway accident in the UK up to that time in terms of numbers killed and the manner of their deaths – the victims were burned beyond recognition. The reaction to the Abergele crash was given added impetus by the major increases in the numbers of men who could vote in elections after the 1867 Reform Act. There was a further meeting in Bangor in 1869 that was rather less deferential to the LNWR than the previous one. The mood was angry about 'the real torture' being experienced. This was not the death and mutilation of the recent victims at Abergele, but rather that at Bangor station where they complained about the need to climb into railway carriages and cross lines.[27] Bulkeley-Hughes MP chaired the meeting and complained that he had twice fallen into an ash pit while attempting to cross the lines. The post-Abergele mood against the LNWR was apparent in his comment that the LNWR was 'the most heedless of public safety of any railway company in existence'. The meeting therefore resolved to obstruct LNWR legislation until Bangor station was improved.[28] The tactic appeared to work. Just two months later there was a report of the new works at the station and no evidence of further meetings: certainly not one to protest about poor Thomas Jones, who was killed during the improvements and removed to the 'dead house of the [Poor Law] Union' (a morgue for those who could not afford funerals) to await an inquest.[29]

Thus, the railway and region's elite began to understand their relative status and obligations and to feel their way towards mechanisms to resolve differences – but there was a long way to go before anything close to equilibrium between them and the LNWR could be achieved. The LNWR remained powerful, while the

20. *In 1869 local MP Bulkeley-Hughes complained of the lack of a bridge over the lines and the danger of falling into an ash pit at Bangor. In 1975 there are no such problems as a class 40 leads an express from Birmingham through the station on its way to Holyhead.* **(Photo: John Hobbs)**

power of landowners in north Wales was in decline after the 1868 election in which the votes of the emerging middle classes were mostly deployed in favour of Gladstone's Liberals. The issue that showed this in north Wales was resistance of the LNWR to the payment of local Poor Rates, that funded poverty relief, which the LNWR had opposed paying from its inception. It considered these local taxes to be a major burden on the CHR as it held some of the most highly rated land in north Wales.

The Reverend William Venables Williams, vicar of Llandrillo yn Rhos (the basis of modern-day Colwyn Bay) from 1869–1893, made it his personal mission to tackle the LNWR on this issue. Matters came to a head in 1871 at Caernarfon Court of Quarter Sessions when the LNWR lost an appeal against the assessment of railway property in the Conway Poor Law Union and was ordered to pay £500 per mile (£60,000) in poor rates – a large increase on the previous rate.[30] Venables Williams and the railway solicitor Richard Preston carried on the argument outside court through the local paper where the Reverend Williams commented: 'as a ratepayer … I am desirous … of having the line placed at its proper assessment; as a shareholder in the [LNWR] I am extremely unwilling that it should be charged more than its due'.[31] Williams became something of a local celebrity, not least because the LNWR contribution reduced demands on other ratepayers.[32] That was an unusual victory for north Wales, which even the local right-leaning *North Wales Chronicle* reckoned was in need of a Daniel O'Connell or a Richard Cobden – leaders of Irish nationalism and the anti-Corn Law movement respectively – to lead them.[33]

Although it was a private company, the LNWR was a key part of the infrastructure of north Wales. It was crucial to the development of Llandudno from 1849 as a high-quality holiday resort: for example in the creation of Marine Drive that opened up the seafront.[34] On the other hand, it opposed acquisition of the gas and water provider by the council in Bangor from whom it obtained preferential rates.[35] It also contested Conwy's Harbour Bill as it affected its own plans on the other side of the estuary.[36] The impression left by these and other exchanges, including the increase in poor rate, is that the area needed the railway more than the railway needed the area. The relationship between railway and region therefore continued to be an unequal one.

This showed itself in 1879 when the CHR was formally dissolved as a legal entity. Local people and businesses wanted the LNWR to apply its generally lower fares and freight charges to the CHR, but the company chose to maintain the higher rates previously charged by the CHR. Those higher charges were based on the cost of constructing the line thirty years earlier, but the LNWR argued that the line was still expensive to maintain and justified higher charges for its use. George Stephenson's exaggerated claims about the cheapness and ease of construction of the CHR from 1840 were thus laid bare. At the heart of the problem, according to local opinion, was the lack of any railway competition in north Wales. Local business interests considered that the LNWR used its monopoly position to compensate for the lower rates they charged in areas where customers had a choice of lines.[37] And there was a national dimension to the argument as some towns in north Wales argued that this was a 'really *Welsh* commercial grievance.'[38]

Ultimately, the LNWR was successful in sustaining its high rates and fares and dissolving the CHR.[39] The CHR had never been fully independent, but its loss removed another local connection (however tenuous) between railway and community. The struggle over the financial relationship between the LNWR and an emerging group of influential people in north Wales, enfranchised by the 1867 Reform Act, marked a change in the nature of the relationship between the region and the railway. The LNWR had probably emerged with the upper hand from its success in sustaining its higher rates and fares, but the local people had also tasted success in the Poor Rates argument.

We have seen that the ability of the better-off to deal with the power of the LNWR was rather limited. For those with less power and little money, it was almost impossible. Employees depended on the company for their livelihood and had to accept the dangers inherent in their work. They coped with poor wages and had to resort to indirect methods to attract public attention to their poor conditions, as 'Pointsman' seemed to have done in May 1871 in a letter to the local paper. He received an indirect reply through the paper, apparently from another on the same line, but probably from the LNWR itself. The latter advised that 'if a servant of the company is aggrieved, he can apply to the directors and can always get redress if he is deserving of it [but] if we have little pay, we are provided with a uniform'.[40] When the Holyhead LNWR carpenters struck in the summer of 1875, they were told by the LNWR chairman, Richard Moon, that they should send a letter to the board. That did not work for them and, in the absence of a settlement, the LNWR then attempted to recruit replacements. When three of those arrived in Holyhead a local carrier refused them transport and they were also subjected to some rough handling, after which a £10 (£1,100) reward was offered for the arrest of those responsible.[41]

It would be inaccurate to suggest that relations between LNWR and its staff in north Wales were always poor. In fact, they appeared to be generally good and the opportunity to work for the company was probably highly prized in a region where alternative employment was scarce and less secure than on the railway. The company supported a CHR Friendly Society that provided benefits to staff and their families.[42] At the regular dinner for company staff at Bangor in January 1879 the staff celebrated the 'good feeling which existed between the management and the large staff … and the kindness of the directorate, during this dullness of trade, in not reducing the wages as had been done by other great companies'.[43]

The LNWR's success in Parliament in 1879 showed that it had power to influence at a national level and could easily overcome local resistance. However, pressure for change was growing. Railways were playing their part in building that resistance, albeit unintentionally, by strengthening the ability of groups to meet in larger numbers. At an Eisteddfod in Anglesey one contributor noted the importance of the gatherings to 'bring us together as Welshmen and *unite us as an ancient nationality*' [my italics]– and added thanks to the LNWR for making the event possible.[44] It seems unlikely that the LNWR hierarchy would have approved, but doubtless the revenue was welcome. Gladstone's Liberals benefited most from this emerging Welsh sense of national identity and he made full use of the changes by using his status as a resident of Wales who had married into a Welsh family. His popularity soared as was clear at Holyhead in October 1877 when Gladstone made his only visit to Ireland. After a telegram was received in the town indicating that he had left Chester on the Irish Mail, the town crier passed on the news to the townspeople so that the prime minister was met by a large crowd who demanded an address from the noted orator. Unfortunately for them there was too little time between the arrival of the train and the departure of the steamer for Dublin.[45] Residents of another north Wales town were more successful in 1882 on one of Gladstone's regular visits to Penmaenmawr. He spoke to a large crowd in the aftermath of the killing of two senior British officials in Phoenix Park, Dublin; and when there was a major war in Egypt. However, the crowd was more concerned with the way the railway obstructed access to the beach from their town than with those major events. Gladstone was most supportive and told them, perhaps a little disingenuously:

> I hope you will obtain consideration from [the LNWR]. It is a company whose management is characterised by great wisdom and liberality, and it is because of these that I am of the opinion that they should give you better access to the beach.[46]

In 1892 Gladstone also expressed support for the creation of a station at Shotton on the CHR to connect with the one planned by his friend and supporter Sir Edward Watkin on what is now known as the Borderlands line from Wrexham to Bidston.[47] The LNWR obliged – but only in 1907 after Gladstone had died.

The LNWR's confidence in its strength in north Wales grew as the century progressed and Richard Preston, the company solicitor – and a man who was always keen to press its case – told an LNWR officers' dinner in 1881 that: 'there was not a single valley where a railway could go in this part of the country in which the trains of the [LNWR] were not running [and he hoped that each employee] should never scruple to bear the mark of the [LNWR] on his collar when he knew it was a passport to society.'[48]

Given his experience of defending his company in court in north Wales, Preston must have known that his statement was at best aspirational. His analysis was contradicted by the jury at an inquest in Holyhead in 1882. It named senior LNWR officials as responsible for the deaths of three passengers walking between ferry

21. *In January 2020, Transport for Wales 175103 approaches the site of the 1950 crash at Penmaenmawr on its way to Birmingham. Crowds here in 1883 appealed to Prime Minister Gladstone to press the LNWR for a bridge to improve beach access. The station main building has changed little, though shelter is sparse as the structure is closed to the public.* (Photo: Phil Lloyd Collection)

and train during reconstruction of the facilities after storm damage. They were duly charged with manslaughter. The case showed tension between management and staff in which the community supported the latter. As usual, the LNWR resisted any suggestion of responsibility on its part and considered that the long service of Ephraim Wood, district superintendent and the most senior defendant, guaranteed he was 'incapable of the culpable negligence of which he was so unjustly accused'.[49] The defendants were all acquitted. Wood and his co-defendants showed little remorse after the incident and there was a spirit of triumphalism when the LNWR officers held their annual dinner in Chester. They presented Wood

22. In 1892 William Gladstone appealed to the LNWR to make a station at industrial Shotton to connect with the Wirral line – which it did in 1907. In August 2020 Shotton looks like a rural halt rather than a centre of industry as 158829 for Holyhead sets off, while above it a class 230 (ex-London Underground) continues training for use on the Borderlands line. (Photo: Phil Lloyd Collection)

with an illuminated congratulatory scroll, commemorating his success in court, despite 'extraordinary efforts to the contrary' – presumably meaning by the local populace.[50] There was no reference to the people who had died in the incident.

Evidence that this incident was part of a wider problem between railway and populace was reinforced in 1885 by serious disorder in Holyhead that was apparently unreported in north Wales but was picked up across the Irish Sea. A 'special reporter' recounted that the LNWR had sent fifteen staff from Chester to replace Welsh staff who were dismissed for pilfering on the basis that 'one Welshman steals therefore all Welshmen are unreliable'. The real reason had been 'prematurely disclosed [by] a principal official [and it was the LNWR's intention] to make "a little English town" of [Holyhead]'. The LNWR sent replacements from Chester and although the local population had: 'no notion of combination, they have a very good idea of moral pressure, and the force of public opinion has been too much for the visitors'.[51] The LNWR was also accused of favouring its own suppliers and putting local traders out of business. It was reported in Manchester that the Chester employees had been duped by a story that there were staff shortages at Holyhead. They had returned home when they found out the facts and after two of them were beaten 'very severely'. That report suggested that: 'the feeling in Holyhead is intense in favour of the discharged men and detrimental to the newcomers'.[52] A further report in Ireland suggested that: 'several of the Saxon invaders [were given] a sound thrashing' and that Frank Harrison (a senior manager) from Euston had been sent to Holyhead to attempt a resolution.[53] Evidence that relations between the LNWR and its workers were strained at this time is suggested by a court case that coincided with the disturbances and

23. *LNWR's alleged intention to make 'a little English town' out of Holyhead caused serious trouble in 1885. Things are much quieter as 37414 couples onto a Crewe-bound train in July 1993 when ferries still docked next to the railway station.* **(Photo: David Sallery, Penmorfa.com)**

may have been linked. It involved Robert Roberts attempting to take control of Number 2 signal box from signalman Frank Wood. Roberts was duly arrested by the railway police and fined sixteen shillings for obstruction.[54]

Industrial and social tensions were not the only issues between company and region: the LNWR's monopoly and its fares and freight charges also caused resentment. Thus in June 1887 there was a meeting in Rhyl to support the construction of a railway that bypassed the LNWR between Chester and Rhyl because the LNWR: 'had a system not so much to accommodate passengers, as a line of communication between England and Ireland to carry Irish traffic'.[55] Issues such as freight charges, fares, monopoly, safety and industrial relations were sources of general tension between the railway companies and communities in Britain in this period. The extra ingredient in north Wales was Welsh nationality. As the right to vote was extended, it became more possible for the Welsh voice to be heard from an emerging group of radical Welsh Liberal MPs. Gladstone tried hard to appear to meet their demands, but the movement was strong and when it combined with the Irish faction, it became a formidable force. The connection between Ireland and Wales became stronger during the 1880s and the radical Porthmadog solicitor, David Lloyd George, caused a stir when he shared a platform with the Irish nationalist Michael Davitt at Blaenau Ffestiniog in 1886.[56]

The difficulties between the LNWR and Welsh nationalism came to a head in 1894 when the company dismissed several staff who spoke only Welsh. Earlier that year the LNWR scored a significant victory over Lloyd George, the Caernarfon Boroughs MP, and the Liberal government over the issue of the Employers Liability Bill. The Bill was intended to provide a basic level of insurance cover for workers who suffered injury at work. The LNWR opposed it because it preferred its own more generous scheme that also gave it a hold over its employees because, if dismissed, they could lose their benefits. Unions and government wanted a scheme that covered all workers rather than sectional schemes for certain industries. The issue was therefore one about the common interest of all workers.

Lloyd George was initially sympathetic to the government but was compromised after he rather unwisely called a meeting of railway workers at the Rechabite Hall in Bangor in January 1894. The LNWR had ensured that its employees backed the company scheme and Lloyd George was forced to oppose his own government, causing a local paper to wonder about MPs 'who are not quite sure whether principles or vote-catching dodges stand higher in the scale of morals'.[57] It is not clear whether this success emboldened the LNWR in its later actions and strengthened Lloyd George's determination to oppose them, but it is the case that a fierce battle ensued between them as the year progressed. When news of the dismissals of Welsh-only speakers reached Llandudno, Lloyd George was summoned to a meeting where he:

> Spoke of the action of the railway company as an act of tyrannical despotism, for which the railway company should suffer. [He] did not hesitate to indicate how the Welsh members should seek their revenge. The [LNWR] will find that their bills will be opposed and blocked in the House of Commons by the representatives of the Welsh people, who are … smarting under the wrong inflicted upon a number of workmen in North Wales.[58]

This time it was Lloyd George who mobilised the workers and the local councils, churches, newspapers and boards of guardians to pass resolutions against the actions of the LNWR which was rather startled by the strength of the response.

Conwy provided an interesting example of how the actions of the LNWR united opinion across the region. The Conway [*sic*] board of guardians – whom we have already noted challenging the LNWR over its Poor Rates payments – was still chaired by the Reverend Venables Williams in 1895 and it considered a motion condemning the LNWR's actions. Venables Williams was unwilling to allow debate unless at least one of the dismissed men had resorted to poor relief in Conwy for his upkeep. Once it was confirmed that one had, the meeting debated the issue and was united in its response. His words against the LNWR for sacking Welsh-speaking employees were unequivocal:

> The action of the railway company appeared to him to be a most iniquitous one, one of the most iniquitous he had ever heard of, and one that must surely recoil upon the company in some form or other, and he felt that they were only doing their duty as Welshmen in protesting against that attempt to put a stigma upon men simply for being Welshmen, and most emphatically he wished to endorse the protest just made by the Board.
>
> As a Welshman himself, his very blood boiled within him to think of a great Company like the London and North-Western, that depended so very much – especially as regarded the Chester and Holyhead section – on the Welsh for its success and wellbeing, acting in such a way … and he hoped it would go forth, and that that protest would have weight to stay the downward course which the [LNWR] were adopting in North Wales.[59]

The LNWR found itself having to answer to shareholders at its meeting in February 1895 when it produced a clumsy response. Chairman Lord Stalbridge said that for some years there had been a rule against employing people who could only speak Welsh, but it had not been enforced. The LNWR decided that passenger safety required that all employees should be able to converse in English, although it was willing to allow one Welsh-only speaker in each work gang. His generally dismissive tone drew laughter from the audience but Bryn Roberts – MP in north Wales and a LNWR shareholder – responded strongly. For him, the fact that:

> The rule had been in abeyance showed that the officials in the past were a good deal wiser than the men who made the rule [and] that there was no real necessity for the rule, because the company had been carrying on its business in Wales for over fifty years [without incident].

He also pointed out that the explanation at the meeting contradicted the first statement from the LNWR six months earlier that the dismissals were seasonal. Stalbridge delivered a most high-handed and tactless retort:

> It must be remembered that before very long there would be nobody in Wales who could not speak English as well as Welsh, for it was one of the conditions of the Education Department that where the Government grant was given to a school, English must be taught. Therefore, in the course of a few years this case would not arise. But he could not repeat too often that people who did not speak English could not be allowed to come in contact with the traffic.[60]

That attitude was a guarantee of further trouble, and Lloyd George duly delivered it with opposition to the LNWR's legislation that was designed to pave the way for additional lines along the route from Chester to Llandudno Junction. The LNWR had to produce a detailed rebuttal of Lloyd George's claims of harassment and anti-Welsh sentiment and suggested that the MP was using the case for political advantage at a time when Welsh nationalism was riding high. But there was another point that was perhaps more important in the longer term, and which Lloyd George used to his advantage at the 1895 election when he claimed that his actions were:

> The first time in the history of [Parliament] that a direct motion had been proposed for the purpose of instituting an enquiry into an act of oppression committed by a company of employers against their servants. Up to that point it had not been considered to be a part of the functions of the House of Commons to protect working men against the tyrannical acts of employers. Mr John Burns [a leading trade unionist] afterwards told him that he

considered the discussion to mark one of the most important epochs in the parliamentary history of labour during the last 30 years.[61]

Lloyd George's campaign served him well in the 1895 election when he retained his seat against the general tide that flowed in favour of the Conservatives. His narrow victory was celebrated at Bangor railway station where he:

> Was compelled to leave the train and address a large crowd of Liberals outside the station, after which he was again carried shoulder high to the train. At each station en route to Chester, especially at Bangor, Conway, and Rhyl [he] received tremendous ovations from the people on the platforms.[62]

The dismissals of railwaymen led to a decision by several Welsh county councils to hold a meeting at Rhyl in 1895. That conference considered the Welsh language grievance largely resolved but decided there were many other issues presented by the LNWR in north Wales that needed resolution, particularly fares and freight rates. The complete monopoly of railway traffic held by the LNWR in north Wales was central to these concerns. The politicians decided to invite other companies to build lines in the region to break the monopoly and one delegate suggested that Sir Edward Watkin should extend his line that crossed the River Dee at Shotton to Conwy or Llandudno, while another suggested a new port to compete with Holyhead. That competition did not materialise and the unity of councils, churches, unions, and MPs in north Wales eroded because of the temptation for councils to make separate settlements with the LNWR. As Flintshire MP Herbert Lewis, a prominent Liberal and Welsh nationalist, observed:

> The public in North Wales had no large and comprehensive organisation to protect their interests in matters of this kind. The railway company, a wealthy and powerful corporation, could fight in detail local bodies. ... They even went to the length of approaching the witnesses brought to London to give evidence against them, finding out their individual grievances and settling with them ... The interests involved were so great that no effort or expense was spared to make the case of the company as complete as possible.[63]

If the people of north Wales hoped that a rival railway would break the LNWR and establish the long-promised route to Ireland from Porth Dinllaen, the new century brought the ultimate disappointment. A light railway was proposed to serve Porth Dinllaen but opponents argued that the council in Caernarfon should resist it because it would preclude standard railway construction. Lloyd George addressed its concerns and recognised the victory of the LNWR as he urged support for the light railway and reflected on the history of the much-touted route to Porth Dinllaen:

> He had heard since the days of his childhood [that] there was a scheme on hand for the development of Lleyn by means of railways. One day, it was the [GWR] and the next the [LNWR], and the next day somebody else. They were told that bills and plans 'had been prepared' and go on, right on to [Porth Dinllaen] and that a steamship company was going to run thence to Ireland. Everybody had heard that during the past 30 or 40 years.[64]

Ultimately, this modest light railway scheme failed: and while the LNWR doubled its route along most of the north coast of Wales, not even a tramway was ever built to Porth Dinllaen.

This chapter has demonstrated the massive impact that the arrival of the CHR had on north Wales. An area that had been a backwater for many centuries was suddenly at the heart of a project of national importance, though its importance related to Ireland rather than to Wales. That did not prevent the line changing the lives of much of the population in the four Welsh counties through which it passed. Most of the changes were appreciated by the population, and perhaps most of all by those who worked for the LNWR in north Wales receiving better wages and conditions than they could have secured by any other means in the region. But there was a price to pay. The LNWR carried with it a sense of superiority – of England over Wales, of capital over labour and profit over service.

The massive power of the LNWR – the largest industrial corporation in the world – created a reaction in north Wales at a time when more men had the vote and could use it to erode the deference of local people built up over nearly four centuries. In 1870 the LNWR chairman, Richard Moon, outlined the strategy for north Wales at a meeting celebrating the completion of the tunnel into the centre of Caernarfon. He told local landowners that the LNWR:

> Had only accomplished in commerce what they had done in feudalism long ago. They had woven a girdle which now completed the circle round Wales, and they had done so in a manner that would neither disturb artists or tourists. Their object had been to bring coal into North Wales and take back slates.[65]

If Moon had expected the kind of deference that the local landowners had enjoyed for centuries in north Wales, he and his successors must have been rather disappointed.

Accidents on the Railway

In the midst of life, we are in death.[1]

As we have seen, the arrival of railways provided a mixture of excitement and awe among those that experienced this revolutionary means of travel that finally moved land transport beyond the realms of the wind and the horse. Railways also created a new source of death and injury. The Chester and Holyhead Railway (CHR) accident returns for the period from 1849–1859 (when it was absorbed by the London and North Western Railway – LNWR) record that there were fifty-eight fatal and twenty-eight non-fatal accidents reported by the CHR. This was not a full return as it tended to focus on accidents to passengers and staff, but the wider picture shows that many others were involved. Within the CHR returns for the period the word 'incautious' occurred quite regularly, indicating that in those early years of operation people in north Wales had no conception of the sheer power of a railway.

These general findings are reinforced by an interesting analysis by F.G.P. Neison in 1853. In a report to the Royal Statistical Society, of which he was the secretary, he found in 1840–1851 the number of railway passengers in the UK was 478,488,607, of whom 237 were killed and 1,416 injured, a ratio of one killed in 2,018,939 miles, and one injured in 337,916. Of engine drivers, stokers and guards, 275 were killed and 274 injured from a total of 40,486: a ratio of one killed in 177 and one injured in 148. The number of porters and other servants was 359,683, of whom 683 were killed and 343 injured: the ratio being one killed in 521, and one injured in 1,058. During the years 1844–1851, 7,044,469,484 miles were travelled by passengers and 176 deaths happened through accidents from all causes: one passenger killed for every 40,025,395 miles travelled. Neison reckoned that if a person were always in motion on a railway and travelling at an average speed of 20mph, including stoppages, that person would travel 175,200 miles yearly, and must constantly travel for 228 years to be killed by an accident on the railway from any cause. He showed that over time the deaths from collisions and from trains running off the line reduced, while deaths from passengers falling from trains had scarcely varied and estimated that deaths from causes beyond the control of the companies at 54.8 per cent of the number of injuries: but the deaths from causes under their control were 10.9 per cent, showing that accidents from failures of management tended to result in injury rather than death.

Neison was keen to shift the focus of public concern away from death and injury to passengers and towards incidents involving staff and the wider public. He analysed deaths to passengers, staff and trespassers and found that falling from trains was the main factor in passenger deaths but that even so, deaths of staff were greater and tended not to reduce in the period of his analysis.[2] The situation appeared to improve little, so that by 1877 a correspondent to the *Star* newspaper complained in verse about William Gladstone's obsession with massacre in Turkey but not that on Britain's railways:

> To slaughter by Turks, it is needless to say,
> I always am willing attention to pay,
> But slaughters by railway on our British soil,
> Of porters and stokers don't make my blood boil.[3]

Death and injury at home or at work were treated as almost commonplace in the nineteenth century, such as the death of sixteen miners at Holywell, but railways brought a different and shocking quality to it.[4] It was not from familiar and local causes such as the home, the sea, the quarry, mine or the farm – but from a dramatic and new source that, at the time, felt alien to the area. This was shown in the fate of driver Robert Brcreton in 1884 at Llandudno Junction that affected his locality profoundly:

> A 'rule book' found in a coat pocket contained Brereton's name, and this was the only means by which [he was] identified. … His sad and untimely death has cast gloom over the whole neighbourhood. He leaves a widow and four small children. … A subscription for their relief has been already opened.[5]

But that was not always the response in the newspapers. Brereton was given extensive and sympathetic support compared to that afforded to John Hughes of Roscolyn in 1885. His death was treated as almost routine:

> On Thursday afternoon he was working on the length between Valley and Holyhead, and to avoid a down goods train stepped into the up line, and was knocked down by the express, death being instantaneous. The jury returned a verdict of accidental death. Inspector Port (Bangor) was present on behalf of the railway company.[6]

Thus, the people of north Wales were confronted with the phenomenon of railways in a dramatic manner that affected individuals, families and communities who had to adapt to the speed, power and impact on the senses of high-speed trains rushing through their region. These trains brought new possibilities and experiences with them, but also new dangers and challenges that affected all classes and ages indiscriminately, though the bulk of impact was on employees and bystanders rather than those who had the means to make use of the railway as passengers. We noted earlier the death of cockle-gatherer Catherine Williams in July 1848, but she was not alone as an early casualty of this new and powerful technology that was inserted into the largely rural landscape of north Wales. Henry Lewis, aged fifteen, was leading his team of horses over the line at 'Sluices' (Llanerch y Mor) and was 'overtaken by the express train and killed on the spot' along with one of the animals after he tried to reverse their direction rather than hurrying forward over the line.[7] People took time to adapt to the massive increase in power and speed that was heralded by railways. But such casualties were not necessarily a high priority for those in authority.

This was highlighted at a public dinner held to mark the departure of local dignitary Edward Cropper from Conwy in 1854. He was the contractor for part of the CHR that included the Penmaenbach tunnel just west of Conwy and he was later responsible for overall maintenance of the track.[8] The chairman of the meeting drew attention to an important point: 'Since Mr Cropper came to reside amongst them – about 9 or 10 years ago – not a single accident of any magnitude had occurred on the line.' But what were the facts?

In August 1846 David Hughes, 'an old miner from Llandudno … a very industrious and well conducted man, with a large family' was killed in a blast, and two colleagues were 'extensively burnt' at the Penmaenbach tunnel for which Cropper was responsible.[9] A similar accident in a neighbouring tunnel demonstrated the risks of using gunpowder in an area lit by candles. The coroner was critical of working practices but recognised 'the benefits those receiving injury to the person derived from [the railway]' – in other words the price was worth paying.[10] In 1846, George Taverner died of fumes while sleeping in a lime kiln near the Penmaenbach works. Another man died in similar circumstances a short time earlier. They were in the kiln to keep warm as they had no lodgings.[11] At Llysfaen, Martin Holoran – 'a poor, aged Irishman' – died from an earth fall in June 1847 on the works of contractors Mackenzie and Brassey.[12] In the same month, James Morris died in a fall at the Bodorgan tunnel on the Betts contract in Anglesey, but at least benefited from a 'fine oak coffin' paid for by the contractor and over £10 (£1,000) collected from workmates for his widow and child.[13] William Lewis died in a nearby cutting just two months later after being crushed by falling stones.[14]

Above: 24. *There was some heavy tunnelling near Bodorgan in 1847: James Morris died when he fell down a shaft during construction but benefited from 'a fine oak coffin'. In February 2020, an Avanti West Coast train clears the tunnels as it rushes to meet the afternoon ferry at Holyhead.* **(Photo: Phil Lloyd Collection)**

Left: 25. *Penmaenrhos (or Llysfaen) tunnel marks the summit of the CHR. An 'aged Irishman' Martin Holoran died here during its construction in 1847 and seven years later an Irish woman was found 'alive but in a most pitiable condition' after falling from a train.* **(Photo: John Alsop Collection)**

The year 1847 was a poor one for the CHR marked by the failure of the Dee Bridge. That collapse came close to ruining the reputation of the CHR and particularly its engineer Robert Stephenson. The toll of shocking death continued into the next year when the wife and child of a labourer died of burns when a steam pipe burst after they secured a lift on an engine in 1848.[15] Just a few weeks before Cropper's dinner in Conwy, an Irish woman on her way home was found in the tunnel near Colwyn Bay: 'alive but in a most pitiable condition', having fallen from a train.[16] The CHR's own returns did not include several of those mentioned here. For those celebrating the success of the CHR and Mr Cropper at the 1854 Conwy dinner, only passenger deaths of people like themselves were relevant.

The one formal memorial to those who died during construction is a tribute to those who lost their lives building the Britannia Tubular Bridge, which took a heavy toll of its workers. Some of them are remembered at the nearby St Mary's Church, including a young girl and an accountant who succumbed to typhus in the poor living and working conditions on and near the site. The figure is likely to be an underestimate as the casualty record from the original construction seem to end in 1850 – for example Hugh Williams died from a fall while roofing the bridge in June 1851 and is not included. Two deaths from the reconstruction of the bridge in 1972–1973 are recorded.

Although there were many collisions in the early years of the railway, one at Chester in 1854 might be considered typical, reflecting the early stages of safety practice. The tunnel near Northgate was under repair and drivers were instructed to stop before entering it. A coal train stopped as required but stalled when given permission to move ahead. The crew detached a portion of the train and proceeded to Chester, intending to return for the remainder. That portion of the train was just out of sight of a passenger train from Bangor which hit the trucks at speed, causing injury to a few passengers and risked the train falling down a high embankment. At a time when people rather than organisations tended to shoulder the blame, the local paper opined that, 'The men in charge of the train and the pointsman are highly culpable, and we should hope their carelessness will be strictly enquired into.'[17]

Speed was the essence of the CHR, so it was no surprise to find casualties from the imperative of the mail getting through on time. William Saunders died in 1850 after falling from the SS *Eblana* as it docked at Holyhead with its doors opened early to speed the transfer of mail bags.[18] And in a portent of the later crash nearby, a porter at Abergele station was killed as he dashed to remove a truck from the line to let the Irish Mail through in June 1858.[19] Another serious accident to the

26. The tunnel under Northgate on the approach to Chester station was the scene of a collision in 1854 after a freight train stalled and staff decided to leave the trucks behind while they collected a more powerful engine. In July 2020 a five-coach Voyager from Holyhead to Crewe enters the tunnel without such difficulties. (Photo: Phil Lloyd Collection)

Irish Mail occurred in January 1861 but achieved remarkably little coverage in the press. The train had just emerged from the tubular bridge onto Anglesey when a wheel broke and derailed the train causing substantial injury to many passengers – especially post-office staff – and two deaths.[20]

But the attitude to such incidents remained remarkably indulgent as the response of the local paper to a serious smash at Menai Bridge in 1865 amply demonstrated. The paper noted that reports were: 'as usual … accompanied by exaggerated

27. *In February 2020 a five-coach Avanti West Coast Voyager passes the road crossing at Llanfair P G and approaches the site of a serious derailment in 1861 when a wheel broke on the Irish Mail. Two passengers died and many more were injured. The building that guards the crossing is the oldest existing signal box on the CHR dating from 1871.* **(Photo: Phil Lloyd Collection)**

statements as to the number of individuals killed and injured'. In fact, the collision between the mail train from Caernarfon and the passenger train from Chester was a severe one. It occurred at high speed and caused both engines to leave the track, destroying several coaches, including the front coach of the Chester train that fortunately was empty. Damage to the engines was extensive but the crews survived by jumping before impact. Eighteen passengers were not so fortunate, and one received a serious facial injury. Two engines and twelve carriages were sent to Bangor for repair. The driver of the mail train was blamed for missing the signal, though he suggested that it was set halfway between clear and danger. The report was keen to point out that this was the first accident 'on this part of the line' and regarded the CHR as: 'one of the best managed lines in the kingdom', while conceding that the junction to Caernarfon might have benefited from some improvement.[21] The paper was soon forced to reconsider its views on the management of the CHR.

A little over three years after the Menai Bridge smash, the worst railway accident in the UK up to that time occurred when the Irish Mail, headed by Problem class engine number 291 *Prince of Wales*, hit paraffin wagons that had rolled onto the track from a siding at Llysfaen (the station there was called Llandulas at the time) in August 1868. The wooden coaches were set on fire and thirty-three people died in the most horrific circumstances. It was the 'only very disastrous railway accident in which there have been no wounded, with the exception of one individual it has been death in the most dreadful form, or entire escape'.[22]

Ultimately, the staff largely escaped censure for the accident though the LNWR tried hard to focus on their conduct. The inspector found that much fault lay

28. *There was a serious smash at Menai Bridge station in 1865 with many passengers injured but little concern expressed about the LNWR's management of this junction with the line towards Caernarfon.* **(Photo: John Alsop Collection)**

with the LNWR tendency to create regulations that gave the impression of sound management, such as that trumpeted by the *North Wales Chronicle* in 1865 but doing little to enforce them if they compromised operational or financial priorities. Remarkably, the inspector found that the siding from which the paraffin wagons slid onto the main line had never been inspected and approved in accordance with Board of Trade requirements and was too short. I think a possible culprit was the former CHR chairman Samuel Peto who had pressured managers to open sidings wherever possible in order to boost revenue on the line when it faced financial pressures in the 1850s, as noted in the previous chapter.[23]

Railway accidents such as Abergele with multiple casualties provide one of the few opportunities to examine the profile of those travelling by train in detail. In the case of the Irish Mail at Abergele, it amounted to a roll-call of the British and Irish upper classes headed by Lord and Lady Farnham, two of the Aylmer family of Walworth Castle, Sir Nicholas and Lady Chinnery, Judge Walter Berwick and his sister from Cork, Captain J. Priestley Edwards (deputy lord-lieutenant of Yorkshire), his son and Caroline and Augusta Lea, who were daughters of the high sheriff of Worcestershire and lived at Astley Hall, Stourport. The casualties included members of the rising middle classes who had made their money from

29. *Llysfaen station was opened in 1862 as Llandulas [sic] and was renamed when the next station east opened in 1889 and took the name. Wagons with paraffin containers rolled down the hill from here into the path of the Irish Mail in August 1868 causing the deaths of thirty-three people. Llysfaen station closed in 1931.* (**Photo:** **John Alsop Collection**)

30. *In August 1868 Arthur Thompson drove the Irish Mail into this bend unaware of runaway trucks of paraffin rolling towards him down the hill from Llanddulas. Here, 152 years later, 158820 eases into the ascent, also on its way to Holyhead. The adjoining A55 now provides the most common route to the port.* **(Photo: Phil Lloyd Collection)**

the new industries, such as William Townend Lund, William Parkinson and Christopher Parkinson from Blackburn. They intended to holiday in Ireland and set off on a connecting train that gave little time to spare if they were to catch the Irish Mail at Chester. A telegram confirmed that they had joined the doomed train – and that was the last their families heard of them.[24]

It was a different experience for Dowager Duchess Abercorn, who would not have attained her great age had it not been for an alteration at Chester in the carriage arrangements of the ill-fated train. She left London with her sons, husband and the Duke and Lords Ernest and Frederick Hamilton. At Chester, three carriages were added to the train and placed between the engine and the carriage in which the Hamilton party were travelling on their way to the Dublin Vice-Regal Lodge, where the Marquess of Abercorn was lord lieutenant. At Abergele, those three carriages were enveloped in flames and their occupants burnt to death.[25] Thus, the bulk of victims of the accident were from a different slice of society than those whose deaths we have considered so far in this chapter. Many were English or wealthy Irish people, mostly landowners or connected to the system of governance in Ireland under the 1801 Act of Union. Those that were not from the middle and upper classes were on the train as servants – such as Caroline Stearn, a dressmaker from London who was a maid. Additionally, there were the two crew members among the dead, William Smith the guard and stoker Joseph Holmes. Driver Arthur Thompson became the thirty-fourth victim in October 1868 when injuries from the crash were considered to have aggravated an existing condition and caused his death.

The impact on the relatives of victims continued for many years as noted on the death of the bard Owain Alaw in 1883:

> He was the author of a cantata of considerable merit, called the 'Prince of Wales', which was performed at the Welsh Eisteddfod held in Chester some years ago. More recently Mr Owen composed, in addition to many songs: an oratorio, 'Jeremiah'. Mrs Owen died some three or four years ago, and this, together with the death of his son in the terrible Abergele railway catastrophe, inflicted a great blow upon the deceased, from which he never appeared to quite recover.[26]

While the LNWR largely escaped the blame and the cost of the Abergele crash, the public's rather indulgent attitude towards the railway operators began to change after this terrible event. At least one person took matters into his own hands when another smash occurred near Holywell two months after Abergele. Mr Edwards-Wood was incensed when his train collided with a goods train and no action was taken. He mounted a private prosecution of George Grimmett, a signalman at Holywell. The court hearing was chaired by the Earl of Denbigh who heard that Grimmett had changed his signal from danger when an approaching train whistled. He did so despite the presence of a goods train. It transpired that this was an informal local arrangement. The driver of this train normally stopped for water at Holywell and Grimmett assumed the whistle was to confirm that he was doing so. In fact, the tender was full on the approaching train and the driver had whistled to check the signal. Grimmett's defence implied that the prosecution was designed to gain some personal reward: Edwards-Wood insisted it was for the

31. *The monument to the thirty-three victims of the Abergele rail crash reminds visitors that: 'In the midst of life we are in death.' The enclosure (Right) contains the remains of those killed on 20 August 1868 – named on the monument in order of social status and then alphabetically. (Photos: Phil Lloyd Collection)*

public good. The bench agreed with him, as they were probably bound to do in the aftermath of the Abergele crash. Grimmett's good work record had not spared him dismissal by the LNWR, and it did not spare him two months in Flint gaol, though his sentence was not accompanied by hard labour.[27]

Remarkably there was another collision close to the Abergele tragedy around its first anniversary:

> A very alarming collision occurred last Friday week at forenoon, near Abergele … which might have resulted in frightful consequences. A passenger train from Bangor, proceeding at a high speed, entered the [Penmaenrhos] tunnel at Colwyn and dashed into a goods train which was [stalled] in the tunnel at the time. The greatest consternation prevailed, and many of the passengers are cut and bruised on the face and body.[28]

Three years later the Irish Mail was still intent on achieving its connection with the mail boats whatever the obstacle. When a telegraphed report indicated that the train was an hour late at Chester, another train of empty trucks left Bangor assuming that there was time to reach Holyhead before the mail train. Unfortunately, the freight train stalled after crossing the Stanley Embankment a few miles short of Holyhead. The signalman at Valley – just behind the stalled train – urged caution on the driver of the Irish Mail as he had not received confirmation that the goods train had reached Holyhead. Undeterred, the driver proceeded at high speed and collided with the trucks after he and the stoker had jumped from the engine. Several passengers were hurt as were five workmen who were struck by a heavy chain while clearing up after the crash.[29] That incident points to the rather lax practices employed among maintenance gangs. A particularly stark example was on the viaduct west of Penmaenmawr in 1895 where a gang of ten painters fell twenty feet when the scaffolding collapsed. Solicitor John Fenna struggled to defend LNWR practice in front of coroner Bodvel-Roberts who was investigating the death of Herbert Lees of Crewe. The jury concluded that the scaffolding had been poorly erected and that had contributed to the death.[30]

PEN Y CLIP VIADUCT.

32. *Herbert Lees from Crewe died when maintenance scaffolding collapsed on the Pen y Clip viaduct in 1895 injuring many of his colleagues. In the 1930s road traffic is using the Pen y Clip tunnel built in 1932 while the train below has just passed Gerazim, where long-serving ticket inspector Edgar Swann fell to his death in 1940.* **(Photo: John Alsop Collection)**

The frequency of accidents on the line reduced markedly as the century ended, reflecting changes such as the introduction of the block system of signalling whereby only one train is allowed in each section of line at a time (that could have prevented the Abergele crash), better braking systems and more robust materials in the building of carriages. But no such changes could compensate for the fundamental problem of the line being built so close to the sea. Despite George Stephenson's optimism about the route, it had been beset by frequent interruptions in service due to high tides and storms. The line passes particularly close to the beach between Conwy and Llanfairfechan, where it was repeatedly damaged by strong seas and where the LNWR spent large amounts of money maintaining the line. There was a near miss in November 1872 when a goods train passed over the line moments before it was washed away. The block system stopped other trains on the line and ensured that the calamity was not greater.[31]

Attempts to produce a permanent repair proved fruitless, and it was on this stretch that a serious accident occurred to the Manchester to Holyhead fast goods after a storm in January 1899. The engine driver was Edward Evans with Owen Jones firing the engine – a DX class 0-6-0 goods engine number 1418. Hugh Charles was in the guard's van with another employee who was returning home. Unknown to them, they were advancing rapidly to disaster after stopping at Llandudno Junction. The embankment near Penmaenbach had been washed away and the line then collapsed under the weight of the train soon after it emerged from the tunnel. The engine and the first five trucks crashed into the sea killing both the engine crew, although initially only the body of the driver was recovered. Remarkably, the two men in the guard's van survived as it stayed on the track and they were able to sound the alarm and prevent further tragedy. At the inquest in Bangor the jury was told of the severity of the weather and the heroic attempts by various employees to avert the disaster and reduce its consequences. The vulnerability of the line was clear from the fact that this portion of the route had been subject to an extensive reinforcement programme over the previous four years that had only just finished. The LNWR had learned at least one lesson from Abergele and ensured a high-level visit to the area by Lord Stalbridge. He was the chairman of the LNWR from 1891 and appeared at the scene soon after the crash, clearly more aware of the need to improve public relations at a time of tragedy than Richard Moon had been in 1868 at Abergele, and his own mauling in 1895 after the sacking of Welsh-only speakers discussed in the previous chapter.

A regular feature of such events was the public appeal on behalf of the victims – in this case launched by Miss Marianne Ridgway of 'Fernbrook' in Penmaenmawr:

33. *In January 1899 the Manchester to Holyhead fast goods cleared the tunnel at Penmaenbach before it crashed onto the beach off a section of line that had been washed away. Only the body of the driver was recovered on the spot while fireman Owen Jones was found by a fisherman on the far coastline (visible in the picture) in March 1899.* **(Photo: John Alsop Collection)**

Hundreds of people have this week come by road in all kinds of vehicles to see the fated spot where two brave Welshmen at their post of duty were in one moment killed. All those who have driven over to see the locale of this terrible tragedy will surely not be satisfied until they can give expression in material form and show the practical sympathy they feel in such a sad and awful event as this which almost heralded the New Year's opening. Evans, the driver – a steady and reliable man – has left a wife and eight children. Owen Jones, 25 years, only a wife and one child. I plead for the poor, old and bereaved father of this only son whose body is not yet found and may be lying under the engine.[32]

The fireman's body was not under the engine: in a rather macabre sequel, the decomposed remains of Owen Jones were discovered in the sea near Deganwy by a Conwy fisherman in March 1899.

34. *The collision at Penmaenmawr in August 1950 was the second most serious on the line. Five people died but individual bravery prevented a worse outcome. The injured fireman on the Irish Mail ran back to warn an approaching train, while two Irish nurses tended the injured and then disappeared – reflecting an age when anonymity was prized more highly than celebrity.* **(Photo: Auk archive, Alamy photo stock)**

The first year of the new century was marked by the queen's heavily publicised April visit to Ireland. A medal was struck for the Irish security forces who guarded her, but one poor railwayman, also on duty for the Royal Train, was just a footnote. William Stephens of Denbigh, proud to be deployed to guard the line near Rhyl as the Royal Train passed during the night, was discovered dead and dismembered after the passing of that train, having been hit by an express heading for London.[33]

Such individual accidents occurred with distressing frequency much as road accidents occur in modern times, drawing just a few lines of newspaper comment. Even the simultaneous deaths of four men working on the line near Mostyn in August 1922 were not covered extensively. Two trains were running at high speed together and four workers stepped away from one train but did not see the other as it was shrouded in smoke: all four were killed instantly.[34] The lack of comment in 1922 may be compared with the tragic death of two men working on the track in south Wales killed by a Great Western express in July 2019. It drew expressions of sympathy and concern from many politicians and public figures including the prime minister herself. That is testimony to the greater levels of public concern over the dangers faced by workers in public services now and the infrequency of such accidents on the modern railway.

Since the drama of the Penmaenbach incident in 1899 there has been only one further high-profile accident on the Chester and Holyhead line, coincidentally just two miles from the previous crash. Five people died and thirty-five were injured on 27 August 1950 when the 1.45 a.m. Irish Mail, packed with holidaymakers returning from Ireland, smashed into a light engine near Penmaenmawr station. The actions of John Williams, the twenty-one-year-old fireman on the Irish Mail, prevented further tragedy as he hurried along the line despite significant injuries and stopped oncoming trains, including one full of explosives. Local people joined rescue teams and first-aid units, and the Grand Hotel provided hundreds of the passengers with blankets and refreshments. The track was ripped up for over 200 yards, and the first five coaches were piled across the rails with personal luggage strewn over a wide area in the manner of modern air accidents. Two Irish nurses who worked tirelessly with the injured and then disappeared were later identified and formally commended by the rail authorities.

An immediate private inquiry was followed by a coroner's inquest and official investigation. The inquest jury found that the crash was caused by the error of the signalman assuming that a light engine was safely in the siding when its whistle was sounded, although the engine driver said he had blown the whistle to signify the opposite. The jury was unwilling to blame one individual for the crash and urged reform of the muddled system of managing traffic between the siding and the main line. The official inquiry found some shortcomings in the work of the signalman and the crew of the light engine and considered that a local informal system had developed for managing traffic between the siding and the main line. This routine tended to ignore Rule 55 (b), requiring engine crew to contact the signal box in the event of undue delay and uncertainty. The inquiry also concluded that Rule 69 covering the use of sound signals from the engine was ambiguous and should be changed. There are echoes of the Abergele smash of 1868 in these events. The importance of not obstructing the progress of the Irish Mail was a factor, the rules were in place to prevent the accident, but informal practices had been allowed to develop. At Abergele, unlike Penmaenmawr, there was no block working of trains whereby only one train was allowed in a section at a time. The 1950 incident shows that even when technology and regulation are improved, human error can still intervene. People undertaking routine manoeuvres play the percentages and occasionally lose, with catastrophic consequences.

Neison's analysis noted earlier stressed that staff and bystanders were at greater risk from rail traffic than passengers, and events discussed in this chapter have shown many examples to support his analysis. One risk to passengers that persisted was the tendency of doors to open easily while the train was moving. A couple of examples illustrate the problem and the tendency to assume that it was the passenger's responsibility to stay in the train rather than that of the operator to keep them there. The first example also demonstrates an issue that was prevalent in the later nineteenth century – the absence of means of communication between passengers and crew. Robert Hughes was travelling with his wife between Colwyn Bay and Llandudno Junction in November 1886 when he accidentally opened the door of the compartment and fell out. When Mrs Hughes arrived at Bangor she notified officials who dispatched an engine and eventually found her husband. There was apparently no effective means to contact the guard and driver via the communication cord before their arrival at Bangor. There was a cord in the compartment, but another passenger reported that he had pulled and pulled on it and had merely got many yards of cord in his hands and no response from anyone.[35]

In most cases, falls from trains were treated routinely, but in March 1901 a coroner's inquest at Prestatyn heard that Irishman Matthew M'Garry met his death by falling from an express train at Prestatyn. He was travelling with three others from Dublin and joined the 2.25 a.m. from Holyhead. Later Matthew M'Garry moved a box that was against one of the doors, the door flew open and he fell from the train. The coroner was concerned that the dead man's brother did not give the alarm until Chester. The brother insisted that he knew nothing about communication cords, a point the coroner seemed unwilling to believe.[36] Subsequently the LNWR officials gave evidence as to the good condition of the doors and the coroner's suspicions were not pursued – with the jury deciding that death was from the fall but could not say how that fall had occurred.[37]

Passengers in premier accommodation were not immune from such incidents. Lennard Lucas was a high-ranking officer in the Royal Navy travelling to Holyhead on the sleeper train in March 1898. He asked the attendant to wake him an hour before the destination, but the attendant was aware of a strong draft from the compartment soon after the train passed Gaerwen. He checked and found the door open and General Lucas missing. The inquest concluded that he had mistaken the carriage door for the lavatory and had fallen onto the track.[38] Lucas was inspector-general of hospitals and fleets and had survived several campaigns and one serious wound while aboard HMS *Tamar* – only to be defeated by the door of a railway carriage.

This stretch of the CHR was the scene of another death of a passenger from a fall but one where the passenger had deliberately left the train. Robert Evans was a theatrical stage carpenter travelling to Holyhead from Crewe but was 'mentally deranged' shortly after joining the train according to one witness at the inquest. That witness had gone to sleep but awoke as the train entered Anglesey and he was aware of a man hanging on to the outside the train trying to smash the window. He said he pulled the communication cord but there was no response and the train continued to Holyhead. Robert Evans was found severely injured in Bodorgan tunnel and died soon afterwards. The jury agreed that this witness had pulled the communication cord even though the LNWR claimed that it had not been used.[39]

Communication between train and lineside was also fraught with danger, as an incident in 1942 demonstrated. The husband of Margaret Hughes of Bangor was working on the line near Conwy and she wished to pass a message to him. She resorted to the unusual means of dropping a weighted note from the window as he worked by the line. When she leaned out of the window to check the success of her efforts she was severely injured as her head hit the stonework of the tubular bridge and she died a week later.[40]

We saw from the Abergele crash in 1868 that the occupants of the Irish Mail were largely the better off, but another accident shows that some less exalted trains were used by a different slice of society. Ten years after the Abergele crash there was an inquest into the death of William Morrissey who was travelling with friends and family to emigrate from Ireland to Australia. He fell from the train in circumstances that aroused the suspicion of the authorities in the subsequent inquest. The evidence of William Evans, platform inspector at Holyhead, provided interesting data about the boat trains. This one met the SS *Earl Spencer* from Dublin North Wall at 1.10 a.m. on 25 June 1878. There were sixteen carriages, of which twelve were passenger carriages containing 495 passengers; 440 were third class passengers in nine carriages. Most of the passengers were Irish and there was a large quantity of emigrant luggage. William Morrissey's body was later found on the track near Prestatyn station by the driver of a Manchester to Holyhead goods at around 4.25 a.m. Inspector John Jones of the Flintshire Police eventually caught up with two of Morrissey's travelling companions who were heading for the *Lusitania* at Gravesend and thence to Australia. They gave an account of the fate of their comrade but had no idea that they ought to have reported it. The best explanation the coroner could offer was that the man had changed his mind about emigration and tried an early exit from the expedition. The authorities agreed

ENTRANCE TO TUBULAR BRIDGE, CONWAY CASTLE

35. *Unlike its counterpart over the Menai Straits, the Conwy tubular bridge has survived since 1848 with only the addition of supporting pillars to cope with the increased weight of trains. The narrowness of the tube entrance contributed to the death of Margaret Hughes of Bangor who hit her head on the masonry in 1942.* (**Photo: Phil Lloyd Collection**)

that the *Lusitania* could be intercepted at Plymouth if foul play were suspected: after some consideration, the jury agreed that William Morrissey's death was accidental.[41]

Michael Kelly's fall and death at the Llandegai tunnel in 1905 had a rather distasteful sequel. John Cooney told the coroner that he and the deceased had been harvesting in Norfolk and were sleeping in a compartment. Suddenly Mr Kelly got up panicking that he was late for work, opened the train door and disappeared into the tunnel, from where his badly mangled body was recovered. Subsequently the LNWR and the local authorities refused to fund the burial of his remains which were put in a fish box. After some unseemly negotiation, the local priest and the Catholic community in Bangor raised enough money for a wreath and a funeral at Glanadda cemetery.[42] There was a similar lack of humanity from the LNWR a year later when two Irish brothers were going home from their jobs in a Wigan colliery. One fell from the train and his brother, Thomas Keenan, asked if he could board another to go back and look for him. The LNWR told him he would have to buy a ticket. Patrick Keenan was subsequently found by the line at Talybont near Bangor, and later died of his injuries. The jury accepted that the death was accidental but demanded that an official explain to them why the deceased's brother was treated so disgracefully.[43]

In 1888 it was sailors using the line to travel from Holyhead to join their ship at Portland when one of their number awoke and in a state of confusion, opened the door and fell from the carriage between Rhyl and Prestatyn. He survived long enough to reach hospital in Chester but died soon afterwards.[44] Another sailor disembarked at Holyhead in 1908 and headed for his next ship at Cardiff by train. Elias Jones died falling from an express shortly after passing Sandycroft. The coroner could offer no explanation, but the fact that Jones left the train close to where his family lived seems to be an unlikely coincidence and may suggest an ill-advised attempt to call home on his way to south Wales.[45]

Equally ill-advised was the trip by several young children of the Luke family of Bagillt who attempted to cross the line at Gronant towards the beach. The eldest

36. *Merchant seaman Elias Jones fell from a train just past Sandycroft on his way from Holyhead to Cardiff in 1908 and may have been attempting a visit to his family who lived close by. In September 2020, the 1.58 p.m. Voyager service from Holyhead is near the same spot while work proceeds in the old Sandycroft sidings. This service terminated at Crewe rather than London – one of the timetable changes made during the COVID-19 pandemic.* (**Photo: Phil Lloyd Collection**)

girl managed to assist her younger brother across the line, but he let go of her hand and rushed back under the wheels of the Irish Mail. The coroner's court passed the usual peremptory accidental death verdict.[46] The children were at least using a recognised crossing, whereas William Roberts – a former porter with the railway – met his death between Ty Croes and Bodorgan while using the line as a short cut until he was hit by a freight train from Holyhead. That stretch of line was particularly prone to this kind of incident as the roads between remote rural settlements in the area were very indirect.[47]

George Wright, an employee of the Great Western Railway (GWR), died on the line east of Abergele in 1893 while travelling to see his father who was dangerously ill. The GWR man was unable to take a train direct to Abergele and so alighted at Rhyl and chose to walk along the line. He got within a quarter of a mile of his destination when he was killed by a passing train. It was reported that there was one consolation for the deceased's wife and seven children: at the time of the accident, he had with him 'a current copy of "Ally Sloper" [an early comic] bearing an insurance coupon value £150' [£19,000].[48]

There is one kind of fatal railway incident that no amount of action from railway operators can prevent – when people decide to use the railway as the means to end their own lives. The tragedy behind such incidents is apparent from three on the CHR that show the underlying mental strain on the deceased and their families. In two examples the anonymity of the deceased was an additional complication. In September 1887 railway officials and police struggled to identify a body found on the railway between Mostyn and Point of Ayr. The only clues were a diary with the entry 'Stage early' on one page, and a programme from a Liverpool theatre. The authorities assumed that he was an actor until forensic police enquiries eventually identified the man as Leon Gabriel of Liverpool. He was not an actor but the son of a prominent member of the Jewish community in the city. The original plan to bury Leon in the churchyard at Mostyn was fortunately prevented and he was subsequently interred in Liverpool in accordance with his faith.[49]

In a somewhat similar case in 1899, Sarah Paul contacted police in Rhyl having read newspaper reports about the mystery of a man's body having been discovered on the railway. She was certain it was her husband with whom she had once kept two hairdressing shops in Liverpool.[50] Other instances were more straightforward. In a particularly shocking event in 1911 George Terry, an ironworker who lived with his mother in Shotton, deliberately stood on the railway nearby and was 'dashed to pieces by the express from Chester to Holyhead'. An unsuspecting victim was the young witness of the tragic incident. He reported that the driver whistled repeatedly but Terry stood between the rails calmly buttoning up his coat.[51] A year later, and just a few miles down the line from Shotton, a nurse who had visited her dying father in Holywell threw herself from the train having left a heartrending note about her intolerable grief.[52] An unusual feature of the tragedy at the Old Colwyn end of the Penmaenrhos tunnel in 1907 was that it involved a North Staffordshire Railway train. That company had running rights on the CHR and its midday express from Stoke to Llandudno killed Joseph Owen, a local carpenter and wheelwright who appeared to cause his own death.[53] Occasionally there was a happier ending, such as in 1895 when a bundle of clothes was found near the line at Rockliffe Hall and it was thought that someone had committed suicide. Eventually the police found that the clothes belonged to an army pensioner who had been taking the cure at Holywell – the Lourdes of Wales. He found his clothes bundle too burdensome on his trip back to Runcorn and threw it out of the train window. It was eventually returned to him.[54]

John Parry Jones, aged fifteen of Aber also met his death in 1908 through a deliberate act, although he did not intend to end his life. He was a porter at Llanfairfechan and had a special pass to travel to and from work. He joined a relief train from Chester that was due to stop at all stations to Bangor. When the driver failed to notice Aber station, where the young man wanted to alight, he took

37. *The North Staffordshire Railway had running rights on the CHR as shown by No 54* John Bramley Moore *hauling a passenger express near Colwyn Bay around the end of the nineteenth century. The train has just passed the point where a North Staffordshire train hit and killed Joseph Owen in 1907.* **(Photo: John Alsop Collection)**

38. *Aber station around the time John Parry Jones – aged just fifteen – of nearby Henfaes cottage, a porter at Llanfairfechan, died after jumping from a train that failed to stop as scheduled at his home station in 1908. In 1960 Aber station was the first of the 1848 stations to close and little trace of it survives.* (Photo: John Alsop Collection)

matters into his own hands and jumped from the train near Glan y Mor but was hit and killed by an oncoming train.[55]

The CHR was a major technological investment in an area that was essentially rural and agricultural. The evidence in this chapter is that some local people and passengers struggled to adjust to the scale and speed of the railway. If that is true of people, how much more so of animals? In 1855 three of farmer Kerfoot's horses broke through fencing and onto the line at Bodhafod Farm, Towyn. The result was inevitable as they 'became terrified and bewildered, and were instantly run over and frightfully mangled'.[56] At Prestatyn in 1896 it was a flock of sheep that felt the force of the railway as they were being herded across the line at Tyn y Morfa farm and twenty-one were killed by two trains. It says something about news reporting priorities that their fate took precedence over a serious injury to a shunter at Prestatyn.[57] At Greenfield in 1889, farmer John Evans of Glan y Don farm chose to bring his herd into the dairy just as the Irish Mail was due and one was 'cut to atoms'.[58] For a song thrush, killed in the same area, there was at least the consolation of preservation for posterity. J.A. Walker was one the best-known drivers on the line and in September 1910 was on the Irish Mail between Bagillt and Holywell when the left-hand glass, through which he was keeping a look-out, was smashed. The fireman looked around for an explanation and discovered a dead thrush on the footplate that had come through glass a quarter of an inch thick and hit the driver in the eye. Walker nonetheless took his train through to Holyhead where he went off duty from the injury, while the thrush was 'sent to Mr Newstead of Chester for preservation'.[59]

The railway solicitors sometimes attempted to manage the behaviour of animal owners near the line, but the court's sympathies were more often with the farmer. So, when John Owen – resident at the railway crossing at Llanfihangel yn Nhowyn – appeared at court in Valley in 1902 for allowing his ponies to stray

39. *Industry and agriculture continue side by side at Talacre with the gas terminal having replaced the colliery. The sheep are still here, just as they were in 1896 when twenty-one were killed by two trains at nearby Tyn y Morfa crossing. In March 2020, a Transport for Wales class 175 for Manchester has just passed the crossing which is now elaborately protected by gates and lights.* (Photo: Phil Lloyd Collection)

he was merely cautioned.[60] The indirect impact of the railway on animals was illustrated in a most extreme manner at Prestatyn in December 1874. John Hughes was a carter for a local grocer and was standing at the door of the Railway Hotel with his horse and cart when the noise of the train starting caused the horse to bolt. Hughes grabbed at the animal but was dragged under the wheels of the cart and died soon afterwards leaving a widow and young children.[61]

For every mishap on the line there must have been many unreported near misses. Some near misses were noted, such as an extraordinary event in July 1883 that could have ended in a serious collision. The signalman at Llandudno Junction was offered a light engine from the Conwy signal box. He was aware of the simultaneous approach of the Irish Mail and so set the signals at danger intending to run the engine into a siding while the express passed. Having changed the signal, he was startled to see the engine pass danger and disappear east through the junction with the express hard on its heels. According to one account, the signalman telegraphed Colwyn Bay to place detonators on the line to wake the crew; the ploy succeeded and the engine was placed in the siding at Colwyn Bay where it was discovered that the fire was out and the boiler dry. A later – and more likely – version suggested that the engine had carried on until it stalled and was discovered at Penmaenrhos beyond Colwyn Bay with the driver and fireman still asleep. They were discharged immediately when it was discovered that they had falsified the length of their shift and had been on duty for over fifteen hours.[62] The incident was sufficiently serious to provoke a question in Parliament and the official version of the event was provided by Joseph Chamberlain of the Board of Trade:

> I have communicated with the [LNWR], and am informed that the engine driver and fireman had worked a special goods train from Chester to Carnarvon, and that, there being no load for them to take back, they were authorized to return to Chester with their engine alone but, in order to obtain this authority, the men, in their anxiety to get home to Chester, wilfully made a misstatement to the effect that they had commenced work at 12.45, instead of 8 o'clock, that morning. I am informed that for this falsehood they have both been dismissed. The signalman at Llandudno Junction exercised great presence of mind when the engine ran through that station in telegraphing to the signalman at Colwyn Bay, as the Colwyn Bay staff [were] thus enabled to take measures for protecting the line.[63]

Another close call occurred at Flint in 1913 when the 6.10 p.m. stopping train to Chester approached the platform. A latecomer rushed from the ticket office and

40. *Fowler class 4F 44389 drifts light through a rural scene near Pabo in August 1964. In 1883 another light engine passed this point having gone through all the danger signals from Llandudno Junction with its crew asleep and the Irish Mail hard on its heels. Alert work by signal staff prevented a disaster and the engine eventually stalled near the CHR summit at Penmaenrhos.* **(Photo: Geoff Smith, Online Transport Archive)**

began to cross the line in front of the train and was seen by porter Owen Roberts. He leapt on top of the man to push him away from the train, saving the life of the errant passenger at great risk to his own.[64] It was not only staff who performed such heroics. Mrs Margaret Irvine of Gadlys House, Bagillt was presented with a silver medal of the Grand Prior of the Order of St John by the Prince of Wales in 1890: 'for rescuing an aged and infirm man from a position of the greatest peril at Bagillt Railway Station'.[65]

The bulk of the incidents in this chapter occurred before 1914, showing that railway safety and public awareness of the dangers improved relatively slowly from the time the line opened in 1848. By the end of the century there had been

41. 175102 for Holyhead pauses at Flint in June 2019 on its way to Holyhead. This is close to the spot where porter Owen Roberts pushed a passenger away from a moving train in 1913. The station buildings at Flint have changed relatively little since it opened in 1848 but all stops between here and Prestatyn have closed, creating the longest gap – fourteen miles – between stations on the CHR. (Photo: Phil Lloyd Collection)

many improvements such as block working rather than time interval signalling, better braking, passenger communication facilities and improved infrastructure. After 1918 there were fewer incidents and less likelihood of reports in the newspapers. For example, in 1903 the relatively minor injury of Evan Williams near Mochdre during the widening scheme was reported, which probably would not have happened after 1918.[66] Even so, some incidents did come to public notice such as the death of Albert Turner who was employed by a firm of wagon repairers. He was hit and killed instantly at Llandudno Junction by the 7.40 a.m. train from Bangor in 1936 as he crossed the line.[67]

In 1965 there were two incidents in Anglesey and one at Connah's Quay that warranted referral to the railway inspectorate. On 25 May a farmer driving his car over Llanddaniel level crossing near Llanfair P G was killed. A diesel multiple unit from Crewe to Holyhead hit the car when the crossing keeper opened the gates after a train from Holyhead had passed through. The gate operator, a Miss Williams, had failed to check the train indicator, which showed that another train was approaching from the opposite direction. The local supervising stationmaster maintained that he reviewed the crossing practice regularly with the two women responsible for it. But the inspector was sceptical because the stationmaster spoke only English, the instructions were all printed in English and Miss Williams – the gatekeeper involved in the incident – spoke only Welsh and could not read or write in either language. Despite the concerns of the LNWR about the Welsh language in 1894 – when it dismissed Welsh-only speakers as noted in the previous chapter – this is the only incident where the Welsh language was mentioned as a factor. It was not the first fatality at this crossing. In August 1918 Mrs Mary Williams was the gatekeeper when her toddler wandered onto the line and Mrs Williams dived in front of the train to save him. She was severely injured in the attempt and the unfortunate child died at the scene.[68]

There was a serious fire near Connah's Quay station in August 1965 when parts of the gearbox of a Metro-Cammell diesel multiple unit became detached and pierced the fuel tank of the train. The spilt fuel was ignited on the exhaust pipe and considerable damage caused. Nine passengers sustained minor injuries and shock and the three crew were slightly injured in their energetic efforts to put out the fire and warn other traffic. The driver's name was Robert Stephenson. By the time the report came out in April 1966 Connah's Quay station was closed.[69] In September 1965 there was another incident on Anglesey when a train struck standing carriages at Holyhead causing the death of Elaine Bell, aged thirteen, a resident of the town who was trapped with friends in the wreckage. The train entered the station too quickly and its crew were inattentive, with driver Davies shouldering most responsibility. For perhaps the last time, reduced visibility from smoke and steam was a factor. But like many incidents reported in this chapter, it was familiarity that bred complacency and blinded the crew to changed circumstances. There are narrow escapes, but eventually serious consequences can result from relatively minor risks taken by train crew or other staff.[70]

There is no suggestion that the CHR was more dangerous than any comparable stretch of line in the UK, although the combination of the rapid trains to Ireland and the slower local services on a busy line probably raised the risk of mishap. Some of that risk was removed after 1900 when four tracks replaced two for much of the route from Chester to Llandudno Junction. But that could not compensate

42. *Llanfair P G station was part of the Beeching-based cull of February 1966 but was saved by the destruction of the Britannia Tubular Bridge in 1970 when it became the southern terminus for rail in Anglesey. The facilities and surroundings in this 1980s shot – with a rare fall of snow in Anglesey – portray a sense of continuing neglect. The crossing at Llanddaniel where a farmer lost his life in 1965 is beyond the bridge.* **(Photo: David Plimmer)**

for chance events such as in 1904 when a lump of piping being carried by one train fell on the line near Talacre and derailed the following train, destroying a part of the new wooden platforms at Talacre in the process. The Irish Mail was closing from the opposite direction and was in danger of ploughing into the wreckage until the guards placed detonators on the line to alert the approaching train.[71]

But Neison's statistics at the start of the chapter show that even when rail accidents were more prevalent, the risk was still relatively low. And the risk should be set alongside the massive loss of life from road accidents, which in any five years in north Wales would probably outnumber all rail accidents on the railway in the region for the whole of its existence. In 2019 there were 18 deaths, 275 serious injuries and 633 minor injuries on north Wales roads at a time when vehicle and road safety is improving.

It was a point picked up by Robert Adley MP, a notable supporter of railways, during a parliamentary debate in 1990 in which he noted 2,500 deaths per year on the roads and 250,000 injured:

Nothing better illustrates [MPs] attitudes to safety matters than the way in which we deal in the House with transport accidents. There has only to be the slightest railway accident – even if one person is killed – for an [MP] with a constituency interest to ask for a private notice question, and very often the request will be granted. Day in and day out our constituents are killed and maimed in road accidents. … However [MPs] do not make demands for private notice questions after road accidents, and we certainly do not see the headlines that we are accustomed to seeing whenever there is a rail problem.[72]

Sadly, the wording on the Abergele memorial to the victims of the 1868 crash noted at the head of the chapter seems more relevant to road transport than it ever did to rail.

43. *Facilities for passengers were improved greatly by the LNWR, including the hotel at Holyhead station which provides the background for the imminent departure of a heavy train when double-heading was still required. The hotel closed in 1955 to be replaced by a smaller office building.* **(Photo: John Alsop Collection)**

5

The Railway and the Crossing to Ireland

The City of Dublin Steam Packet Company [DSP] have never lost a life yet in the conveyance of mails and passengers to Ireland. But the same cannot be said for the London and North Western. They have lost very many lives, and some of the boats too.[1]

Although this book is primarily about the railway from Chester to Holyhead, it is important to recall the words of Robert Peel from 1848 in Chapter 2. His government of 1841–1846 had:

> Always looked upon the railway as a great national undertaking the terminus of which was not, in fact, Holyhead, but Dublin, [so that they] had departed from the ordinary rules and granted a sum of money to assist in carrying it out.[2]

The money provided by government was in the form of revenue funding that guaranteed a profit to the railway company for carrying the mail, and capital funding to improve the harbour at Holyhead. We have noticed in Chapter 1 that the battle for the railway route was essentially one about which harbour would be favoured – Holyhead or Porth Dinllaen. Once the decision had been taken in favour of the former, government had to address the shortcomings of the harbour at Holyhead, particularly its unsuitability for larger ships and its vulnerability to adverse weather. It also wished to provide a refuge for the vast shipping traffic heading to and from Liverpool that was frequently affected by the adverse weather conditions. So, government committed to a massive capital project that began at the same time as the railway construction but was not finished until 1873. As with almost all aspects of the Chester and Holyhead Railway (CHR) project, it was beset with challenges, accidents and incidents.

In September 1844 William Rickford Collett, the first chairman of the CHR, reported the proposed line had 'few natural difficulties' apart from having to divert around the Bishop of Bangor's property and crossing the Menai Straits at great expense. Moreover, government had agreed major expenditure on harbour improvements at Holyhead.[3] The importance of the sea crossing was underlined by the appointment of a seaman – Captain Constantine Moorsom – to direct the CHR project. Collett was a rather unstable figure who agreed that the CHR would contribute £200,000 (£27m) to the harbour and by 1849 he had disappeared to Africa surrounded by a fog of suspicion around share dealings, leaving Moorsom to chair the CHR and later the LNWR.

Work commenced on the harbour in January 1848 and by 1851 was in full flow. The mail was processed through the Admiralty Pier half a mile or so from the main station and connected by a branch line. Admiralty Pier station opened in May 1851 to speed up the process of shifting the mail between boats and the railway. The London and North Western Railway (LNWR) developed its station including the Royal Hotel which employed Leonora Hibbert as manager after she gained national celebrity chef status for her handling of the Refreshment Rooms at Wolverton station, with *Herapath's Railway Journal* expressing the hope that 'her pork pies [will be] as excellent as the trumpet of fame has proclaimed'.[4]

The breakwater was on an entirely different scale and it took a year to create an infrastructure of railways, quarries and scaffolding that employed 1,100 workers. The broad gauge may have been defeated in 1846 but it was used on the breakwater construction because it was more efficient, and three railway lines were created that enabled stone to be brought from Holyhead Mountain.[5] The process encountered significant difficulties beginning with the death of Captain Hutchison in March 1851. He oversaw one of the many 'monster blasts' in the quarry that attracted much interest. Despite standing far away from the explosion, Hutchison took a direct hit from a large piece of stone and was killed instantly.[6]

In May 1851 there were serious disturbances on the works because of resentment by Welsh workers about the employment of Irish labour – like the disturbances at Penmaenmawr in 1846. The Reverend Jones of Holyhead was the chief rabble-rouser, adding his own anti-Catholic sentiment to Welsh nationalist resentment of the Irish workers. Betts and Peto, the contractors, acted firmly in resisting the objection to Irish labour and only allowed work to recommence when those workers could return. The paddle gunboat HMS *Lucifer* was at the ready to assist with tackling the mob before peace prevailed and blame was heaped on workers from Flintshire and Denbighshire rather than on the locals.[7]

It was no surprise that there were numerous casualties among the construction workers given the complexity of the operations and the presence of gunpowder and rock. The railway delivering stone was the scene of a notable accident

44. The breakwater railway operated until 1980 and 01002 was the last locomotive to work it. The earlier railway on the breakwater was broad gauge but this engine was a standard gauge locomotive. In November 1976 it was carrying materials for the repair of this structure that is 1.7 miles long. (Photo: John Hobbs)

when a locomotive tipped off the line into the water while bringing a load to the works, causing the death of driver Peter Wynne at Soldier's Point in March 1851- very soon after the death of Captain Hutchison.[8] In September 1854 the Marquis of Chandos visited the works as chairman of the LNWR – underlining the predominance of his company over the nominally independent CHR – to urge progress because of the threat to Irish traffic from the Great Western Railway's (GWR's) progress towards Dublin from south Wales. He showed no signs of concerning himself with the coincidental death of 18-year-old Hugh Evans, crushed by falling equipment: Evans' brother had died in an identical manner three years earlier. Another man was buried by stone and narrowly escaped death a day or two before Chandos arrived.[9]

By 1864 attention was turning to developing the facilities for the LNWR trains with the old dock being excavated to allow steamers to berth within the station complex at all states of the tide. The station was expanded to increase accommodation for passengers and freight and provision made for repair facilities for the LNWR's fleet to avoid steamers being sent to Liverpool.[10] The main works on the breakwater were declared complete twenty-five years after starting when the Prince of Wales visited the town for the opening ceremony in 1873. Despite the extreme cost and complexity of the project – more than twice the cost of the Britannia Tubular Bridge – the event was rather low-key so that the 'prince acknowledged the addresses with a bow, and the few hundred people who witnessed the ceremony gave a cheer'.[11]

There was a much larger ceremony in 1880 when the Prince of Wales returned, almost as a private guest of the LNWR, in order to open the new station, hotel and harbour works that provided the company with greatly improved facilities to exploit growing traffic to and from Holyhead. The event did not go well in the eyes of the local people because of the LNWR's behaviour towards them during the ceremony. Some of the reporting suggested that the company treated local people with contempt:

> Loyal citizens feel a little sore that the railway people are going to keep His Royal Highness to themselves, that they will not let him budge beyond their own premises, that they have brought a division of the Metropolitan Police to keep all but a privileged few at arm's length and that they have stuck glass along the surrounding walls to punish enthusiastic persons who may presume to peep over.[12]

The response of some Holyhead's residents to the LNWR's arrangements for the royal visit was predictable:

> The oldest inhabitant and his friends were unanimously of the opinion that Holyhead had been badly treated and were proportionately grumpy [as it is] eminently unsatisfying for a loyal Welshman [to be] met at every passage … by the dismal Welsh legend 'Dim Mynediad' [no entry] and to be cuffed about on his own streets by London Policemen while strangers from all parts of England and Ireland were being treated with Royal smiles and iced champagne.[13]

The LNWR had at least departed from its usual practice by using the Welsh language – but only to declare its exclusion of local people from the event. The negative impression was reinforced by the LNWR chairman Richard Moon, who used the occasion to boast of fifty years of railway dominance in the UK by his company since the opening of the Liverpool and Manchester Railway, and of the LNWR's supreme power and wealth within the industry. He showed little concern for local anger at the freight rates and fares charged by the company in north Wales when he complained of traders who ignored the achievements of railways and: 'thought [the LNWR] ought to carry their traffic for nothing'.[14] He also underlined the exclusion of Wales from the occasion by declaring that the new harbour was: 'a great blessing and a connecting link between the *two* [my italics] countries [England and Ireland]'.[15]

Whatever he might have wanted or been prepared to do, it appears the royal visitor was entirely in the hands of the LNWR. When political leaders in Rhyl wrote and asked him to stop at their town on his way home, they were told by his secretary that the prince would have been pleased to do so but that: '*railway arrangements* will not allow of the train being stopped [so] it is *not in his power to comply* with the request' (my italics).[16]

The harbour at Holyhead and the 'steam bridge' across the Irish Sea were clearly part of the CHR as Peel had hoped – at least until the first motor car ferry left Holyhead in 1965, at which point the terminus of the line became Holyhead – except for the few foot passengers who continued to use the ferries. We saw that government granted the CHR the exceptional power to operate its own steamships, but then rather perversely gave the mail contract to the DSP. That created a tension that featured in the operation of the service between London and Dublin for many years. The LNWR and the DSP had to work together for decades with the former constantly aiming to win the contract off the Irish company. The dispute became a feature of the political battles for Irish Home Rule as the LNWR was often aggressively English in its dealings with Irish (and Welsh) national sentiment, acting almost as an extension of the London government.

After the initial decision in favour of the DSP, a major flashpoint in the dispute occurred in 1883 when the Gladstone government appeared to be on the brink of switching the mail contract to the LNWR. The subsequent uproar caused a change of heart and the DSP won the day, probably influenced in part by Gladstone's desire to placate Irish interests as he moved towards support for Home Rule. The LNWR had acquired powerful new steamers and aimed to demonstrate its superiority to the DSP as an operator, so its disappointment was intense. A curious incident in 1883 demonstrated the intensity of feeling between the parties:

> For some days past the [LNWR] have been contrasting the speed of their vessels with that of the Royal Mail steamers of the [DSP]. It was generally understood that yesterday the final test would be tried as to the merits of the respective steamers and their sailing powers, and although no official sanction

was given to the affair and no regular match arranged, the officers and servants of both companies entered with enthusiasm and spirit on the trip and looked with anxiety to the issue. … The crowd composed every part from the hottest and best-known Nationalists to the strongest and most aristocratic supporters of the Tory Party. … The female portion of the fashionable assembly which lined both piers were equally demonstrative in showing which way their feelings ran. … The steamers running were the *Munster* of the home company and the *Lily* – the fastest boat of the powerful LNWR.[17]

The result was a clear victory for Captain Slaughter and his officers and crew on the DSP vessel who completed the crossing in 209 minutes compared to 220 minutes for the *Lily*. Both crossing times compare favourably with 2020 timings.

In 1898, Parliament debated whether the LNWR should have the power to run vessels between Holyhead and Dublin without any further review by Parliament. That incensed Irish MPs who considered that government was unable to control the LNWR, and that it was the LNWR that controlled the government. During the debate one Irish MP made an interesting point about the two operators across the Irish Sea:

There have been many accidents upon their [LNWR] boats – unfortunately too many. I am not afraid to say what none of the Gentlemen who have spoken on the other side can say, that I have not a shilling in either Company, and I can therefore say this for the City of Dublin Steam Packet Company with a clear conscience … they have never lost a life yet in the conveyance of mails and passengers to Ireland. But the same cannot be said for the London and North Western. They have lost very many lives, and some of the boats too.[18]

That statement from Patrick O'Brien was all too accurate. The parliamentary investigations into the poor performance of the mail contract in 1853 was critical of the railway and maritime arrangements, and especially the terrible conditions on the boats of both companies. The government's priority was the rapid delivery of the mail, as shown by the arrangements for a 'fog bell' on the cliffs above Holyhead in 1853. In fog it was to sound every half-hour ahead of the arrival of the passenger ferry, but every quarter-hour before the mail boat arrived.[19] It was clearly mail before people.

The 1860 launch of the *Admiral Moorsom*, named after Constantine Moorsom of the old CHR company, who also chaired the LNWR and had lived latterly at Menai Bridge, marked an attempt by the LNWR to improve conditions on the boats. This boat was more powerful and had: 'a peculiarity in the construction of the fore-deck house of this steamer, which gives complete shelter to the cattle and deck passengers', thus going some way to meet the 1853 criticisms.[20] That ship's arrival came soon after the difficulties of perhaps the most famous ship ever to enter the harbour at Holyhead. As we have seen, Brunel had plans to reach Holyhead by rail in 1845–1846 but was thwarted by the Gauge Commission. In October 1859, a month after Brunel's death, it was the weather that ruined the visit to Holyhead of his ship the *Great Eastern*. The LNWR had taken advantage of the visit by advertising trips to see the ship. Queen Victoria also visited with Prince Albert. Unfortunately, the *Great Eastern*'s arrival coincided with the storm that sank the *Royal Charter* off Anglesey and wrecked the CHR railway line at various points along the coast of north Wales.

Four years later, one of the LNWR's own steamers, the *Telegraph,* with Captain Warren in charge, hit rocks near South Stack lighthouse in thick fog, only managing to rescue the 400 livestock and 250 passengers after a perilous operation with much damage caused to the ship.[21] Worse was to follow when the *St Columba,* with about 250 passengers plus crew and a large deck cargo of cattle and sheep, hit rocks near the Skerries lighthouse in June 1873. The boats were lowered, capsized due to overcrowding but eventually managed to get ashore. As the steamer broke up, the livestock fell into the sea and the passengers were sheltered by the lighthouse crew. Next day another vessel – the *Rook Light* – completed the rescue, at a cost of one person drowned. This event was reported just as the LNWR steamer *Duchess of Sutherland* hit a reef ten miles out of Dublin in thick fog. There was panic on board, and further alarming incidents before the much-damaged ship arrived in Holyhead amidst wild celebrations from the relieved passengers.[22] The tale of woe continued for two LNWR steamers on 8 September 1875 when the *Edith*, heading for Greenore under the command of Captain Richard Owen, collided with Captain Beaumont's *Duchess of Sutherland* – recently restored from its 1873 mishap – returning from North Wall, Dublin. The *Edith* sank quickly, and two lives were lost. The loss of the latter ship caused the *Cambria* (one of the original LNWR fleet) to be brought back into service when clearly not fit for purpose. John Roberts was killed while loading the *Cambria* when a rotten mast fell onto his head – the jury asking the LNWR to: 'take into consideration the circumstances of his poor, blind widow now left destitute'.[23] When the Board of Trade inquiry into the earlier collision concluded, it found that Richard Owen of the *Edith* was at fault for attempting to pass the other ship on the wrong side.[24] In the same month as that inquest, the LNWR *Earl Spencer* collided with and sank a schooner near Holyhead.

None of these mishaps inhibited the growth of the LNWR operation at Holyhead so that in 1877 the steamer *Isabella* was launched at Lairds' shipyard in Birkenhead. It was an entirely steel vessel, much of which was manufactured at the LNWR's works at Crewe. That brought the total of LNWR steamers at Holyhead to thirteen.[25] The *Cambria* was among them and still associated with tragic accidents. It sustained damage on a crossing to Dublin in December 1877 and James Williams of Holyhead was the carpenter sent to repair it. He lost his footing and fell into the Liffey, apparently ignored a lifebuoy that was thrown to him and drowned – leaving a wife and two children.[26]

At the start of the 1880s the LNWR added the *Violet* and the *Lily* to its fleet; two powerful steamers that could still not outrun the DSP as we saw in the unofficial race of 1883. Later that year fifteen lives were lost when the LNWR steamer *Holyhead*, carrying passengers and livestock, sank after colliding with a German coal carrier. The *Liverpool Mercury* report included the surprising statement that: 'It is most unusual for accidents to occur with the [LNWR] boats, and this collision is unprecedented, with the exception of that when the *Edith* sank in Holyhead harbour some years ago.'[27] To call that assessment generous would be an understatement. That became clear in January 1885 when the *Admiral Moorsom*, by then regarded as 'old and somewhat slow', sank with the loss of five lives after a collision with the *Santa Clara*, an American steamer. The *Santa Clara* eventually docked in Holyhead carrying fourteen survivors. Captain Weekes of the LNWR ship and his crew had been transferred to the *Admiral Moorsom* after their previous ship had collided with another vessel in Holyhead harbour the previous day. The collision demonstrated the difficulties of navigating a channel from west to east when there is significant traffic from north to south. Weekes had altered course to avoid one ship but in doing so was hit in the side, and his old paddle ship was destroyed. He was among those killed in the incident.[28]

The catalogue of accidents continued into 1887 when the LNWR steamer *Banshee* ran onto the rocks in fog in Holyhead Bay: the *Eleanor* was sent to assist but also ran aground at Penrhos. Fortunately, there were no casualties.[29] In June of the same year, the LNWR steamer *Shamrock* ran over a fishing boat and killed two occupants: an accidental death according to the coroner's jury which nonetheless said Captain Darling could have done much more to avoid the collision.[30] Almost exactly a year after the spectacular double grounding and in similar foggy conditions, it was the *Earl Spencer* that tested the strength of the new breakwater with a hefty collision after which the terrified passengers had to be rescued by coastguards.[31]

But it was not all bad news for the LNWR steamers. In November 1888 captain John Owen of the *Isabella* was sailing to Holyhead from Greenore and encountered the *Robert Burns* carrying a cargo of wheat, but adrift with no rudder. Owen towed the ship to port in difficult conditions after three times losing connection. Subsequently, he received an inscribed clock from the owners of the other ship and a letter that alluded to the risky nature of seafaring at that time. It wished that Owen: 'may long be spared to ornament that profession in which rests the security of our little island and of which foreign nations envy us so much'.[32] But the warm glow from that incident did not last and as the decade came to an end, two LNWR ships collided in thick fog. Once again, the *Banshee* was involved when it was struck amidships by the *Irene* and sustained serious damage to its paddle box. There was panic among the 500 passengers which continued even when it finally reached Holyhead: 'One woman swooned away from the intense excitement to which she bad been subjected. Another passenger who sat with his back to the [collision] received such a shock to his nerves that he was not able to proceed until mid-day.'[33]

In the light of the serious loss of life and shipping around Holyhead it was no surprise that a third lifeboat was established at the start of the 1890s. The LNWR started the decade with improvements to some of its vessels, notably the application of the 'triple expansion system' to the engines of *Violet* and the *Lily* which increased power significantly.[34] That technological advance did little for the accident record of the LNWR as the *Lily* struck a vessel and killed one of its occupants on its way from the shipyard at Birkenhead to Holyhead in August 1891. The victim failed to respond to medical treatment after being brought aboard the *Lily*. The LNWR might have been in difficulty at the coroner's hearing but a verdict of accidental death was returned. Whether Admiral Dent's assurance that the other occupant of the boat would be 'returned home with some money in his pocket' influenced that result is not known, but it was consistent with the LNWR's machinations in avoiding embarrassing outcomes in court.[35]

Dent retired in November of the following year from his post as superintendent of shipping at Holyhead. In light of the LNWR record at sea under his leadership, it is probably appropriate that in the same paper that recorded this fact it was also noted that the *Violet* collided with an Irish trawler in Dublin Port and ran aground, and that the *Edith* was three hours late at Holyhead due to the fog.[36] While the 1890s seemed to have been a better decade for the LNWR at sea, it did not escape criticism for some of its practices. In 1896 a boy named Holmes of the Limerick City Artillery died of rheumatic fever after his passage from Holyhead on one of the LNWR cattle boats reserved for the accommodation of soldiers, but which had little shelter aboard. He apparently had insufficient money to afford the four shillings required by anyone below the rank of sergeant for a passage on the ordinary steamer. The attitude and culpability of the company was asserted by one correspondent who considered that the LNWR was 'directly answerable for his death' but thought it 'idle to make representations on the subject to the directors' and appealed to LNWR shareholders to take the matter up.[37]

It is unclear whether any improvements were made for the carriage of soldiers, but in 1897 the LNWR took delivery of the *Cambria,* its first twin-screw steamer. It boasted warm accommodation, on-board catering and improved safety facilities that were apparently so good that they were unlikely to be 'put to use, except as a drill for the crew'.[38] No doubt soldier Holmes would have been impressed had he survived his own experience of LNWR hospitality, although the commission for the steamer *South Stack* in 1900 was not reassuring. It was built by Laird Brothers at Birkenhead and was of: 'a distinctly new type and has been designed to meet the largely increased cargo and cattle trade of the company [and] can be *readily adapted to carry troops*' (my emphasis).[39] For civilian passengers, a ship of similar design to the *Cambria* was added in 1899 with the launch of the *Hibernia* by Denny Brothers of Dumbarton. The launch ceremony was an occasion for celebration by the LNWR as it reached the peak of its powers, with its route to Dublin at the fore. Peter Denny opened proceedings for the shipbuilders with a summary of the state of the LNWR at the close of the century:

> There was no one present, he said, but knew of the vastness of the [LNWR]. Like a spider's web, it had caught nearly all England [*sic*] in its iron thread. It never seemed to know where to end, and now it had taken it into its head to girdle the ocean also (laughter and applause). Where the railway would stop [Houldsworth a senior director] would be able to let them know, but in the meantime, there did not seem to be any signs of the traffic in rails for them stopping. The Company having determined to extend and quicken its cross-channel service, had been good enough to entrust the means of doing so to the hands of his firm, and they had built for them three steamers, which ran between Holyhead and Greenore, and also the *Cambria*. Lately there were placed in their hands two steamers, the *Hibernia* and the *Anglia*, the first of which they had seen launched that day.[40]

Houldsworth, who defended the right of the LNWR to dismiss workers who spoke only Welsh in 1894, did not minimise the power of his company and made clear that the mission of the route from London to Dublin was still in line with what Peel had set out in 1844:

> Although the directors were bound in all they did, whether on their own railway or in the vessels which belonged to them, to first of all consult the interests of the shareholders, and not less the interests of the travelling public, still he must claim more for the Company, because he believed in addition to meeting the wants of the travelling public and doing some good to the shareholders, in developing this service to the highest pitch of perfection they were doing something of a national work, for they were doing something to unite Ireland and England [*sic*] in closer bonds (applause). The condition of Ireland at the present time would have been very different had it not been for the silver stream between the two countries but all they could do to bridge over that stream was in the direction of doing good.[41]

Houldsworth had nothing to say about the safety record of the LNWR at sea, but the pattern soon reasserted itself in June 1900 when there was a collision between two LNWR steamers – the nearly new *Connemara* and the accident-prone *Eleanor* carrying around 700 harvesters. Fortunately, no lives were lost although both ships were damaged.[42] The *Anglia* was next up when it struck the rocks near North Stack in thick fog in June 1907. Captain Mahood was in command with 500 passengers and crew aboard and approached Holyhead very slowly to the sound of the fog gun on the cliffs above the area where the ship ran aground. Lifebelts were distributed, lifeboats prepared, and the passengers calmed with some difficulty before the ship finally made port only thirty-five minutes late. There was significant damage to the hull necessitating the *Anglia* being taken out of service for repair.[43]

By comparison, the collision between the *Connemara* and a Glasgow steamer in January 1908 was a minor one that Captain Nash considered was entirely caused by the lack of lights on the latter vessel.[44] There was no defence for Captain Lanfesty on the same ship with 200 passengers in August 1908 when he was held responsible for a collision with the *Avon* of Grangemouth. One crew member of the *Avon* was injured and Lanfesty was suspended for three months for his failure to observe Article 19 of the regulations to prevent collisions at sea.[45] Some indication of the experience of passengers may be gleaned from a note on the back of a postcard of SS *Cambria* sent from Holyhead by James Paterson on 7 January 1909 to his daughter Phyllis in Liverpool. The purpose of his trip was not stated, but it was clearly not for pleasure: 'I suppose I'm in for a trouble, wind is high, and I am low, but it has to be faced. "I'll take it lying down." Will try to cheat the elements by getting a good start in my bunk before the boat sails.'[46]

45. *On the back of this postcard James Paterson wrote to his daughter in Liverpool in January 1909, 'I suppose I'm in for a trouble, wind is high, and I am low, but it has to be faced.' Unlike many LNWR ships, the SS* **Cambria** *had a good safety record, survived active service in the First World War, returned to the LNWR in 1918 and was renamed* **Arvonia** *in 1920.* **(Photo: Phil Lloyd Collection)**

As the decade ended the *Galtee More* operating on the Holyhead to Greenore route for the LNWR ran ashore at Bellagan Point near the Haulbowline light in thick fog with many passengers rescued by the lifeboat and the *Greenore*, another of the LNWR's ships.[47] The *Connemara* was in the news again in March 1910 when it sank the steamer *Marquis of Bute* – on a voyage from Liverpool to Newport – near the Skerries but with no loss of life.[48]

Technology had a part to play in improving the accident record of shipping – as it had done for trains – and enhancing the prospect of survival when there was a problem. The LNWR secured the use of radio communication as war approached in 1914 but was soon mired in controversy again when its chosen supplier, the Helsby Wireless Telegraph Company, was immediately sued for breach of patent by Marconi.[49] The early stages of the war were relatively quiet at Holyhead, but from 1915 the presence of submarines began to make life difficult. The *Greenore* was involved in transporting survivors from the sinking of the *Lusitania* in May 1915, and there was much work for the railway officials at Holyhead in returning survivors to their homes.[50] The most significant loss for the LNWR was not the result of enemy action. The somewhat accident-prone *Connemara* finally went down after colliding with a coal carrier called the *Retriever* on 3 November 1916, four days short of twenty years since the LNWR ship's launch. Initial reports suggested a death toll of 300 but that was cut to 97. There was only one survivor from both ships so that it was difficult to establish what had happened. The *Connemara* was left floating bottom-up near Carlingford Bar.[51]

The final years of the war were marked with several disasters for Holyhead traffic. On the credit side the *Slieve Bloom* assisted in saving passengers from the large White Star Line liner *Celtic* that hit a mine near the Isle of Man in February 1917; 1918 was less successful for LNWR ships. In March, the *Rathmore* sank after a collision with a naval trawler with the loss of four lives and much livestock, although remarkably was raised and stayed in service for another five years.[52] But there was no second chance for the *Slieve Bloom* which collided with another vessel in April and sank, although all passengers were saved by the other ship, which it later transpired was an American naval vessel on anti-submarine duties.[53]

The greatest loss of the war in the Irish Sea was reserved for thirty-two days before the end of the conflict and for once did not involve a ship of the LNWR but one belonging to its rival the DSP. The DSP had already lost the *Cork* to a German submarine off Point Lynas in Anglesey in January 1918; then the *Leinster* was struck by torpedoes in October 1918 and sank with the loss of at least 501 crew and passengers, second only to the *Lusitania* in loss of life on a UK civilian ship, and the most casualties in a single incident in the Irish Sea.[54]

There was a hint of a conspiracy against the Irish company in the speech made by the DSP chairman at its meeting in May 1919 when he said that the board was:

> Satisfied that the *Leinster* was lost through the culpable—he might say the willful [*sic*] – negligence of those responsible for her safety, and what surprised him was that the *Ulster* and *Munster* were still afloat. If the authorities had desired to lose the mail packets, they could hardly have acted differently than they did. If the company had any say in the matter the *Leinster* would not have been allowed to leave Kingstown on October 10. There is no doubt that escorts would have saved her. Escorts were provided for the Stranraer route and could have been given to the Holyhead.[55]

Conspiracy or not, the LNWR finally won the contract to carry the mail from November 1920 and the DSP ceased trading four years later. The success for the British company had taken over seventy years to achieve and officially was because of a lower tender from the LNWR. The LNWR seemed to anticipate the change a year earlier when it accepted delivery of the *Anglia*, the first of four new vessels that focused almost entirely on passengers and mail and had: 'the most up-to-date safety appliances … including the Stone-Lloyd system of watertight gear, submarine signalling, wireless telegraphy and an emergency dynamo capable of lighting the whole ship in case of failure of the main dynamos. Practically no cargo will be carried'.[56] Nonetheless, the *Cambria* sank a vessel on its maiden voyage in December 1921 while carrying, among others, the Irish delegates who had been negotiating an end to the Irish War of Independence. Early in 1922 there was a severe storm at Holyhead, and the *Hibernia* broke from the moorings in the inner harbour and drifted towards the breakwater before being saved at the second attempt by the *Rostrevor,* another LNWR ship.[57]

The record of railway owned ships sailing from Holyhead did improve after the London Midland and Scottish Railway (LMS) took over in 1923. In 1925 the new company arranged for passengers to and from Dun Laoghaire (formerly Kingstown) to use the inner harbour rather than the Admiralty Pier and thereby

46. *For the first hundred years of operation the CHR was at the heart of the mail and passenger traffic between Britain and Ireland. This is a typical scene when the Irish Mail arrived at Holyhead. The dress styles, rolling stock and steamer suggest that this is a picture from the inter-war years.* (Photo: John Alsop Collection)

enjoy complete shelter when moving between train and ship.[58] There were few serious incidents to report with the LMS in charge, apart from the air attack on the *Cambria* in December 1940 that resulted in the death from machine-gun fire of third officer William Jones of Holyhead. The speed of the ship and the skill of its captain ensured the eventual failure of the attack by a German bomber.[59]

After the end of the war in 1945 the fate of railway owned ships followed the trajectory of the railway itself: a brief upsurge followed by a steady decline as the car and the lorry stole an increasing share of the market in goods and passengers. Key dates were 1965, when the first car ferries connected Holyhead and Dublin, and 1970 when the Britannia Tubular Bridge was destroyed and began its transformation into the Britannia road bridge, with a railway beneath it – literally and metaphorically. That loss of the railway connection hastened the decline of foot passenger numbers, while the improved road connection strengthened the hold of road traffic on the route along the A55. It made sense to give the railway power to operate ships in 1848, and it probably made equal sense to remove the ships from the railways in 1984. Problems were few while services were operated by the LMS or British Railways, in contrast to the accident-prone shipping operations run by the LNWR. Given that the LNWR was mostly a well-managed company it is hard to explain its record on the sea at Holyhead, but the list of accidents and incidents in this chapter make it hard to argue with the judgement of MP Patrick O'Brien at the head of this chapter – the LNWR had indeed 'lost very many lives, and some of the boats too'.

6

The Railway and Conflict

The coast of North Wales from Rhyl to Conway has been fairly bristling with Volunteer bayonets.[1]

The origins of the Chester and Holyhead Railway (CHR) show that it was built to help address one of the most troublesome dilemmas for the British Empire during the nineteenth century – the relationship between the British government and Ireland. As noted already, the line was actually intended to reduce conflict, based on the idea that all that was needed to settle Ireland was to manage it more effectively from London, and that required more efficient means of communication. More rapid decisions could then be made, and Irish people brought into a closer relationship with the rest of the UK. As history has proved, that was a rather naïve assessment.

During the second half of the nineteenth century, it became clear that the tensions could not be resolved so easily, but the CHR remained important as a means of transport between Ireland and mainland Britain for mail, government papers and MPs of all persuasions. As such, it became a symbol of British rule and was embroiled in the overall political questions of the day. The people of north Wales also flexed their muscles as nationalism grew from the late 1860s. Again, the services of the railway company were used by the authorities to deal with issues such as the tithe agitation that spread across the region. Railways were vital to the military in both world wars and the line to Holyhead played its part. North Wales was a useful place to train troops, develop technology and store the materials of war out of the reach of later German bombs.

It did not take long after the opening of the Liverpool and Manchester Railway (LMR) in 1830 for the authorities to recognise the value of railways in military deployment. The calculation was that if troops could be moved quickly then fewer would be needed to maintain order. Ireland provided an early example:

The *Jupiter* steam-vessel, having on board the headquarter division of the 71st Light Infantry, consisting of six companies, under the command of Major Levenge, arrived at Kingstown Harbour yesterday from Glasgow. The troops disembarked in the afternoon and took their seats in a train of the Dublin and Kingstown Railway carriages, which were prepared for them, and were conveyed to town, five miles and a half, in fifteen or sixteen minutes. It was a most novel sight to see a regiment, flying as it were along the line of railway, and set down in the heart of the city as if by magic.[2]

This advantage was consolidated by the government creating a regulation in 1845 that required railways to carry troops for a fixed fee whenever required to do so.[3] In the case of Ireland troops were sent directly from London or from Scotland rather than Holyhead or Liverpool as one commentator noted:

We have frequently recorded instances of rapid passages from port to port, of our steam-vessels sailing out of the Thames. We find that the celerity of movement in the Irish seas between Ireland and Scotland has likewise of late been remarkable, and that a body of troops could be conveyed from Greenock to Dublin now in the same space of time as is frequently occupied in taking them from Liverpool to Dublin.[4]

The port at Holyhead was not suited to large-scale troop and supply movements – it was a first-class route focused on speed rather than volume. It was essential to governance and as such became vulnerable when Irish discontent rose again as it did from the 1860s with the emergence of the Fenian movement. Early in 1866 passengers on the station at Holyhead witnessed the conveyance of convicted Fenians from Cork and other areas of Ireland complete with military guard. They were escorted to the station by troops and there met by warders who handcuffed them and put them in a special third-class carriage attached to the back of the limited-stop mail train. The local paper noted rather unkindly that, 'there was nothing in their appearance ... that could raise any apprehension of danger. One of them was hunchbacked and all the others had very repulsive appearances'.[5]

By the end of the year large numbers were fleeing the problems in Ireland and crowded the steamers and the trains at Holyhead even during a severe gale.[6] There was certainly justification for alarm in February 1867 when credible intelligence was received at Chester that a force of around 1,500 Fenians from Ireland, America and France would assemble in the city, storm the local garrison in order to steal the cache of arms and then capture the Irish Mail train and take it to Holyhead. The plan was to destroy track and telegraph connections behind them to delay the authorities. At Holyhead they planned to capture a steamer and launch a full-scale rebellion on arrival in Dublin.[7] Reinforcements were brought in and the plot was foiled.

47. *All is calm at Chester in June 2017 as the* **Gerald of Wales** *sets off for Holyhead in the evening sunshine. It was more hectic 150 years earlier when Fenians planned to capture a train here and head for Dublin with a cache of arms stolen from Chester Castle. The plot was foiled but a sense of nervousness about attacks on the railway remained for many years.* (**Photo: Phil Lloyd Collection**)

There was another significant response from the authorities in November 1867 when word was received by telegraph in Holyhead that a squad was heading to the town to release a recently captured Fenian by the name of Nugent. When the next train arrived, it was searched with no result apart from the capture of a drover who ran from the train to secure a cabin on the ship and was arrested as a suspect. Attention then turned to the incoming LNWR steamer, and the naval turret ship HMS *Wivern* was deployed to stop and search the vessel arriving from Dublin, again with no result.[8] Things appeared to have reached a crisis in December 1868 when railway staff reported being fired at from the windows of the Irish Mail near Mostyn. The report shows that there had been a suspicion that the Abergele crash and conflagration in August 1868 was the work of Fenians and the

December incident could be related.[9] In fact, the explanation was rather simpler as a newspaper correspondent confirmed:

> It is a curious but indisputable fact that a young friend of mine, ten years old … came by that identical train from Holyhead and amused himself by snapping off caps at passing trains and other objects of interest. On leaving school for the Christmas holidays, he had been presented with a toy gun, guiltless of powder and shot, but fitted with percussion lock for caps. It is not a deadly weapon, when you examine it closely as I did; but can make a noise, and from a distance looks formidable.[10]

The line was not assailed by any similar drama until 1880 when a failed attempt to place dynamite in front of the Irish Mail near London was discovered. Nervousness about the security of the vital Irish link led to measures to protect the Britannia Tubular Bridge from attack in 1881:

> Consequent upon the Fenian 'scare' special precautions are being taken on the Chester and Holyhead section of the [LNWR] as to the safety of the Menai bridges. Watchmen are stationed at both ends, and no person, not even a company's servant, is allowed to pass through, save under the strictest surveillance, being accompanied by an escort. The precaution is identical with that employed at the time of the last Fenian 'scare', and locally is greatly ridiculed.[11]

A more radical breakaway faction of the Irish Republican Brotherhood, calling itself the Irish National Invincibles, carried out the Phoenix Park killings of Lord Frederick Cavendish and Thomas Burke – two senior Dublin Castle officials – in May 1882. Security was tightened again at Holyhead in the aftermath, and at least one person was apprehended in possession of a gun. Having satisfied the police with his story he was allowed to proceed but was then stopped again at Valley station and charged with the rather less serious matter of riding in a first-class compartment with a second-class ticket.[12]

Official anxiety remained and it created quite a stir at Queensferry station in December 1883 when:

> A contingent of Flintshire constables arrived on Monday night at Hawarden [Prime Minister William Gladstone's home], from Queensferry Railway Station, in evident haste. Inspector Aplin from Rhyl, who was the first to arrive with two constables, upon reaching the station, immediately hurried into the

stable yard of the adjoining hotel and, securing a horse and conveyance, drove rapidly to Hawarden Castle, a mile and half distant. By the next train there arrived at Queensferry half-a-dozen more constables, all of whom left in the same hurried manner. ... Rumours were meantime current in Hawarden to the effect that the Premier's life had been threatened, that Invincibles were coming down from London to murder him.[13]

In 1887 there was more drama – and a suspicion that Fenianism was again at the root of it. Platelayers discovered four boxes of dynamite in one of the sidings at Flint station. It was suggested that a box was thrown out of one of the expresses passing through the station and the authorities began an investigation without much result.[14]

In earlier chapters we noted some tension between the LNWR and the local population in north Wales that may in part be explained by a sense among some Welsh people that the LNWR was part of an anglicised establishment. As such it might be considered alongside landowners and the established Church as a bastion

48. *Inspector Aplin arrived at Queensferry in December 1883 and hurried to Hawarden with armed officers to protect Prime Minister Gladstone. By the summer of 1965 motor traffic is building towards the Dee crossing but there are few signs of life on the station as it awaits its fate after the Beeching Report before closing in February 1966. (Copyright: The Francis Frith Collection)*

of Englishness, and liable to the kind of response seen after the dismissal of Welsh-speaking workers in 1894 discussed in earlier chapters. The alignment of the LNWR with the state against the emerging Welsh nationalist agenda was suspected locally in 1887 when the authorities struggled to contain a tithe riot in the Mochdre district of north Wales: a place famous in railway terms previously only for the construction of the world's first water troughs in 1860 that assisted fast running of the Irish Mail. The tithe was a charge against residents that was paid to the Church of England and was deeply resented by the majority of Welsh people who were nonconformist in religion. Many refused to pay and were then visited by bailiffs intent on removing property, often livestock, to pay the debt. Many areas were accessible by rail, which in north Wales meant mostly the LNWR. Trains were used to carry officials, police and the military to the sites for distraint of goods.

In the case of Mochdre, between Colwyn Bay and Llandudno Junction, soldiers and police transported to the site by rail found it difficult to alight without the special help of the LNWR as there was no station.[15] A major riot occurred once the process of distrainment began and property was returned to the train in payment for outstanding debts. In 1889, the LNWR constructed a station at Mochdre, though the local traffic did not warrant it. It seems most likely that it was constructed largely to aid local policing of the area because of the events here during the so-called Tithe Wars. As an aside, we may note that the presence of the station might also have encouraged Ephraim Wood, whom we have encountered as superintendent of the line, to retire with his second wife and a large group of servants to Pabo Hall – just a short distance from Mochdre and Pabo station. There he was able to enjoy the commanding view of the passing trains until his death in 1915. The exact location of the station is now lost beneath the A55 because of the realignment of the railway when the dual carriageway was built in the 1980s.

Events covered so far in this chapter concern domestic matters in Ireland and Wales. However, events in the wider world occasionally affected operations on the CHR. During the American Civil War diplomats from the Confederacy were removed from the UK mail ship *Trent* and Britain came close to war with the Federal states in 1861. Their response to the British ultimatum reached London from Holyhead in just short of six hours via a special train hauled by 229 *Watt* and war was averted. From the 1880s onward there were further international concerns that prompted the UK government to create and train a new army of volunteers for the battles anticipated initially across the Empire but then in Europe and the wider world. North Wales proved to be a popular location to train these new forces. One early report shows how vital the railway was to their work, with camps at many coastal locations on the line:

49. *Mochdre and Pabo station was opened in 1889, two years after the area was at the centre of a major disturbance over tithe payments by local nonconformists to the established Church – during which the LNWR struggled to unload troops and police. The station had no goods facilities, was little used and closed in 1931. The site now lies below the A55. This picture features LMS Claughton class 5998 heading west through the empty wooden station on the fast line in the 1920s.* (**Photo: John Alsop Collection**)

The coast of North Wales from Rhyl to Conway has been fairly bristling with Volunteer bayonets. … From the railway we caught sight of the tents of the 2nd Volunteer Battalions of the Lancashire Fusiliers, whose camp appeared almost on the seashore at Pensarn, held close to the railway. … At Colwyn we found the Lancashire (2nd Manchester), green coated corps, similarly employed. Their tents were pitched in a field below Pwllcrochan Hotel, at which hostelry the officers held their mess. … We moved from here to Deganwy, near Llandudno Junction, where the 11th Lancashire, a very strong battalion, numbering over a thousand bayonets, were encamped on a picturesque slope. … The ferry boat brought us across the Conway River to the camp of the 1st Volunteer Battalion of the Lancashire Fusiliers. … There is plenty of space here for all and an excellent supply of water. At the Deganwy camp, what is known as the 'arrow' field system [of trenches] was employed. … We were led to the conclusion that camps by the sea are not more expensive than those held nearer home, and that the additional advantage of a bracing sea air, getting the men clear away from their friends and other attractions to giving their undivided attention to military duties.[16]

By 1891 there were more volunteer soldiers on the coast than ever, with 11,000 at Rhyl, 1,800 at Conwy Morfa and four camps of artillery specialists at Llandudno. The only way the railway could accommodate such traffic from the North and Midlands was to run trains through the night so that many volunteers were arriving in camp in the early hours of the morning.[17] A year later the *Liverpool Mercury* considered that the north Wales coast from Rhyl to Bangor had the appearance of a 'garrison town' during the Whitsuntide holidays due to the number of volunteers under training, all brought there by train.[18]

In these circumstances it would have been surprising if there had not been a mishap. And one duly occurred in August 1892 at Penmaenmawr. Volunteers from the Welsh border country arrived by train for the Morfa Conwy camp and some got off at Conwy for a short march. Officers sent the train forward to

50. *In 1883 it was reported that 'the coast of North Wales from Rhyl to Conway has been fairly bristling with Volunteer bayonets'. Conwy Morfa was one of the main sites with its own station from 1894, enlarged in 1901 and benefiting from a signal box from nearby Penmaenbach which can be seen behind the platform.* (**Photo: John Alsop Collection**)

Penmaenmawr to bring it back on the up line and stop near the camp to unload the heavy equipment that remained on board. The train was ordered into a siding at Penmaenmawr and on hearing a whistle, the signalman assumed that the train had cleared the main line and allowed a cattle train from Holyhead to proceed from the signal post west of the station. In fact, the troop train was still straddling the main line and a collision followed in which three coaches were close to being thrown into the sea. In an awful repeat of the Abergele smash of 1868, the coaches started to burn, cartridges exploded, bullets flew, and it was only by strenuous efforts from the soldiers and local villagers that the situation was contained. It had its funny side when one soldier apparently seriously wounded called for help only to be told that the stains on his uniform were not blood but redcurrant jam. The impact on signalman David Evans was more serious as he was suspended after twenty-one years of flawless service, much to the annoyance of the local populace.[19] A glance at the events causing the fatal 1950 smash at Penmaenmawr shows almost exactly the same level of misunderstanding of the meaning of a whistle from the engine that was in the process of entering the siding at the same location. In 1894, discussion between the LNWR, local council and the army led to the creation of a platform at the western edge of the camping area of the Morfa. The potentially catastrophic crash of 1892 was not specifically mentioned as a reason for this change though it would be surprising if it had not been considered:

> The Corporation of Conway have recognised the growing importance of the recurring mobilisation of citizen soldiers in their midst by extending the facilities for the supply of pure water, and the various battalions, whose encampment has brought so much increased trade, have in their turn given indications of stability and permanence by erecting substantial mess rooms, cooking ranges and store houses. A conference has been held between the military and railway authorities, which has resulted in the erection of a platform at the western extremity of the camp, and this concession on the part of the railway company will be of distinct advantage to the Volunteers [who] have more than once experienced the effects of a long and dreary march through the drenching rain to the camping ground, arriving there in a wretched and miserable condition. This will now be altered.[20]

Conwy Morfa station was re-sited to a more convenient position in 1901 and was equipped with its own signal box which was 'carried bodily' from nearby Penmaenbach.[21]

The volunteers for these camps on the north Wales coast were mainly from the English industrial heartlands of the north-west and west Midlands. There appeared to be an underlying concern that not enough recruits were coming forward from north Wales. The authorities attempted to remedy this situation in September 1892 when regular soldiers of the Royal Welch [sic] Fusiliers based at the Curragh, west of Dublin, left Kingstown (Dun Laoghaire) for Holyhead and then took the train for Llanfair P G where they were met at the station by large crowds. They were addressed by local dignitaries before the soldiers marched to Bangor and subsequently toured the region on foot and by train. There seemed to be some mystification among those who addressed the crowds about why recruitment was so poor in north Wales, though there was a clue in the fact that Colonel Blyth, who could 'not yet speak Welsh', had to implore those who could understand English in the crowd to pass the message on to those who could not. It is not recorded how successful the campaign was, or whether Colonel Blyth ever learned Welsh, but the support of the LNWR for the authorities was again in evidence in the offer of cheap tickets for all to attend the final 'smoking concert' at Denbigh Castle, which was specially illuminated for the occasion.[22]

There was no shortage of patriotic zeal when hostilities broke out with the Boers of South Africa around the turn of the century; and there was a clear role

51. *Lord Dundonald of Gwrych Castle returned from the Boer War to a mass welcome at Abergele and Pensarn station in December 1900 as the 'Hero of Ladysmith'. The station buildings have not changed much since LNWR days as a nuclear flask train passes through behind 25212 in May 1984.* (**Photo: David Sallery, Penmorfa.com**)

for the railway as the social medium of its day. The residents of Bagillt learned about the famous relief of Mafeking in May 1900, 'by the arrival of a message at the Railway Station signal box and slightly later by the postal telegraph'.[23] Great as were the celebrations in Bagillt in May, they were even greater at Abergele in December when Lord Dundonald of Gwrych Castle returned from the war as the 'Hero of Ladysmith' having relieved that South African town in March 1900. The railway station was at the centre of the events of a general holiday declared in Abergele to mark the occasion. The hero's return was delayed because of the mass of extra packed trains that descended on the station, and area manager Francis Dent ensured that the station was festooned in evergreens and banners that conveyed the special joy and pride felt locally for this national hero.[24] Dent was well versed in military protocol as he was the son of Admiral Charles Dent who was the superintendent of the Marine Department of the LNWR at Holyhead after he retired from the navy in 1888.

52. In May 1900, the residents of Bagillt learned of the famous Relief of Mafeking via the signal box. Huge celebrations followed. There are still signs of Bagillt station (closed in 1966) in this picture from October 1975: The signal box has now disappeared. (Photo: John Hobbs)

A much greater challenge than the Boer War awaited the volunteers by 1914, but just four days before the greatest conflict the world had yet seen there was no hint of anything other than a holiday atmosphere among troops from Coventry arriving at Old Colwyn:

The march from the railway station will be easy, as the distance [to the camp] is within a quarter of a mile. Lovely weather favoured the arrival of the party, and it looks as though a turn has been taken for delightful camping conditions. It is by no means an isolated camp [being] bounded by roads on three sides and within easy reach of the town …There were many indications of a large influx of general visitors to their favourite North Wales seaside resorts, for there were piles of advance luggage at all the stations.[25]

The arrival of a world war on 4 August 1914 created a vast demand for soldiers and other personnel. By the second year of the war, it was apparent that it had impacted on the staffing of the CHR. At the start of the war Britain relied on volunteers for the army and many north Wales railwaymen responded to the call. Reports

53. *Old Colwyn station opened in 1884 and had narrow escapes from fire in 1898 and 1902 – the latter when a passing train set fire to the creosoted railings. Troops arriving here in late July 1914 and preparing for war had to mingle with holidaymakers. The station closed in December 1952.* (Photo: John Alsop Collection)

in 1915 showed that within the traffic and goods departments some 145 men had volunteered by March from stations along the line. The data are what one might expect, with the larger stations providing the bulk of recruits. Porters and clerks, who might be the most expendable in terms of maintaining the operation of the railway, made up the bulk of the recruits. Bangor contributed its share through the Bangor Railway Institute's Boys Corps with twenty-one past members listed as having enlisted and twenty-five current members. Their roles in the LNWR were not listed but the units they joined were. Most joined battalions of the Royal Welch Fusiliers (RWF) and there were quite a few in the artillery and the Royal Engineers, with only two in the navy. The LNWR's contribution to the Royal Navy was significant because four ships – *Cambria*, *Scotia*, *Tara (Hibernia)* and *Anglia* were requisitioned along with their crews of sixty-four, sixty-six, sixty-eight and fifty-five, respectively.[26]

Thus, within six or seven months of the war starting the CHR had contributed 435 recruits towards the war effort, plus four ships. The company also contributed its management expertise. L.B. Shoppee was a senior manager at Chester before the war and was mentioned in despatches in 1917 for devotion to duty during his service in the Railway Operating Division of the Royal Engineers. Mr C.H. Tait, another senior manager, was commissioned as staff captain in the Army Transport Corps (General Headquarters Staff). But most significant was the honour bestowed on Francis Dent, whom we met welcoming back the hero of Ladysmith at Abergele in 1900. He was knighted in 1916.[27] He had risen to assistant superintendent of the CHR before leaving for the South-Eastern and Chatham Railway. He was made an officer of the Legion of Honour by the French government for his management of railways in the war zone in July 1915.

The railway also provided those writing home with an example that helped to describe their experiences at the front. Thus, Private Carr of Shotton, serving with the 1/5th RWF described how, 'the big guns are roaring almost night and day. When the shells whizz over us it reminds me of the 10 am express rushing through Flint station'.

Inevitably, there were casualties. Private Isaac Jones, a porter at Chester who was in the 1915 list of recruits and was with the 1/5th RWF died at Gallipoli in September 1915; another from the list was Second Lieutenant T.F. Walker who served in the draughtsman's office at Bangor. He was wounded on the Somme in 1916. One of the many artillery recruits was Private Jesse Ayres of the Royal Field Artillery, who died on the Somme in 1917 and had seen service as a relief stationmaster at several locations on the CHR. Perhaps the most unfortunate was Sapper Evan H. Roberts of the Railway Operating Division, who was on

54. 'When the shells whizz over us it reminds me of the 10 am express rushing through Flint station' said Private Carr, writing from the Western Front in 1915. In 2019 a mocked up Irish Mail tries to repeat the trick at Flint with Carnforth's 45690 Leander in charge. (Photo: Phil Lloyd Collection)

the railway staff at Bangor and joined the Royal Engineers in September 1914. He survived service in Gallipoli and Palestine and was due for demobilisation until transferred to Egypt because of civil disturbances. There he became a victim of the worldwide influenza epidemic and died five months after the war ended.

Two incidents stood out for their impact on the railway community in north Wales: the loss of the HMS *Tara* and HMHS *Anglia* within a few days of each other in November 1915. The *Tara* (previously the *Hibernia* in the LNWR fleet) was torpedoed and sunk off the north African coast. Survivors who got ashore were handed over to locals by the Germans and were marched across the desert to a prisoner of war camp; around fifteen crew from Holyhead died. The *Anglia* sank after it struck a mine at the mouth of Folkestone Harbour. These ships were fast steamers on the Holyhead to Ireland route until commandeered by the Royal Navy. Among around 170 deaths on the *Anglia* were twenty-five crew of whom twenty-three were from Holyhead. These examples were just a small part of the sacrifice that was made by railway employees in north Wales during the war. The death toll was enough for there to be a large memorial service devoted to the region's railway workers in Bangor in May 1919 when the bishop commented:

> They were met together to honour a body of men whose work was unknown to those who lived in past centuries. Of the 186,475 railwaymen of Great Britain and Ireland who joined the forces, 18,957 were killed in action or died of wounds. Some of them were attached to regiments, but a section of them went out as railwaymen and as railwaymen they died. There were days when railways were unpopular in the land [but] railwaymen showed what great use they could be in time of national emergency.[28]

No figures were given for the number of CHR staff killed or injured in the war, but the national figure of 10 per cent deaths of those that served suggests that it would have been a significant number. The service for all casualties in north Wales was held in October 1919 at Bangor but severely disrupted by that rarest of events on the CHR – a railway strike. It was part of a national action and meant that local MP David Lloyd George, who also happened to be the prime minister – and effectively the manager of the railways which were still in government hands – could not attend.[29]

There was a more recent sequel to the story of the service of railway staff of north Wales in the First World War. In January 2020 Network Rail moved a memorial plaque from a local church that had closed. It was dedicated to members of the Bangor Railway Institute Boys Corps who died in the conflict and has been relocated at Bangor station. The plaque shows the names of sixteen soldiers with two from the Cooil family, whose father was also employed by the railway company as a bridge inspector. Private John Dentith Cooil died in November 1917 and is buried in the Tyne Cot Cemetery in Belgium where there are many casualties from the Passchendaele battle. His brother Caesar Alfred Cooil is buried in Bangor after fighting through most of the major battles of the war only to die at home from the combined effects of gas and pneumonia on the very last day of the war, 11 November 1918.[30]

55. Exactly fifty years after the start of the First World War, 45353 sets off from Bangor to Llandudno on 4 August 1964. In 2020 a memorial to members of the Bangor Railway Institute who lost their lives in that conflict was relocated to the station. (Photo: John Worley, Online Transport Archive)

As it had a heavy traffic in military personnel, it is no surprise that the CHR was also the scene of casualties during the conflict. One was Private John Sullivan, an Irish born member of the Australian Imperial Force who fought on the Somme. The unfortunate soldier had been wounded and was returning to the front from Ireland in 1916 when he leaned out of the window to be sick and hit his head on a bridge between Gaerwen and Bodorgan. He was bandaged by the guard and taken to Bangor military hospital but died later.[31]

There was an interesting postscript to the return of the service personnel to duty after the war that indicated how railway service had changed during the conflict. The North Wales Federation of Discharged and Demobilised Sailors and Soldiers met at Colwyn Bay in April 1919. There they decided to draw to the attention of the LNWR: 'that there appeared to be women in their employ occupying positions which were previously held by men prior to the war, and respectfully asking that these women be replaced by unemployed ex-servicemen (in great numbers these

L. & N. W. Station and Harbour

HOLYHEAD

56. *Holyhead was a major port for war movements between 1914 and 1918. On the back of this card soldier 'Bob' wrote home in November 1917, 'Arrived at Holyhead, embark tonight. ... The weather is frightfully cold, but we are making the best of it.' The clock commemorating the opening of the new station in 1880 by the Prince of Wales now stands on the station approach.* (**Photo: Phil Lloyd Collection**)

days) thereby assisting in the great reconstruction work which is to take place in the near future'.[32]

One significant conflict that featured around this time echoed the origins of the CHR as a mechanism to tackle the governance of Ireland. The Irish demand for Home Rule was left simmering at the beginning of the war in 1914. The conflict boiled over in 1916 with the Easter Rising in Dublin. The rising was over by 29 April and on 4 May around 400 prisoners arrived at Holyhead for transport by rail under heavy guard, probably to Frongoch camp near Bala, which had good rail links.[33]

The hostilities were resumed soon after the First World War and did not end until July 1921. During the crucial peace negotiations the London to Dublin shuttle of delegates was undertaken by the LNWR but its misfortunes at sea continued when they carried three Sinn Fein representatives from Holyhead in December 1921 using the *Cambria* on its maiden voyage. The ship struck a smaller vessel and had to return to Holyhead so that the passengers could be transferred to the *Hibernia*.

This perhaps marked a fitting end to the role of the of the CHR and its managing company in the governance of Ireland. The line had been built to help to secure British rule in Ireland, but it was a task that proved beyond even the power of the nineteenth century's most powerful imperial technology. The twenty-six southern counties of Ireland achieved independence in the form of the Irish Free State from 7 January 1922, and just under a year later the LNWR ceased to exist. There was a final curious incident in the saga of Irish independence in 1923 when a courier arrived at Holyhead from Dublin with important papers for London and found the train leaving the station as he arrived on the platform. He leapt onto the footboard of the guard's van and pointed a revolver at the LNWR official – after which the guard halted the train, and the papers were accepted. This was certainly a novel way to assert the new nation's independence.[34]

The years before the Second World War saw rather less activity on the CHR than the four decades before 1920. The camps in the 1930s were not military but haphazard holiday shanty towns of old buses and railway carriages that appeared at places like Talacre and the environs of Rhyl. This was much to the dismay of local people and especially businesses who objected to this shift to holidays in which people lived cheaply and did not generate much profit in towns along the coast. Kinmel Bay military camp, which had closed and been cleared, was revived under the name 16th Searchlight Militia Depot, but only in the summer of 1939 when war was imminent. It is unclear whether the railway played a major role in serving the camp as the account of its reconstruction emphasises road rather than rail access, and its purpose appears less labour intensive than the infantry exercises of earlier years.[35]

The station at Kinmel Bay had a chequered history; opened in 1885 as Foryd to replace a similar named station on the Clwyd branch, closed in 1917, reopened in 1919 but closed again in 1931, before a final reopening in July 1938 as Kinmel Bay Halt that ended on 1 September 1939, two days before war broke out.

As war approached, training intensified and the CHR was involved tangentially with at least two incidents arising from preparations for war. In September 1937, an Avro Anson K6227 crashed into the sea close to the CHR at Penmaenbach on its way from the Penrhos bombing school to RAF Bircham Newton in East Anglia. The crash was spotted first by platelayer Joseph Speakman who telephoned for help to Llanfairfechan and Conwy stations. There were no survivors from the crash.[36]

The major drama of HMS *Thetis* unfolded in June 1939 and carried on into the final months of the year. *Thetis* was a submarine built at Birkenhead and tested in Liverpool Bay. It developed a fault that meant that it could not surface,

57. Kinmel Bay was an important volunteer training camp before the First World War but afterwards the area tended to cater for holidaymakers. Foryd station closed here in 1931: it reopened in 1938 as Kinmel Bay Halt. The platform can be seen bottom right of this picture which was taken in 1939 as both war and the final closure of the halt approached. (Copyright: The Francis Frith Collection)

and a dramatic rescue began. Sadly, ninety-nine naval personnel and civilian workers on board died. The ship was salvaged near Moelfre in Anglesey, and the bodies of the victims were brought to Holyhead where the London Midland and Scottish (LMS) railway and harbour facilities were the centre of funeral arrangements:

> If the submarine *Thetis* is successfully raised it is understood that it will be towed into the [LMS] dock at Holyhead, and at Holyhead a combined naval and civic funeral will take place. Should relatives of any victims prefer a private burial nearer their own homes [then] the bodies can be sent to any railway station. … If the interment takes place at Holyhead all the funeral expenses would be paid by the authorities and each family would receive two third class return tickets. For private interments, the cost of the

coffin and its transport to the home railway station would be paid by the authorities.[37]

Generally, there was much less publicity about military activity than in the 1914–1918 period, with all details of troop movements kept secret once war started. For example, in the aftermath of Dunkirk evacuation some troops were moved to north Wales, but this report is very vague about where and when:

> Residents of a North Wales holiday resort stayed up late last night to give members the [British Expeditionary Force], who have returned from Northern France, a tremendous welcome. The soldiers who, it is understood, have been sent to North Wales for a holiday, were loudly cheered as they left the station after being greeted by members of the local Urban Council.[38]

The extent of the region's activity was made clear when hostilities in Europe ended and the 'Invasion of North Wales' was revealed in the LMS staff newsletter reported in the *Chester Chronicle*. Around 5,000 staff and their families appeared 'almost overnight' to serve the Ministry of Food establishment at Colwyn Bay with a further 2,000 at the Inland Revenue in Llandudno. While most left quickly after the war ended, the railway officials expected to get a steady business from many of them returning for holidays. The LMS also reported taking thousands of troops every week for battle training and Chester was the headquarters of Western Command. The Royal Navy commandeered Snowdon as a meteorology station and there were new airfields whose occupants arrived and left by train – notably Sealand near Chester and Valley in Anglesey. At the latter place, the LMS delivered one huge train of petrol every day and:

> There were several shadowy factories, bomb dumps, the Mulberry Harbour and Bailey Bridges [that] meant many more thousands travelling to and fro on the LMS, but the ample bosom North Wales folded all this warlike effort amongst its valleys so secretly that the thousands of weary war-worn folk, debarred from most other coasts, who came for short spells to holiday in North Wales … found an incredible peace and a quite unspoiled beauty.[39]

Inevitably the departure of this civilian army from north Wales was enacted at the railway station. In December 1945 as the first batch left Colwyn Bay:

58. *In Colwyn Bay 5,000 people appeared 'almost overnight' in 1940 to carry out vital war work. In December 1945: 'there were tears and laughter on the crowded platforms as good-byes were said'. This scene is of holiday traffic in 1925.* (**Photo: John Alsop Collection**)

> There were tears and laughter on the crowded platforms as good-byes were said by landladies, colleagues in the Ministry [of Food] who are remaining, and others who had come to say God-speed. Among those on the platform were Councillor C. Palmer, who as Mayor of the borough welcomed them five years ago last June and gave the new arrivals a shock by telling them they had come to a town in which there were more churches and chapels than pubs.[40]

As in the First World War, the railway contributed many staff to the armed forces, and it had to rely on older employees or ex-employees to cover duties. In the case of Edgar Swann, a man who was well known to the travelling public along the CHR, it did not end well. He was born in Shropshire and after his father died, his mother married Joseph Oakley, stationmaster at Tattenhall on the Chester and Crewe line, where Edgar lived before joining the railway company himself. He started his lengthy career at Llandudno Junction and worked from Rhyl where he lived in 1911. He was checking tickets as usual on the CHR in

June 1940 as the national crisis reached its height and suddenly disappeared. His body was discovered on the line at Gerazim near Llanfairfechan, though how he came to fall, as with many other such instances that we have considered, remained a mystery.[41]

After the accounts of conflicts in which the CHR has been involved since it opened fully in 1850, it is appropriate to close the chapter on a brighter note that relates to the politics of Ireland. It concerns the words spoken in Parliament in 1991 in support of the Irish Peace Train that moved beyond its shuttle between Belfast and Dublin through Holyhead to London, as Harry Barnes MP explained:

> For the past two years, the peace train has run between Dublin and Belfast. This year, it has travelled from Belfast to Dublin and then, on the 'immigrant route', through Holyhead to Euston. It arrived here today, and we have had a meeting in the Grand Committee Room and a press conference in the Jubilee Room to mark the occasion. ...The peace train is a protest against... the prospect of job losses on the railways, which have almost been in danger of folding up as a result of the paramilitaries' activities. It is also a symbol of the growing peace movement – a protest against all forms of paramilitary activity in, and emanating from, Northern Ireland, no matter whom they involve. ... The people who support the peace train do so irrespective of their views on the border, and irrespective of their political differences on other matters. They are united in saying that such matters should be dealt with through the normal political processes of democracy, participation, and involvement. The movement has quickly gained momentum, and both its support and the scope of its activities have grown.
>
> The peace train left Belfast at 11 am yesterday and, following a ferry crossing, finally arrived at Euston at 7.14 am today. The people on the peace train then boarded two double-decker buses with open tops and came to Westminster. The buses were driven by an Irish Catholic and a Northern Ireland Protestant, to demonstrate unity. We had a fantastic rally in the Grand Committee Room and an effective press conference in the Jubilee Room.[42]

It was to be hoped that this marks the end of the involvement of the railway line from Chester to Holyhead in Irish politics in any but the most positive manner.

7

The Railway and Tourism

Croeso i Gymru: Welcome to Wales.[1]

Anybody looking at the north Wales coast today with its string of resorts from Talacre to Llanfairfechan might consider that the purpose of the railway along the coast was to serve this once-booming trade. In fact, the Chester and Holyhead Railway (CHR) had no interest in tourism when it was conceived. Its proprietors argued that without a government subsidy the line would not pay because after Mostyn it passed through countryside with a small population and little industry or potential for industry. There was a relatively small tripping trade among better-off people – with tourism seen as something for those with the leisure time and resources to undertake a substantial and expensive tour. It was hardly seen as proper that poorer people should embark on such ventures. In September 1830 as the Liverpool and Manchester Railway (LMR) opened for business and paved the way for mass tourism there was a view of the so-called 'lower-class person' – referred to as a '*Blanketeer*' after the protesters at Peterloo – copying his betters in north Wales:

The keepers of hotels and inns throughout the Principality complain loudly of the annoyance they experience from a new species of the genus *Tourist*, of which the following is a pretty correct description. It is of the male gender, is clad in blue jacket and trousers, in the pocket of which latter garment is generally to be found … the remaining change from the single sovereign which the animal had provided itself in order procure subsistence during a pedestrian tour in North Wales. … The tout ensemble of the creature resembles a dandified chimney sweep. [It deceives the landlord into thinking] it is a 'real gentleman'. … As, however, they are generally runaway schoolboys, shop boys, or slap dashers [plasterers' assistants], we think it were better to have them pounded like strays and confined till reclaimed by their parents, teachers, or masters.[2]

But as often happens, technology deployed for one purpose ends up creating an unrelated, larger and more lucrative business. So, within twenty years of these disparaging comments the hotel and innkeepers of north Wales were competing frantically for the business of these ordinary tourists, and the north Wales economy gradually came to rely on them. For the directors of the CHR and their government sponsors, the railway to Holyhead was concerned primarily with speeding communication with Ireland to boost the capacity of the London government to control events on the other side of the Irish Sea, as discussed in earlier chapters. By contrast this chapter examines how the proximity of the railway to the coast gradually spawned a whole new industry in north Wales and one that came to define the region.

Before the railway era, north Wales was generally inaccessible and regarded as a challenging area to visit, such that those who toured the area found it worthwhile to publish details of their exploits:

> TOUR ROUND NORTH WALES, made during the Summer of 1798; containing not only the Description and Local History of the Country, but also, a Sketch of the History of the Welsh Bards; an Essay on the Language; Observations on the Manners and Customs of the inhabitants.[3]

The north coast had little interest for the tourist, being industrial from Queensferry to Mostyn and largely empty from there through to Bangor, with the notable exception of the castle at Conwy. Such traffic as there was along the coast was largely by ship and appeared to be for commercial and personal reasons rather than for holidays:

> [The] HERCULES, sails from Rhyl and Rhyddlan [*sic*] and from Mostyn Quay … at high water. She sails from Liverpool every Wednesday for Mostyn Quay; and every Monday and Thursday, to Rhyl and Rhyddlan; thereby affording conveyance for goods and passengers three times in the week between Liverpool and Wales.[4]

By 1840 day-tripping was in full swing by boat from Liverpool on the steamers *Snowden* [*sic*] and *The Spirit of Opposition*:

> For several summers past two rival steam packets, offering sixty miles cruising for a low fare, and eventually free of charge for deck passengers – no doubt subsidised by the innkeepers and publicans who enjoyed 'immense benefit' from the visitors.[5]

The demand was there even if those arguing for railways in north Wales were not yet aware of it. Beyond government and the railway industry some astute individuals had already spotted the potential of the line by 1849. The Mostyn family advertised land for sale for the creation of a new town on the coast of north Wales at Great Ormeshead, now called Llandudno. Once the CHR opened for business it was soon clear that trips along the coast were accessible to a wide range of people, something that did not meet with the approval of at least one person who gave an interesting insight into early tourism while complaining – in similar vein to the earlier comment from 1830 – that:

> The common trains, from some strange mismanagement, stop twice at the sub stations, putting down goods at one place and passengers at another; in the meantime, some persons get out and walk on the station, without remonstrance, while the like conduct in others is menaced with fines; the guards and servants of the company fetch porter for the passengers, and hob-nob with them in old-fashioned gossip, after the manner of the heavy coaches and their Jehus [coach drivers] of the olden time. This may be all very agreeable to a few jolly fellows and tourists, who are determined to hold facetious company with everybody, and enjoy everything; but it is not quite so suitable for pleasure parties with ladies, who neither smoke, nor chat with the stokers, nor quaff with the jokers, nor take *cwrw da* [good beer] or British compounds of malt and Spanish juice, at every village on the line. There requires a little more official surveillance on the part of the Holyhead Company touching these doings, though we are no advocates of excessive stringency even in such matters, for we like to see all classes of people enjoy themselves in their own way. One train a day would be sufficient for stoppages of this description.[6]

While government and railway managers could see little traffic on the CHR at the outset, the perspective of the latter changed quite quickly. The heavy capital cost of the railway, particularly the crossings of the river at Conwy and the Menai Straits and the heavy tunnelling from Conwy to Bangor, increased the pressure to boost revenues. The railway even made money from selling trips on the line to see the Britannia Tubular Bridge, with the local scenery as an afterthought:

> The celebrated Britannia Tubular and Suspension Bridges over the Menai Straits and North Wales ... Arrangements having been made to afford parties an opportunity of visiting the above interesting objects and the magnificent scenery of North Wales, tickets will be issued at the Euston Station, available for One Week from the date of issue, by any train, according to class, allowing the

holder to stop at Chester, or any station on the Chester and Holyhead Railway, but not to travel twice over the same portion of the railway in one direction.[7]

This foray into tourist tickets was a positive move by the CHR and the arrangements seem quite straightforward. By 1857 ticket purchase was remarkably like the present day in its impenetrable complexity:

> The Holyhead line, direct from Chester, offers peculiar facilities. We find the company continue to issue 'Seaside Tickets' for families to go and return from the chief resort, within a given period, but have ceased to the issue 'periodical tickets' for the heads of families taking the first-named tickets, to pass to and fro, at greatly reduced rates. The company, however, issue 'Welsh Tourist Tickets', available for 28 days, for something less than one fare and a half at the ordinary rate whilst every Saturday afternoon at 4.15 from Birkenhead there are 'Cheap Excursions for the People' by 'Stanley' return tickets to most parts of Wales, returnable till the fourth day (not till the fourteenth day as formerly).[8]

Perhaps galvanised by the public interest in the bridge, the CHR decided to try to exploit the tourist potential of north Wales, and in doing so demonstrated a distinct lack of knowledge of its host country. Of all the places available in the region to place an expensive hotel, it selected the banks of the Menai Straits between the two bridges as part of a drive to make Bangor the 'Brighton of Wales'.[9] A year later their plans were moving ahead:

> The opening afforded by [the CHR] to the shores of North Wales, and the beautiful and interesting Menai Straits which are now … reached with the greatest facility from all parts of Britain and from the accelerated route to and from Ireland – call for immediate accommodation for visitors to North Wales, in a more advantageous position, and with superior accommodation than at present, and for that purpose a beautiful and extensive site has been secured between the two celebrated bridges over the Menai.[10]

Despite the notoriously dangerous currents and lack of beaches in the Menai Straits, the company advertised the benefits of sea-bathing from the hotel to the guests and large returns on capital for the investors. None of these benefits was realised and the scheme was a complete failure.

The growth of the tourist industry in north Wales happened irrespective of misguided efforts by the CHR. Once the railway was in place people could not fail to notice the attractive coastline and make use of rapid travel to get there, as was clear by 1857 when fine weather brought a: 'multitude almost beyond number [who created] a scene of bustle and animation' at Chester station:

> Birmingham, with the other portion of the iron districts, has contributed thousands of passengers for Wales, whilst Manchester and the populous manufacturing districts surrounding it, have been as equally liberal in their contributions to the towns and villages on the Welsh coast. Rhyl, the largest populated sea-bathing place on the Chester and Holyhead line, is crowded to excess and, within the last few days, many instance have occurred in which tired and jaded visitors, after journeying a hundred or so of miles, with all the excitement of travelling in quest of the picturesque, have been doomed to get no better accommodation in that town than the railway station could afford, and compelled to go miles farther to get a bed. The bye-ways and mountain passes of North Wales which some years ago were inaccessible to the population are now trodden by thousands [and] amid this active locomotion hotel-keepers are reaping a bountiful harvest [and the people] are making themselves acquainted with a portion of the kingdom until recently but imperfectly understood.[11]

It was not only the hoteliers who were cashing in on this boom in 1857. The LNWR offered cheap tickets from London to Llandudno with the option to break the journey at Manchester to visit the Art Treasures Exhibition.[12] Liverpool residents were reminded in the same year of the changes that had taken place in travelling to north Wales and the options available to them:

> *Doctor Syntax* [a cartoon figure of the early nineteenth century who searched in vain for the picturesque] in search of the Picturesque would certainly not have far to seek for it in Wales, when once he got there. Since the Doctor's time, economical facilities for getting there have so multiplied that – except for the old Holyhead road from Chester – one seldom or never sees a tourist mounted on steed and saddlebags, nowadays. [The] modern mediums of reaching the very heart of Welsh scenery are mainly three: – steamers from Liverpool; the railway to Holyhead or Carnarvon; coaches from Llangollen-road station to Carnarvon but occupying two days.[13]

It is possible to get an insight into how the LNWR facilitated travel to north Wales by looking at one example from 1859 – the annual holiday of the members of Wigan's

Mechanics' Institution. This organisation was unwilling to accept the financial risk of booking for 300 people in advance so Mr Marcus of the LNWR accepted the risk and contributed a donation of two guineas (£253). Even though some had been put off by the weather, at 6.00 a.m. on a damp June day, the group of close to the required number set of in a train of seventeen carriages. They travelled via Warrington and Chester to the coast and were soon impressed by the spectacle of the sea close by on one side and the mountains on the other. About thirty of the group opted to get off at Conwy while the rest continued to Bangor where they struggled with the Welsh language. The group's main aim was to see the tubular bridge across the 'Mania' straits as many of their number called it, and they had the good fortune to witness a train passing through overseen by a railway policeman who whistled to his counterpart at the other end of the tunnel. He provided them with many details about the bridge and received a few tips in return before the party returned to Bangor and an hour or two in the local hostelry out of the rain. Some visited Beaumaris or took a train to join their colleagues at Conwy. The return journey began at 6.30 p.m. and reached Wigan at 11 p.m. and the tourists were cheered by evening sun and high tides that improved the sea view.[14]

59. *In June 1859, the Wigan Mechanics' Institution visited north Wales on its annual day trip. The party of 300 split between Bangor and Conwy which emerged as a popular tourist destination. In July 1990, the modern tourist road traffic problems around Conwy are apparent as 47206 enters Llandudno Junction yard with petroleum coke wagons.* **(Photo: David Sallery, Penmorfa.com)**

By 1864 the growth of tourism was in full swing so that:

In all parts of the country, along the coasts, amid the valleys and glens, and on the mountain tops, travellers from the manufacturing districts of the northern and midland counties, as well as from the 'great metropolis' and the surrounding counties, have for months past been giving busy life and activity to the hotels and inns ... A new era in locomotion seems to be opening up for the benefit of the inhabitants of North Wales. The beautiful railway from Chester to Holyhead, running along the seacoast the greater part of the distance, has directed the attention of enterprising men to further railway projects, for the purpose of throwing open to the public at large the central portions of North Wales.[15]

The growth in tourism in this period was enough for one commentator to suggest that north Wales was by 1866 'almost as well-known at Fleet-street or the Strand' and no place was more popular other than the Highlands of Scotland during the shooting season.[16] But tourists are notorious for demanding new experiences and by the 1870s there was a sense north Wales was not keeping up with more glamorous rivals in England such as Blackpool and Scarborough. Yes, it had better scenery, but tourists were only prepared to enjoy that for part of their time away – they wanted more excitement and variety as well. The LNWR was not slow to recognise this demand and became directly engaged with local boards and councils to improve the attractiveness of the resorts from which they made money. For example, it put its considerable weight behind the construction of the Marine Drive around the Great Orme at Llandudno in 1871.[17] But there remained a sense that the LNWR was primarily concerned with Irish traffic and the needs of the local economy were a secondary issue. Dissatisfaction with railway monopoly was growing, fuelled by the belief that the LNWR was overcharging in north Wales after the formal dissolution of the CHR company in 1879.

After two poor years during the recession at the end of the 1870s, 1880 proved to be a bumper year during which the railways poured people into places like Rhyl: 'where overcrowding resulted in many sleeping on the streets, in bathing huts or in railway carriages' – causing the *North Wales Chronicle* to urge potential tourists to the region to stay at home.[18] But tourism was by then becoming the driving force of the north Wales economy and a boon to the railway company – and both needed to develop together. By the summer of 1882 the LNWR was offering comprehensive coach tours from major stations on its north coast route.[19] Its efforts were assisted by political celebrities choosing resorts along the line, most notably John Bright at Llandudno and William Gladstone at Penmaenmawr – where he urged the LNWR to construct a bridge to enable people to get to the beach from the town because the route was obstructed by the railway.[20] Not content to rely on these affirmations from notable figures, the LNWR issued its own extensive booklet about touring in north Wales with links to hotels and tours.

Such initiatives were clearly successful so that by the end of the decade the LNWR was facing bigger challenges as visitor numbers increased.

The train service from Llandudno Junction was of character which most severely tested the resources of the [LNWR]. As a matter of fact, the long delays at the junction and the miserable accommodation at Llandudno have long served as serious complaints against the railway company and tended to the advantage of the steamer from Liverpool.[21]

Faced by these problems and acutely aware of the pressure from local businesses and politicians and an emerging threat from Sir Edward Watkin's line from

60. In 1890 'the train service from Llandudno Junction was of character which most severely tested the resources of the [LNWR]'. This picture illustrates the point – but a solution was at hand in the construction of an extensive new station on a site to the top right of this picture. (Photo: KGPA Ltd: Alamy photo stock)

Wrexham to Liverpool which might have formed a branch heading west, the LNWR began to develop plans to boost its tourist trade. It wished to maintain the lucrative, fast Irish traffic and eliminate any possibility of a rival railway benefiting from the booming tourist trade.[22] Minor changes were made, such as acceding to the 1892 request of the Colwyn Bay Local Board for a subway under the railway to connect the town with the beach, the opening of which was an occasion for a full day local holiday and celebration.[23] But the comprehensive solution for the LNWR was to increase its tracks from two to four along most of the route from Chester to Llandudno Junction. That would provide two tracks for rapid mail traffic and freight to Ireland – allowing it through the congested tourist area, while the slow tracks would provide the facility for stopping trains at the various resorts along the line, rapidly recouping the company's considerable investment.

In May 1896 there was a leaked report that the Sir Edward Watkin's Manchester, Sheffield and Lincolnshire Railway was to extend from its Dee crossing near Hawarden to Porth Dinllaen, though there seemed little substance to it. In the same month, the London and North Western Railway Bill came before a committee of the House of Commons despite local fury at the issue of higher freight rates and passenger fares on the CHR than for the rest of its system. Rather than face obstruction from its political opponents, the LNWR withdrew the portion of the Bill concerned with the widening scheme, to the evident surprise of local businesses and politicians, especially the Conservatives who blamed Liberals such as Lloyd George and Flint MP Herbert Lewis.[24] It seemed evident that this was a political ruse by the LNWR to discomfort its opponents as by November the company was publishing plans to acquire land in Flintshire in order to run four tracks instead of two.[25] Even before the formal passage of the legislation for the whole scheme the LNWR was busy. By February 1897 it had begun a series of loop lines from Flint westwards and was developing its stations at Prestatyn and Llandudno Junction.[26]

Early in 1899 the LNWR propaganda campaign was in full swing and it was clear that cashing in on the holiday traffic, beating off any rival incursions into north Wales, and keeping the Irish traffic moving fast were high on the agenda in an article that received wide circulation in the bigger national papers and was repeated in local journals. It made the case that the north Wales route was vital for relations with Ireland but also increasingly for the:

Residents of the big cities of the three kingdoms, for it enables them to spend their hours at recreation and relaxation in the pleasant places along the shores and in the bays and vales of Gwynedd [that had brought] capital and business into a hitherto impoverished country and raised into affluence many Welsh families.[27]

61. This 1899 photograph is an early view of the enlargement of Llandudno Junction. It was completed in 1897 as part of the massive widening scheme that covered much of the CHR from Chester to this junction. (Photo: John Alsop Collection)

The newspaper article outlined how for years: 'wherever additional land was required, and it could be obtained by private negotiation it has been bought, and every inch of ground to which the company could lay just claim has been fenced in'. The work had been done in sections by creating loop lines onto which goods traffic could be diverted to avoid obstructing faster trains. At the same time new bridges and stations were built with a view to the loops being opened out and eventually creating a four-track route for the whole distance from Chester to Bangor, although the initial focus was on the section east of Llandudno. The most extensive works were in crossing the Clwyd river and a large station at Rhyl on the scale of the works at Llandudno Junction. The author concluded that:

At present the [LNWR] is supreme in North Wales, and the policy sketched above is intended to maintain and establish their supremacy for all time. They are not without rivals, however, and it is suspected that another great British railway corporation, which has already got its outworks firmly laid down in the country, means, when an opportunity is offered, to make a bold attempt to share the Irish traffic. This is the Great Central Company, who have contemplated making a railway from Mold, across Denbighshire and Carnarvonshire, [*sic*] to the Lleyn Peninsula, where the finest natural port on the coast awaits development.[28]

The extent of the work on the CHR and the detail of its organisation were apparent before the end of the century especially in the Deeside area:

> The widening of the railroad on the Chester and Holyhead section of the [LNWR] in order to accommodate the increased traffic has led to an enormous amount of work and expenditure of capital all along the route. Apart from the mere doubling of the sets of rails which has necessitated the acquiring of land alongside the railway and the building up of the embankments for the foundation and level of the railway track, the alterations have farther necessitated the construction of numerous bridges in place of the level crossings, and rights of way over the railway ... The contract includes five large bridges at Holywell, Mostyn, Morfa (Point of Ayr), Gronant, and Nant (Prestatyn), and the enlargement of the new station at Rhyl; they are also erecting two bridges, now nearing completion, at Sandycroft and Saltney. ... As the work proceeds, Holywell Station premises will be made the general depot for the whole of the work and from there will be turned out all material required. Workshops, for iron and woodwork, are already in course of erection for the purpose.[29]

Hidden within the reports was a detail that probably drew little attention at the time when the main rivalry was thought to come from other railway companies. An account of the works at Llandudno Junction recorded that 'a siding is being made near the level crossing for an American oil firm's use. A large tank is to be put down for the storage of petroleum, which is thence to be carried about the country in bulk'.[30] Unknown to the author of this report, petroleum and the motors that used it would ultimately end the 'supremacy for all time' anticipated by the LNWR in north Wales.

By 1903 formal legislation had been acquired and much of the widening work completed, such as the doubling of the bridge over the Dee next to Chester Racecourse, the heavy works at Saltney cutting, the four tracks from

62. *The scale of the new station is clear at Rhyl in this picture. It was probably taken when it was under construction in the late 1890s as there appears to be building material at the bottom right. The position of those working on the station canopy looks precarious with ladders over the main line.* **(Photo: John Alsop Collection)**

63. *Adding extra lines to much of the route from Chester to Llandudno Junction was vital if the LNWR was to extract full value from the tourist industry. The headquarters for this operation were at Holywell which is shown here at the turn of the century after it had benefited from the upgrade.* **(Photo: John Alsop Collection)**

64. *Adding extra lines at Bagillt required complex work with the pools on the site. In May 1974 the pools are still prominent as 40124 passes the old station buildings. These class 40s were a regular feature of the CHR: this one was withdrawn in 1984.* (Photo: John Hobbs)

65. *The extensive bridge at Mold Junction, seen here around 1910, is an example of what had to be done once the LNWR decided to add extra tracks to the CHR between Chester and Llandudno Junction. Saltney Ferry station on the line to Mold – next to the engine shed – opened in 1891 and closed in 1962. (Copyright: The Francis Frith Collection)*

there past Queensferry station, and from Bagillt to Abergele and Pensarn. A new station was underway at Colwyn Bay with a goods yard in the adjacent quarry. Quadruple track was in place for much of the route from Colwyn Bay to Llandudno Junction.[31] By the LNWR shareholder meeting of 1904 the company was able to report that twenty-three miles of four-track railway was in place between Chester and Abergele and the section from Colwyn Bay to Llandudno Junction would be in use for the summer traffic – which was clearly its main purpose.[32] The work between Flint and Bagillt was especially complicated because of its closeness to the coast and the limited space in which to work. But by 1907 that too was almost complete with Bagillt providing an example of what was involved:

> At Bagillt, the work of widening has been an extensive and laborious operation. … There was extensive work in constructing a permanent way where pools once existed. The station premises at Bagillt on the down side have not as yet been improved, but the new waiting rooms on the up platform are convenient, and the greater part of the platform is glass roofed … New gates, automatically operated from the signal box, have been placed on the level crossing from Station Road to the wharf. Several new signal boxes have been erected, under Bedol, at the Station and at Dee Bank. … At one time the stopping trains [at Bagillt] will pull up at No. 1 platform, another time at No. 2 platform; the consequence has been that people have time after time stepped out on the wrong side of the carriage and landed on the rails below instead of on the platform. … Possibly as the [LNWR] have now a Bill in Parliament for the electrification of the system it may be in course of time that electric light will displace the flickering gas, and even oil lamps, that grace the platforms of some of the stations of this great and powerful company.[33]

Improvements were also made where the line could not be widened such as at Conwy. There the LNWR blasted rock from the south side of the station to squeeze in a wider platform just inside the town walls. It replaced a dark and inconvenient bridge with one that was lighted and covered. It did not please everyone. A correspondent to a local paper noted that the bridge was higher than necessary in order to provide an exit to Rosemary Lane that would be:

> A great public convenience, as it would enable passengers to step directly into the town from the station, instead of having to walk … 200 yards round

the station approach. No doorway has, however, been made [so people climb the extra height for no purpose]. The objection to [the exit] appears to be that a second collector would have to be employed. [Public convenience] calls for this expense to be incurred by the company as a consequence of their own action.[34]

The hard work and cost of creating all this additional capacity along the whole line was accompanied by a drive for the additional passengers that would make it pay. In August 1900 the LNWR advertised 'convenient and fast expresses for families and tourists' from London along with facilities to travel freely around the region during a two-week stay.[35] By 1904 there was a package holiday arranged between the LNWR, the Queen's Hotel and the Claremont Hydro in Rhyl combining hotel accommodation and railway tickets from Manchester, Liverpool and Birmingham.[36] More generally, tourists enjoyed enhanced facilities, employees

66. *A classic view of Conwy station from the early 1900s. Note the high footbridge built as part of extensive improvements in 1900. The covered bridge was raised to the level of Rosemary Lane to provide direct access to the town, though that part of the scheme was never implemented.* (**Photo: John Alsop Collection**)

were given a reading room and meeting place at Holyhead and passengers could access typing facilities at Euston. New stations were opened, among them the wooden structure at Talacre created in 1903 and originally to be called Morfa Crossing.[37]

The LNWR also boosted its tourist trade with a series of picture postcards of the 'Premier Line' as they liked to be called. Behind this optimism stood a growing realisation that the balance of power was shifting, and that the railway now needed the public as much, or more, than the public needed the railway. Was the money in infrastructure and advertising invested wisely? Figures from the *Liverpool Daily Post* at the end of the 1906 tourist season suggested that it was. It estimated that there had been 7.95m visitors to the region between June and August with each visitor spending an average of fifteen shillings (£93) per week. The bulk of these were to resorts along the improved stretch of line – Rhyl (1m visitors), Colwyn Bay (375,000) and Llandudno just beyond the much improved Llandudno Junction (attracting over 4m visitors).[38] Beyond the most popular resorts on the north coast, the LNWR recognised the potential to open up new areas for tourism.

67. *The Irish Mail is about to collect bags just east of Rhyl in the early 1900s. The Claremont Hydro in the background had an arrangement with the LNWR to sell joint rail and accommodation tickets in 1904. This crossing was the scene of a notable tragedy in 1931 when a couple were found dead amid rumours of a pact between them.* (Photo: John Alsop Collection)

68. Talacre station opened in 1903 and was a wooden structure – originally to be called 'Morfa Crossing' – that was partly destroyed in a train crash in 1904. By the time it closed in 1966 it had more substantial platforms that were still there in September 2020 as Manchester-bound Transport for Wales 175007 speeds through on the old fast line. (Photo: Phil Lloyd Collection)

Anglesey became more popular for tourists towards the close of the century and the LNWR joined with local interests to block the creation of a dynamite factory near the Trewan Sands crossing beyond Rhosneigr, citing the tourist potential of the area.[39] Ten years later they opened a new station at Rhosneigr.

There was growing competition between the various resorts along the coastline that hindered the LNWR's attempts to present the case for the north Wales region as a whole – so even when it provided a 'Welsh Tourist Racer' with non-stop travel from Euston to Rhyl – 209 miles in 305 minutes in 1908 – this was presented as a threat to Llandudno. This innovation employed the latest

69. *Rhosneigr was one of the last new stations opened on the CHR when it welcomed its first passengers in 1907 and this photograph was probably taken soon afterwards. There is a fine collection of hats as this holiday crowd awaits the train from Holyhead. The station is some distance from the town and the beach and became vulnerable to road competition after 1918.* **(Photo: John Alsop Collection)**

technology and considerable organisational power. The first train had eight composite coaches, a dining car and guards van and was headed by Precursor class 4-4-0 *Alaric*, numbered 282, the product of the work of chief engineer George Whale as he moved away from the use of Webb's compound engines and the need to double-head heavy express trains. The local paper recorded that:

> This is the first time in the history of the LNWR that Colwyn Bay has been reached from London in four hours and twenty-four minutes; Llandudno in four hours and fifty minutes; Bangor in four hours and forty-four minutes, and Carnarvon in five hours and ten minutes.[40]

The first decade of the new century saw a boom in popularity of the resorts in north Wales that stretched beyond the summer season. At Easter 1908 Colwyn Bay saw:

> Between six and seven thousand arriving by the trains. Although the new station is in progress, which necessarily hampers existing regulations, Mr Noble had arranged everything so well that there was not a hitch in the

Easter business. Many fresh arrivals were seen on Wednesday, which seems as though the town is in for a good season, with an early commencement.[41]

In 1909 the LNWR made clear that it intended:

During the coming tourist season to make a feature of its plans [to popularise] North Wales as a district for holiday folk. The company realises that the climatic conditions and scenic charms of North Wales are thoroughly calculated to recommend that part of the country to people who go away for health and pleasure'[42] The company backed its plans with the publication of descriptive booklets that maintained 'the company's standard of excellence ... nearly 150 pages are devoted to description of the various resorts, and the illustrations are profuse and of unusual excellence, including beautifully coloured plates'.[43]

70. *LNWR locomotive types: top right is the Problem class locomotive also known as the Lady of Lake class. Number 229* **Watt** *covered the first leg of the famous dash to London with the communique from the American government during the* **Trent** *incident in 1862. From 1904 the Precursor class engine designed by George Whale was introduced and 282* **Alaric** *reached Colwyn Bay from London in a then record four hours and forty minutes in 1908.* (**Photo: Phil Lloyd Collection**)

But, as noted earlier, there was a tension at the heart of the campaign because while it was in the interests of the LNWR to market 'North Wales' as a concept, each individual town was competing against the others for business and so wanted to be emphasised ahead of them, hence the occasional disputes about the number and timing of trains. The LNWR attempted to tackle this issue through a conference at Colwyn Bay at the end of the 1909 season, chaired by L.A.P. Warner, its district superintendent. Letters were sent out to find out how much each resort would contribute to a general campaign, but few responses were received and only the larger towns committed money.[44] The LNWR's campaigns extended to the small portion of the line in England with the special trains to the Chester Races. Its 1910 advertisement perhaps summarised its transformation from regarding the CHR as primarily for Irish traffic – it had become the 'Business and Pleasure Line'.[45]

This boom in holiday travel continued up to the outbreak of the First World War in August 1914. By then the different resorts had begun to cooperate under the auspices of the North Wales Advertising Board, while remaining keen rivals. In the final few months of peace there was no sign of the horrors to come. The LNWR commenced a series of films about the attractions of north Wales which may have contributed to the record crowds at Colwyn Bay at Easter. At Llandudno, also at Easter, the:

> Rash young promenaders braved 'the searching wind', against which one could hardly stand … The gods which specially watch over rash young men and women were throwing their cloaks round the youthful promenaders and keeping them free from what any average doctor would be certain to predict for them.[46]

Soon there would be more than a 'searching wind' assailing the brave young men, and the gods would be doing little to protect them. But meanwhile people continued to take holidays in north Wales in large numbers right up to the eve of the war, with the LNWR offering the people of Birmingham a special trip from New Street station 'at 12.20 am on August 2nd (midnight). This trip has been put to suit the convenience of businesspeople who cannot get away on Saturday until late at night and is likely to very popular'.[47] By 4 August the country was at war.

During the 1914–1918 war holiday traffic in north Wales continued in a similar manner as in the pre-war years but appearances disguised subtle changes that took place and had a long-term impact on the pattern of holiday travel in the region. The initial impact was predictable:

Despite the restricted railway arrangements Rhyl has seldom experienced such a holiday. Visitors were this morning pouring into the town both by rail and road, a continuous stream of cars and motorcycles passing through the main street. ... No one would think war was on to look at the sands or the promenade.[48]

The railway was a key instrument of war, but in its absence, people had begun taking to the road, a process that once started would prove unstoppable. Thus, in June 1916, two weeks before the start of the slaughter on the Somme it was 'business as usual' on the north Wales coast, and while car travel was reduced, travel by motorcycle and sidecar was reportedly extensive. Rail travel was not mentioned.[49] The first ever 'beerless bank holiday' occurred in 1917. Even so, north Wales was flooded with visitors and large fare increases did not keep people off the few trains that ran. Some 1,750 people travelled just from Coventry by train to the three largest north Wales resorts and the motor traffic from that city was also reported as considerable.[50] The following year the exodus from the same city was the largest ever seen by the railway officials, with north Wales only just behind Blackpool in popularity.

The end of the war demonstrated the increased trend towards road travel: at the Whitsun holiday in Chester the papers reported on the 'Ubiquitous Charabanc' noting that:

while many excursionists availed themselves of the special railway facilities, it was apparent that the motor charabanc is rapidly growing in popularity as an alternative mode of travel. Thousands of Bank Holiday visitors to Chester chose it as their means of conveyance ... Motor traffic in general showed increased volume.[51]

The war had created a large industry to manufacture motor vehicles that had the capacity to do so for civilian use at the end of the war. War vehicles were also adapted for civilian use so that railways generally faced more difficult trading conditions. This was felt in north Wales as elsewhere and the LNWR reduced its fares in the face of competition from coach firms who then responded in kind:

With the advent of cheap day excursion, motor coach proprietors at Rhyl promptly dropped their fares, for long distance journeys, but the most sensational cut of all has now been made by the running of a day trip from Rhyl to Snowdon at ten shillings [£24]. The railway day excursion fare is 9s

3d. Before the cheap fares were started the fare was 19s. 6d. Other tours have also been cut to meet the railway drop.[52]

The LNWR marketed the region intensively, for example producing a full-page advertisement making the case for north Wales as the destination for a winter holiday – aided by the introduction of the innovative observation car in 1922.[53]

Rationalisation of the railway companies in 1923 reduced overheads and created greater potential for more economies of scale. So, from 1 January 1923 the CHR was operated by the London Midland and Scottish Railway (LMS). By the summer it was lauded as one of Britain's 'enterprising railways' for the number and variety of excursions it offered to the various seaside areas including north Wales.[54] The LMS picked up where the LNWR had left off with the North Wales Advertising Board so that in 1924 in: 'that season's joint advertising scheme with the [LMS] £1,000 [£61,000] was spent'. Of this £700 was on newspaper advertising, which experience proved was the best medium of reaching intending visitors. In common with many holiday resorts, north Wales felt the effect of the British Empire Exhibition.[55] The LMS also pursued its own advertising campaign with some gusto and in 1925 distributed 750,000 free holiday booklets during the summer months, as well as handbills, timetables and local publications about north Wales.[56]

But the shift to road could not be halted and fate intervened with events such as the General Strike of May 1926 that affected the number of trains and made road travel more popular, for example from the Potteries:

> The number who travelled on Friday and Saturday by train was no more than the number travelling an ordinary weekend; in fact, many of the trains could have been dispensed with. More people travelled on Sunday and Monday, as special excursions were run to Blackpool, Liverpool and the North Wales resorts. What railways lost through curtailed services the open road gained [as] the number of motors was greater than ever.[57]

The irreversible nature of the change was demonstrated later in the same year when the LMS arranged to collect passengers for the resorts at their local stations rather than at Stoke and were helped by:

> The reduction in the number of passengers [that] made the task of the railway officials a comparatively light one … and the probability is that never again, even in normal times, will such congestion be experienced at Stoke station.[58]

71. *The continued importance of the CHR was indicated by the top-quality motive power used on the line when the LMS replaced the LNWR in 1923. Here LMS Fowler Royal Scot class 6161* **King's Own** *hurtles through Bodorgan towards London in February 1932 – just two years after its construction at Derby.* **(Photo: Phil Lloyd Collection)**

The connection between Stoke and the north Wales coast has a long history, including permissions for the North Staffordshire Railway to run on LNWR rail lines to Llandudno, so this apparent weakening was significant – though even in modern times Rhyl is sometimes known as 'Stoke-on-Sea'.

In 1927 the company introduced a note of spontaneity by announcing short-notice trips such as a non-stop run from Burnley to the bigger resorts that allowed six hours' stay on the coast.[59] But by 1928 it was clear that the monopoly on holiday traffic enjoyed by the old LNWR in north Wales had not been inherited by the LMS and the position in that year was neatly summarised by the *Western Mail* in the most positive terms:

North Wales depends for much of its prosperity on the wonderful scenery and the numerous holiday centres. … Modern motors have made the most remote areas readily accessible, and the motor charabanc or bus provides facilities for those who cannot afford a motor of their own. Progress in this direction has been very great in recent years, and new life has been given to inland towns and villages that had for generations shown declining population. If the motor has robbed the railways of traffic in the more populous areas, and oil has encroached on the kingdom of coal, there is no doubt that the advent of oil has renewed life for the remoter and opened up to all and sundry beauty spots that formerly could only be enjoyed by the few.[60]

The response of the LMS in north Wales was a novel one of trying to establish bus services of its own. It was a re-run of the 1847–1848 argument about railway companies running steam ships which was thought then to be monopolistic. That was not something that appealed to politicians nationally, who had spotted where the public preference was going and the way it conflicted with the intentions of the railway companies. Arthur Dixey, MP for Penrith, articulated this point:

> I suggest that the main object of the railway companies in bringing forward this Bill [to buy bus companies] is plain. They realise that the present motor bus services are cutting too deeply into their passenger traffic receipts. They realise that people today prefer the motor bus, which drops them at their doorsteps, to the slow trains and the spasmodic service to which some of us are accustomed. ... It is perfectly obvious that the railway companies desire to drive people back to the railways. That is what is at the back of their minds. They have their permanent way to keep up and long stretches of lines which are of little use locally for passenger traffic. Undoubtedly, in the minds of the promoters of this Bill is the desire to force people, if possible, to use the railways instead of the roads. To do that they have first to eliminate private competition. If they start motorbus services and drive passengers off the roads, bit by bit, they can withdraw their own bus services or run very attenuated services, and then force the people generally to use the railways.[61]

Nonetheless, the LMS did advance its interest in road transport in north Wales by the significant act of purchasing Crosville buses in 1929, it being the company posing the greatest threat to its traffic in the region. It ran 150 different services over 1,250 route miles in an area with 4m people and around 500 towns and villages that embraced the whole of north Wales. The days of rail competition were clearly over as the purchase was made jointly with the newly expanded Great Western Railway (GWR) at a cost of nearly £400,000 (£25.5m), which was 27 shillings and sixpence (137.5p) for every one pound share.[62] Such measures were augmented by attempts to play to the railways' advantage over road transport in frequency, comfort, safety and speed. The LMS introduced 1,200 extra services in the summer of 1929 that included extra trains to the north Wales resorts.[63] North Wales was also among the subjects offered in the LMS series of free lantern slides in August 1929. It was a generous offer because, 'not only are slides loaned free, but in certain cases where an audience of at least 100 or more is expected, an official lecturer is provided free of cost'.[64]

The acquisition of the White Rose Bus Company and its ninety vehicles in Flint, in 1930, represented 'a further stage in a comprehensive scheme for the co-ordination of rail and road services throughout North Wales'.[65] It was an impressive strategy to tackle the threat of road competition, but it could not stop demand draining slowly away from the railway, even with a radio programme taking listeners 'behind the scenes at a North Wales railway station' in 1937;[66] the provision of camping coaches in the region, for example at Aber, from 1934;[67] and a £250,000 (£17m) joint venture with Thomas Cook to build a holiday camp at Prestatyn in 1938.[68] Nonetheless, one newspaper correspondent wrote in 1932 that:

> The express railway services to North Wales take a circuitous route, and involve two or three changes, whilst the road machine, taking its own direct course to any of the rendezvous named, has the railway passenger beaten every time.[69]

Figures for the 1936 August Bank Holiday demonstrate the mixed picture that emerged in the 1930s. Period bookings were up by 1,723 and totalled 17,839 while day tickets were down 1,000 to 19,839. Railway travel was still predominant for holidaymakers, especially for longer stays.[70] This report of conditions at Llandudno on the eve of war in 1939 gives a sense of the emerging pattern:

> Thousands of holidaymakers invaded Llandudno by road, rail, and sea, and the promenade and beach were thronged from an early hour. More than thirty special trains brought excursionists from all parts of the country, and the railway passenger traffic, including short-term visitors, showed a considerable increase over the figures for Whitsun last year. So many motorists came into the town that parking was a real problem. Along the three-mile front was an unbroken line of cars, and practically every street was used for parking.[71]

Following the outbreak of the Second World War, there was a concerted effort to move children, primarily by rail, from large cities to areas such as north Wales and there was an increased sensitivity about the vulnerability of all coastlines in the autumn of 1940. Nonetheless, visits to the coast continued and there was a tendency away from concentrating all holidays into a few weeks – a process referred to as 'spread-over' to avoid interruptions to industrial production.

By 1941 the situation had eased and in April at Liverpool there was considerable movement on the railways, mainly in the London and north Wales directions. The Welsh resorts claimed many visitors from Merseyside, including some 'who travelled to Caernarvonshire especially to see the German bomber brought down there early yesterday' – probably Heinkel He-111 F4801 that crashed on Llwytmor on 14 April.[72] There seemed to be little evidence of people heeding the request to travel only when necessary. Petrol rationing did not halt the rush to the coast and caused tremendous additional pressure on the railway:

> Despite warnings from all the North Wales resorts that accommodation was simply unobtainable, visitors flocked to Prestatyn, Rhyl, Colwyn Bay and Llandudno and other North Wales watering places over the weekend. While most holidaymakers had previously secured accommodation, large numbers arrived on the 'off chance' and a railway journey, most of which was spent standing in corridors, was followed by a trek around the towns in the quest for accommodation.[73]

It was the same story in 1944 and 1945 as the end of war beckoned and victory became more certain. In August 1944 trains to the north Wales coast were well filled, but additional trains prevented the station crowds becoming unmanageable during a: 'war-time record for most of the resorts'.[74] The 1945 holiday season was especially heavy with the LMS carrying 600,000 passengers to north Wales resorts in July and August alone.[75]

All this traffic with little investment meant there was a growing tension over the state of the railways, and nationalisation of the network in 1948 was aimed to tackle this. Services in north Wales were no exception as Emrys Roberts, MP for Merionethshire, noted in the debate in Parliament:

> In the rural areas the railways have not been efficient; they have established a monopoly, and their service, particularly in North Wales, has deteriorated. Rolling stock is often in an appalling condition; in some parts of North Wales carriages run by the London Midland and Scottish Railway still carry the name 'London North Western Railway,' and still have the same old seats. There was an overwhelming case for bringing those monopolies – for monopolies they were – within public ownership, and for making them responsible to a Minister, and to this House.[76]

Even so, improvement was slow, and one MP reckoned that a year after nationalisation the trains on the north coast of Wales were slower than when the line was built by Stephenson.[77]

From the end of the war up to 1955, which perhaps marked the peak of the post-war railway boom in north Wales, passenger numbers were high and the overall operating difficulty for the line was the massive disparity in its use in the tourist season compared to the rest of the year. In the days when the Irish traffic was vital to the national interest and tourism secondary, this issue did not matter. But by the 1950s tourism was the overwhelming purpose of the line so that spending large amounts of money to remove bottlenecks that only occurred in the summer months was deemed inappropriate. It had been the intention of the LNWR to provide four tracks from Chester to Llandudno Junction (and eventually to Bangor) but two key sections from Connah's Quay to Flint and Llanddulas to Colwyn Bay had never been completed and these were heavily congested at peak holiday times.

The switch from rail to road continued and was intensified by events such as the national rail strike of 1955 but also because of wider changes in society.

72. *Bangor station and shed were fully occupied in 1956 with a variety of engines and traffic types. The only identifiable locomotive is 40003 in the foreground – a Fowler 2-6-2 tank engine from the 1930s. Change is underway - represented by the diesel multiple unit amidst this gallery of steam.* (Photo: R.E. Vincent Transport Library)

The 'never had it so good' years as proclaimed by Prime Minister Harold Macmillan in 1957, with increased motor car ownership, were moving people inexorably towards a less communal and more personal style of holiday with more choice and flexibility. The change began to show where there were pinchpoints on the road. But unlike the case of the railways, there was investment available to ease congestion such as the new road bridge at Conwy in 1958 costing £500,000 (£12m) that replaced the one provided by Telford in the 1820s. By 1964 there were 1,000 cars an hour passing over the bridge at Queensferry into north Wales and a half-hour wait at Conwy despite the new bridge. By then, drastic action had been taken by government to tackle the decline in rail use and the increasing financial deficit of the rail system. The infamous Beeching Report had arrived.

While Beeching's report had some impact on the CHR, the reality was that the decline in the rail network in north Wales had been happening over many years. By the time of Beeching a number of stations on the line had been closed during the era of nationalisation; Llandulas (*sic*) and Old Colwyn in 1952, Aber in 1960 and Sandycroft in 1961. Beeching proposed closing Bagillt, Connah's Quay, Conway (*sic*), Flint, Gaerwen, Holywell Junction, Llanfairfechan, Llanfair P G, Menai Bridge, Mostyn, Penmaenmawr, Prestatyn, Queensferry, Shotton Low Level, Talacre and Valley. Only Flint, Llanfairfechan, Penmaenmawr and Prestatyn from that list survived the closure programme of 1966.

The logic behind these changes was spelled out in the relatively brief section of the report that dealt with holiday traffic. It compared peak summer traffic on the whole network in 1951 with that in 1961, demonstrating that in 1951 it was 48 per cent higher in June, 96 per cent in July, 43 per cent in August and 44 per cent in September. In 1961 the corresponding figures were 18 per cent, 47 per cent, 43 per cent and 21 per cent. The analysis was damning for a line such as the CHR that was primarily a holiday line by 1963:

> The summer peak has diminished, in spite of developments of holidays with pay, greater general affluence, and overwhelming evidence of greater holiday travel. There can be no doubt that the decline in the rail peak is almost entirely due to the increase in family motoring, and the trend is likely to continue.[78]

The debate had a sense of inevitability about it; the world had moved on from railways and it was time to embrace modernity. Not eveyone agreed and Thomas Jones MP for Merionethshire spoke for many in the region:

73. *In June 1966 BR Standard 73006 meets Stanier class 5MT 44981 just west of Prestatyn station which was identified for closure by Beeching. Many other CHR stations closed in February 1966 – but Prestatyn survived.* **(Photo: John Hobbs)**

If I stopped a train, I would be fined £5 [£105]. Beeching stops a third of the railway system and gets a cheque for £24,000 [£506,000]. That is the only difference. On the law of averages, as I should be fined £5, the Minister should be deported. I speak tonight as a Welshman. I am concerned principally with Wales. What will the proposals mean to Wales? For practical purposes, Wales will be denuded of all its railway system. It is true that there will be a train running from Chester to Holyhead and one from Bristol to Fishguard, but it is interesting to note that those lines will be retained to serve a country which is not even a member of the British Commonwealth of Nations.[79]

There was some hope that the arrival of a Labour government in October 1964 might stem the tide of closures but despite hints of a reprieve for some lines, the process continued unabated. In July 1966, a few weeks after the closure of many stations on the line, the question in Parliament concerned how to get the road over the railway at Llandudno Junction rather than the loss of stations and services. The answer was that work had started in June 1966 and the cost was a mere £624,000 (£12m).[80] The CHR had adapted from serving Britain's policy in Ireland to meeting the needs of holidaymakers in the UK. Its purpose after Beeching seemed uncertain; then bored boys went into the Britannia Tubular Bridge in May 1970, struck a match and ended up accidentally destroying this symbol of the power of the CHR in a devastating fire. So even the link to Ireland was in jeopardy – and with it the entire future of the line.

The Railway and the People of North Wales

'Success to the Chester and Holyhead Railway' – a toast at the marriage of an aristocrat in 1853.[1]

Technology designed and applied to one purpose often ends up serving many others. The railway was no exception. In the case of the Chester and Holyhead Railway (CHR) it was clearly built to assist the government in managing the perennial problem of governing Ireland. But once it was in place local people were not slow to recognise its potential to meet their own needs. North Wales was a remote, almost forgotten, region of the UK in the mid-nineteenth century. Around the time the CHR was built, George Borrow published a book called *Wild Wales* in which he toured the country, including many areas served by the CHR, and found a populace that mostly spoke Welsh, were largely engaged in rural pursuits and industry and knew little of life outside their own village. There had been little serious infrastructure investment since Edward I built his string of castles along the coast; the roads that Telford built to Holyhead from Shrewsbury and from Chester had only been completed in the late 1820s and were quickly overtaken by the power and speed of the railway. In previous chapters the extensive political impact of the railway was considered while in this chapter we will see how the railway featured in many aspects of community life, in religion, in culture and in business.

Not everyone could easily afford to use the railway, or used the railway improperly, and so the chapter also considers how far crime featured in its operation, either through crimes against the railway, the use of the railway for crime – and even misdemeanours committed by the railway and its employees.

In the CHR's many engagements in the courts, one person was invariably on hand to protect the interests of the CHR and later the London and North Western Railway (LNWR) until 1891 – Richard Montague Preston. Born in 1827, the son of the Reverend George Preston of Westminster, he was involved with the legal aspect of railway work all his life and became an authority on it. He was appointed as solicitor to the CHR in 1854 and later with the LNWR, where he remained until his death in 1891.

In the week that the railway opened in Anglesey there were large celebrations in Holyhead but a less favourable outcome for at least one person. Grace Roberts pleaded not guilty to stealing a plank of timber, a hammer and an iron bolt, the property of Edward Ladd Betts, a contractor on the CHR. Her husband was a waggoner employed by the contractor and was probably the offender, but the family could ill-afford to lose his income. The articles were found in the cottage where the defendant lived and she explained that she had found the plank in an adjoining wheat field, and the other articles were brought to the cottage by an unnamed boy. Her position was not helped by the defence of the learned counsel that the poor were free to assume ownership of property they found. The magistrate rejected this attack on the notion of property and after a plea not to separate her from her two children, sentenced her to three months in prison. The foreman of the jury was W.O. Stanley – a local aristocrat, campaigner for the railway and a great beneficiary from its construction; and the man whose family gave its name to the

74. The CHR shared the Stanley Embankment with Telford's road to cross from Anglesey to Holy Island and Holyhead. The company had to build a wall eight feet high to protect W.O. Stanley's view from nearby Penrhos. In this picture 40111 and 40007 lead a Euston-bound express into Anglesey on a glorious day in May 1979. (Photo: John Hobbs)

Stanley Embankment that links mainland Anglesey to Holy Island and Holyhead – and on which he insisted on an eight-foot-high wall so his view from his extensive mansion at Penrhos would not be spoiled. The odds were clearly stacked against poor Grace Roberts.[2]

John Pritchard, facing far more serious charges, fared rather better in March 1849 when he appeared at Bangor charged with murdering a fellow watchman at the works on the Britannia Tubular Bridge. A model of the bridge with the stage where the alleged crime had occurred was presented to the court for the hearing. His defence was that a third party had attacked them for the purposes of theft; Pritchard escaped but John Rowlands was killed by the intruder and found beneath the stage. The jury found that there was insufficient evidence for Pritchard to face trial, much to the surprise of the local paper that appeared to consider that concern over application of the death penalty may have swayed its consideration of the compelling evidence of guilt.[3]

The CHR was created as a corporate body with certain powers to control the actions of individuals on its property, and it established a police force to implement these powers. It had the authority to bring matters to court where its interests were affected, and operated in criminal and civil courts. The most common issue was non-payment of fare, but this sometimes appeared in strange guises as in the case of Alfred Easton who was charged with riding from Chester to Bangor without paying his fare. The defendant, who claimed to be a vet, booked a parcel for Bangor, at the same time borrowing eight shillings and sixpence from the clerk to pay his fare. The parcel was to be sent after him and the sum borrowed to be charged upon it. The defendant was later caught coming off the mail train but was permitted to pass after he explained how he would pay when collecting the parcel – and he gave a respectable reference in Chester. The parcel remained uncollected and when opened contained a pile of dirty rags. Easton was fined £1 (£135) plus costs with three months in jail in default.[4] Such ingenuity in fare-dodging was a consistent feature in newspaper reporting, especially when there was an interesting angle. In 1932 Ernest Sinclair of Conwy was fined £2 (£137) and an additional fifteen shillings costs for travelling several times on the line without a ticket. He deployed various methods, including buying a newspaper and waving it confidently at the ticket inspector to suggest he had merely left the platform to buy it, and on another occasion handing the ticket collector a cigar before boarding a train that was just leaving.[5]

Among the railway police powers was a significant power to detain people. Its rule book indicated how that power was to be applied.

With great caution, and never when the address of the party is known, or adequate security offered for his appearance to answer the charge. …

Detention shall not continue for a longer period than is absolutely necessary, but he shall be conveyed before a Magistrate with as little delay as possible.[6]

The reality was sometimes different, as in the case of cabman Richard Jones from the Castle Hotel, Holyhead, who was simply attacked by two railway policemen until, 'blood gushed from his mouth, nose and ears'.[7] But the railway police were also on the receiving end such as in the case of Thomas Porter of Flint who was convicted of stabbing Richard Hughes in March 1859. Hughes was a railway police officer in the service of the LNWR and was in the King's Head in Flint when the fight started. He supported the landlord but was stabbed in the process, later took the case to court and successfully prosecuted Porter who served nine months with hard labour.[8]

The variety of offences made possible by the existence of a railway was demonstrated in its early years by the case of Richard Lawson of Bagillt, aged eleven, who was accused in 1853 of placing a large stone on the railway line which had disturbed but not derailed the 11.00 a.m. Bangor to Chester train. Driver Thomas Bardsley had spotted the 'urchin' and slowed the train so that its life-preserver deflected the stone safely from the line. It was noted that putting items on the line had become a common practice and the company felt it imperative to prosecute offenders as a deterrence.[9] If so, the memory of it had long gone by 1881 when one boy aged ten and two aged thirteen were in court at Prestatyn for placing bolts on the track at Ffynnongroyw between Mostyn and Talacre. Richard Preston withdrew the charges against one boy who then gave evidence against the others which was enough to convict them. The result was a painful one:

After Mr George (the clerk) explaining the law relating to the punishment of juvenile offenders, the Chairman (Mr T.G. Dixon) severely reprimanded the boys and sentenced them to be birched – Joseph Henry Hughes to receive twelve strokes and John Hughes six strokes. The boys were brought to Rhyl to be punished.[10]

While most offenders against the railway were from the poorer sector of society, there were occasional cases that featured the better-off, and in one case a member of the Irish aristocracy who was in trouble at Chester for trespassing in the Northgate tunnel in 1860:

On Sunday [the Earl of Kingston] went on the Holyhead line of railway and persisted in walking through a tunnel. The policemen there would not allow him and took him to the police office. After being kept there for a few hours he was set free. [He said] he was going to his lawyer, Lord Chelmsford, to enter an action against the Holyhead Railway Company for £100,000, for insulting him. … Two medical gentlemen of the city having certified that he was of unsound mind, the magistrates signed an order for his removal to the County Asylum.[11]

The failings of the early versions of the communication cord were noted in the section on accidents in relation to people falling accidentally from carriages. In one case in 1875 there were similar issues when a man felt obliged to jump after of an altercation with fellow passengers, which was reckoned as a possible attempted murder and in which the communication cord had failed. It involved James Aulds of the Protestant London City Mission who travelled from London with his wife and two children. They were joined in the compartment at Crewe by three cattle traders heading for Ireland. They were apparently arguing among themselves and then turned their attention to the Aulds family and wanted to know their religion. As Aulds tried to pull the cord he was pushed and left hanging from an open door from which he chose to jump to safety about three quarters of a mile beyond Prestatyn station. The cord failed to alert anybody, and it was only at Bangor that Mrs Aulds raised the alarm before a more reliable communication, the electric telegraph, helped to secure the arrest of the men at Holyhead. Joseph Finnigan was charged and appeared at Rhyl where he was contrite and made clear that he had no intention of harming Aulds, still less of killing him. The fact that the bench only convicted him of disorderly behaviour and imposed a fine suggests that there may have been some mitigation. Whether the Protestant Aulds had attempted his missionary activity on his Catholic fellow travellers is unknown but could certainly have inflamed the situation. The magistrates reserved their strongest condemnation for the LNWR, telling their solicitor, inevitably it was Mr Preston, that it was disgraceful that the company allowed drunken people to board trains.[12]

There were signs that the functioning of the communication cord had improved by the late 1880s. The Bowker family were between Mold Junction and Sandycroft in November 1889 when the train suddenly braked hard and slowed to a stop at the latter station where a distraught Mrs Bowker leapt onto the platform screaming for the safety of her child. Her husband had apparently lost his temper to such an extent that Mrs Bowker felt obliged stop the train. Mr Bowker was restrained by two men while he calmed himself and his wife and children returned home.[13]

The LNWR does not appear to have acted on the advice of the bench in the earlier case because drink also played a part in another (but lesser) 'railway outrage' a year later – which also involved an offender being arrested at Holyhead. A sailor named McCure was riding the train from London to join his ship at Holyhead. He had drunk heavily and was fast asleep in the compartment. A fellow traveller named Hayes, returning from Oldham to Dublin, had recently purchased implements for his trade in clipping horses – and decided to try two of them out on the unfortunate sailor. His efforts left the poor mariner without a beard, apart from a small tuft on his chin, and with no hair on his head. His scalp was also damaged. Hayes then spent seventeen hours in custody at Holyhead until it was found that no magistrate was available to try the case and he was released after admitting his offence, which the railway police considered trivial. What McCure thought was not recorded.[14] In 1937, a conviction and a fine for damaging a railway carriage and interfering with the comfort of passengers seemed to be a generous outcome for another drunken man. John Davies, a café owner from Rhyl, apparently tried to strangle his wife in a railway compartment at Chester and was only restrained from doing so by another passenger. Davies thought his actions had been 'ungentlemanly' but that the whole incident had been exaggerated.[15]

Alcohol was not only an issue for passengers. It is evident that railway employees were sometimes prone to excessive drinking. The Station Hotel at Llandudno Junction was said to be known as 'The Killer' and one explanation is that it was a place that staff attended before going on duty, sometimes with fatal consequences. Whether that is the real reason for the nickname of the pub or not, there is ample evidence of a problem among railway staff. The CHR provided cheap tickets to a general temperance event in Holyhead as early as 1854. It took another thirty years for real signs that the movement was taking hold in an industry with an established connection to the brewing trade. In 1884 there were 5,470 railway employees in the railway temperance movement, but the LNWR had only 93 compared to 420 in the Great Eastern Railway and 668 in the Great Northern.[16] The Bangor branch of the Railway Temperance Union opened in 1885 and acquired its own hall in February 1893, which was opened by Alice Pennant, daughter of the local slate quarry owner. The opening coincided with a rant against 'teetotal fanatics' from Captain Harry Harwood of the Bangor Licensed Victuallers Association, so the railway movement for sobriety had a tough task on its hands.[17] The cause was sufficiently important to have an association football trophy dedicated to it – the LNWR Temperance Union Shield. In 1910, Llandudno Junction reached the final after winning a second semi-final replay 1–0 against Northampton at Crewe, before losing 3–0 to Liverpool at Bangor.[18]

While most cases of dishonesty involved passengers, occasionally it was employees of the railway who were involved. The nearest the line saw to a 'Great Train Robbery' was probably at Bangor in 1869. In July, Chief Justice Bovill heard that William Owen Hughes, a milliner, and Alfred Gilchrist Wilson, a railway porter, had stolen 27 gold watches, 107 silver watches, 106 gold chains and a lot of other jewellery. Hughes was also indicted for receiving the goods, knowing them to have been stolen. Mr Aaronson, a local jeweller, told the court that he regularly sent boxes of valuable goods to Southampton for export and did not alert railway staff to the contents, nor did he insure them. The boxes in question were worth about £600 (£72,000). As usual, Mr Preston was present to instruct the barrister, and both Wilson and Hughes were convicted, receiving five years' and three years' imprisonment, respectively.[19]

In the same issue of the *North Wales Chronicle*, the LNWR was reported to be the victim of another significant crime, albeit by a passenger rather than an employee. Henry Ford from Manchester contacted the LNWR after the Abergele crash of August 1868 and claimed to have been in a first-class compartment on the fateful train and to have suffered significant injuries. When seen, he was reported to be living in lodgings as an invalid, 'his legs being wrapped in blankets, and medicine bottles and galvanic apparatus being in his room'. Mr Binger representing the LNWR – Mr Preston was perhaps on leave – was suspicious of the delay in the claim, and he sought prosecution for fraud once Ford had failed to follow up his threats to sue the company when it declined to settle out of court for £4,000 (£480,000). Subsequently, Ford received eighteen months imprisonment and a further six months for furniture he had obtained and then sold after convincing the merchant that he was due a big settlement from the LNWR.[20]

The CHR was also peripherally involved in a remarkable attempted fraud by Violet Charlesworth in 1909. She was from humble background but managed to become part of a wealthy group of people who lived near Mold. She developed a fascination with motor cars and was highly competent at driving them. She was less competent at managing money and ran up large debts. Her route out of these problems was a daring disappearance that she staged on the north Wales coast near Penmaenmawr. She was with a chauffeur and her sister when they were involved in an 'accident' on a sharp bend in the road near Pen-y-Clip. The car hung over the precipice and Violet was thrown off the cliff and into the sea – or at least that is what it was she intended people to believe. The local police were suspicious from the start, especially when an inspector at Holyhead station reported seeing her heading for Ireland.[21] That sighting proved to be inaccurate and the truth was that she had faked the accident, walked to Conwy station, and taken a train to Crewe and from there to Glasgow. She eventually served a term of imprisonment for her trouble.

Cases fought by the railway in court did not always concern crime. An early example from February 1857 involved a postal clerk called Allen who was sorting letters on the night mail from Chester to Holyhead on 10 May 1856. Ahead of it was a double-headed coal and cattle train travelling at about half the speed of the Irish Mail. When it reached Aber one of the engines failed, and instead of taking care to signal the danger to the following train or shunting into a siding, the freight train carried on at a much-reduced speed. This was at a time when the interval system – where one train followed another at a 'reasonable' interval – was used rather than block working that stopped one train entering a section until the previous one had left. So, there was no means to prevent the mail train from catching up the freight train, which it did at Llandegai tunnel near Bangor. In the resulting smash Allen claimed to have received injuries that subsequently caused several debilitating symptoms for which he sought compensation. Preston put up a strong defence in court and in doing so gave an insight into the frequency of this type of claim, noting that 'whenever an accident occurs, the railway is besieged by claims for compensation'. He told the court that no other passenger or crew member had reported an injury and Allen had made his claim many months after the incident. He claimed various injuries and sensory loss and yet had penned a perfectly written and lucid claim. Nonetheless, Allen won his case and compensation of £1,400 (£160,000).[22]

The LNWR was generally keen to see all accidents as a product of personal rather than corporate failure, such as in its response to the Abergele smash in 1868. But it could also be supportive of its staff. In 1867 there was a serious incident when the driver of a Llanrwst-bound goods train carrying railway sleepers crashed into a guard's van and goods trucks at Mold Junction. These had been separated from the rest of a train and left on the main line during shunting operations. The driver of the Llanrwst train was found by the coroner's court to be responsible for the death of Thomas Plevin and sent for trial for manslaughter. Mr J.O. Binger, general manager of the Chester to Holyhead district, was in court and undertook to organise bail for driver Joseph Burrows. At the subsequent trial it was alleged by the signalman that the signal was set at danger to protect the goods train, but five witnesses gave evidence that Burrows had whistled as he approached and that the signal was clear. The judge ordered the jury to find in favour of the driver but what the LNWR did with the recalcitrant signalman is not recorded.[23]

The most serious of the crimes committed on the line involved a clerk at Bangor station who was acting up as temporary stationmaster at Aber. In February 1878, John Prytherch jumped into a compartment with Mrs Margaret Owen, who was heading for Holyhead having visited her family at Aber. He then sexually assaulted her which she reported at Bangor. Prytherch tried to pay off the family to avoid prosecution but they and the LNWR proceeded despite the initial defence from Prytherch's lawyer that the court could not rely on the uncorroborated evidence of a woman. When the matter reached a very crowded court at Caernarfon in March, the judge noted that such an offence, particularly if proved against a railway official, must be regarded as a serious breach of the trust the public should have when travelling by train. Once again, Mr Preston was present to instruct the barrister in a successful prosecution – at the end of which the judge regretted that he was limited to a sentence of two years imprisonment with hard labour. Today it is notoriously difficult to secure prosecutions in such cases, and so the determination of the LNWR and the consideration it gave to the victim despite the reputational damage to itself seems remarkable, especially by the standards that prevailed in 1878.[24]

Another case in 1896 at Abergele points to this approach of protecting women on trains perhaps being an LNWR policy. John Davies from Abergele entered a compartment occupied by five young women and sat on the knee of one of them and proceeded to act in a 'lewd' manner towards the occupants. They complained at the next station and Davies was removed from the train and charged. Mr Fenna, acting for the LNWR, told Abergele Petty Sessions that:

> The case was fortunately one which rarely came under the notice of the company, but they did not know how many cases were allowed to go unpunished on account of ladies not wishing to appear in the police court. He had a couple of ladies who had pluckily come to court, in that case, and he asked that the bench would not permit their names to transpire.

The court agreed and committed Davies for trial where he was convicted and received two months imprisonment.[25]

These cases underlined the importance of women passengers to the railways. Women had secured a much greater freedom to travel because of railways and mostly felt safe to travel alone. Both cases against women described here secured the best available response from the railway company and the court by extending support to the victims and ensuring that the offenders were dealt with effectively. The two years maximum term for a serious sexual assault given to Prytherch should be compared with the five years hard labour given to one of those convicted for jewellery theft at Bangor in 1869 to illustrate the relative importance afforded to offences.

Prosecutions were occasionally to make a point such as the need for passengers to wait for the train to stop before entering or leaving a carriage. Mr Preston confirmed this approach at Valley in March 1887 when dealing with Owen Owen from Amlwch who jumped off a moving train at Ty Croes station. He stumbled badly and was saved from further harm by the quick work of porter Owen Thomas.

The elaborate nature of such railway prosecutions was clear from the fact that the line superintendent Ephraim Wood had written to Owen's employers to confirm the story he had offered to the LNWR officials. Preston wanted an example made of Owen and told the magistrates that bye-law 11 allowed them to fine him up to £2 (£265). They opted for twenty-five shillings (£140) instead and warned Owen about his future behaviour.[26] The incident had an unfortunate sequel in the fate of the unlucky Owen Thomas who was himself injured at Ty Croes in November 1891 and sent to a doctor at Llangefni. He missed the doctor and the return train that called at Ty Croes, and so caught one that stopped at Bodorgan and set off walking home along the line in the dark. Shortly after setting off he missed his way at a bridge, fell over the parapet to his death and was found by platelayers the next morning. He had been a porter at Ty Croes for sixteen years and 'left a widow and six children unprovided for'.[27]

On other occasions the LNWR was keen to distance itself as much as possible from legal proceedings. Thus, in 1868 when an LNWR employee fished a dead body from the harbour at Holyhead its manager and solicitor reacted quickly. The coroner's court heard that an employee pulling on a rope in the harbour found it to be unusually heavy. When he pulled on it further, he noted 'the body of a man with his legs upwards'. With the help of PC Owen, the body was moved to an LNWR barracks that was usually reserved for troops passing through the port. Later, LNWR Marine Superintendent Dent hired Richard Rowlands' donkey cart to take the body of John Hollahan to the police station but the police refused to accept it. Mr Preston was again to the fore in arguing that the body was nothing to do with the LNWR, even though Hollahan had travelled to Holyhead by train and had apparently boarded the LNWR ship and then returned to the town for a drink. There was a testy exchange between Preston and Dent on the one side, who asserted that the LNWR had no responsibility in the matter and should not have had the body left on its premises, and Superintendent Owen and the coroner who thought the LNWR irresponsible in the matter. The jury agreed with the latter and the LNWR was advised to give better lighting and guidance to passengers boarding its ships for night-time sailings, the assumption being that Hollahan had missed his footing on the gangway and fallen into the harbour.[28]

This section on legal proceedings and the railway in north Wales and Chester would not be complete without considering the fitting end to Mr Preston's career in 1891:

On Wednesday morning Mr Preston, in the course of his duties … left Chester by the 8.45 train for Carnarvon and conducted a case at the County Court there. He returned to Chester by the Bangor express, due at Chester at 5.15. He hurried to his offices in the station, and leaving his bag and umbrella went out. It was generally believed at the office that he had gone to the County Court offices, and as his family understood he was to dine at Hoole that evening, his protracted disappearance caused no anxiety. At midnight, however, his absence gave rise to considerable uneasiness, and his son, Mr Arthur Preston, having roused Mr Fenna (his chief clerk), at Hoole, went to the Railway Station, and having forced open the door of one of the apartments in the office found Mr Preston lying unconscious on the floor and breathing heavily. He was first removed to the Ladies' first-class waiting-room, and afterwards to the Queen's Hotel opposite. Dr Archer, and subsequently Dr Dobie … found that the patient was suffering from apoplexy. Death resulted at noon on Thursday from haemorrhage on the brain.[29]

Preston was the quintessential LNWR man who lived in Rhyl and served on the local Board of Commissioners where he could both defend and promote the company's interests:

In politics he was a Conservative, and in religion a Churchman [Church of England]. Although strangers may have thought Mr Preston from his calm, judicial manner rather an austere, even ascetic man, it was more apparent than real. Those who knew him ultimately realised the goodness of his heart, and the poor who benefited by his charity can testify in how many ways he 'did good by stealth and blushed to find it fame'.[30]

A week later he was buried in Rhyl where many legal colleagues were present, although Ephraim Wood, the line superintendent, was unable to attend because of a meeting of directors. It was always business first for the LNWR. Doubtless Richard Montague Preston, who died in harness, would have agreed.

While court cases of the various types described above caught the attention of the newspapers, they were but a small part of the railway's relationship with the people of north Wales. In the era before motor cars, radio, television and the internet the railway was the window and the road into the outside world for a region that had been a backwater for centuries. While this connection did much to extend the use of English ways and the English language in north Wales it also, for a time, strengthened the sense of Welshness. This was clearly seen in the earlier discussion about politics, but it was also evident in the culture and religion of the region.

One institution that received a notable boost from the arrival of railways was the Eisteddfod – a cultural and quasi-political event that was a feature of many communities in north Wales. The impact was apparent from the earliest operation of the CHR when the LNWR offered an excursion from London to Rhyl and Bangor so that people could visit the Britannia Tubular Bridge and the Royal Eisteddfod at Rhuddlan in 1850. The sheer numbers leaving a local train at Holywell station on return from the Eisteddfod caused some injury. The train had stopped at the station and the passengers rushed the waiting omnibuses. Several were cut and bruised after they tripped and fell on the rails in the poor light. Given the revenue the railway had earned from the event, the correspondent reporting these events hoped that the company would contribute liberally in future to various Eisteddfodau.[31]

Whether it did or not is unclear, but the importance of the new form of travel was acknowledged at the event by the award of a prize for the best song in Welsh about the railway. Eisteddfodau were occasions to value the Welsh language and culture – and the arrival of the railway was seen by some as a threat because it was a vital form of communication conducted almost entirely in English. Those holding such views were not helped by the opinion expressed by the Bard John Jones 'Talhaiarn' at the Denbigh Eisteddfod in 1860. He asserted that English was the language of money and success and it was a deprivation for Welsh people not to learn it: and he was supported by at least one correspondent to the local paper, who saw that railways were evidence of the superiority of the English over the Welsh, with the Britannia Tubular Bridge offered as the best example.[32]

The National Eisteddfod three years later seemed to back this position with a prominent banner wishing 'Success to Railway Enterprise'.[33] The CHR was certainly succeeding and had the opportunity to benefit from the first Eisteddfod held outside Wales in 1866, based as it was on the Roodee adjacent to the line in Chester. But the event was apparently rather spoiled by the weather and the 'niggardly disposition of the railway authorities' – though no details of what that entailed were provided. They performed better for the event at Mold in 1873 where the comments from the committee were positive:

The thanks of the committee are especially due to the railway authorities, who worked the system without a hitch. Not a single accident of any kind took place, nor have we learned that a single disappointment occurred on any part of the system and we are the more ready to make this testimony, seeing that only a fortnight previously we had to speak our mind pretty plainly regarding the mismanagement on the day of the cattle show at Rhyl.[34]

The last comment concerned the failure of the LNWR to deliver some potentially prize-winning cattle belonging to Lieutenant Colonel Cooke. That remark demonstrates how vital railway facilities were to almost any event before the First World War, though as at Rhyl satisfaction was not always guaranteed. In 1869 the residents of the north Wales coast responded well to an LNWR trip to the Belle Vue gardens in Manchester – to the obvious discomfort of some of their compatriots:

> On Monday morning last many scores of passengers at Holywell, Bagillt, Flint … who had booked by the first train to Chester, were detained till 11 o'clock, on account of every train being crammed with passengers for Belle Vue, Manchester. Four immense long trains passed from 8 to 10 o'clock, but none of them could pick a single passenger at any of the above stations. Great discontent was shown, and not without reason.[35]

And it was not just lack of space that was a problem, the fares did not always suit the locals either; with the Wepre and Golftyn Calvinistic Methodist Sunday Schools deciding to abandon its trip to Llangollen in 1891 because of the cost of tickets offered by the LNWR.[36]

The railway was supreme in north Wales in the second half of the nineteenth century, as it was in the rest of the UK. That supremacy continued for a time after 1900 so that by the first Christmas of the new century traffic and travel along the line was reported to be at its highest ever. There were tens of thousands of mail bags, thousands of parcels and hampers. Livestock and meat were carried in record quantities and extra staff were employed at Holyhead and Dublin to deal with trains from London that arrived with three or four sections all completely full, and special trains ran from Lancashire, Yorkshire and the Midlands almost entirely devoted to the carriage of Irish traffic.[37]

Because north Wales was a largely agricultural area, the relationship with the farmers who relied on it was especially important. It was not always an easy one as farmers complained about the charges levied by the railway and other issues such as cattle plague carried in trucks and injuries caused to animals in carriage. There was an early sign of the importance of the CHR to the local economy in the area around Bodorgan on Anglesey. When the local landlord was married in 1853 there was a celebration that involved the important local people, including the Bodorgan stationmaster Robert Powell who responded to the toast, 'Success to the Chester and Holyhead Railway'. He was followed by a speech that spelled out the joy of the local landowners and farmers at the arrival of the CHR in their district. He acknowledged that the railway was a great benefit to the whole country and:

The original shareholders deserve the public gratitude for the spirit which they evinced in encouraging its formation. It is not only of importance to the neighbouring farmers, as enabling them to bring manure to their land, and to despatch their produce cheaply and readily to the best markets, but it opens up the hitherto only partially developed mineral wealth of the counties of Denbighshire, Flintshire [and] Carnarvonshire [*sic*] ... [that] abound with lead, copper, and coal mines, stone and slate quarries.[38]

The railway company recognised the benefits of its relationship with farmers and even offered concessionary travel to events such as the Anglesey Agricultural Society Show in 1890.[39] Relations were not always so cordial. Farmer Gratton of Foryd Farm took the LNWR to court at St Asaph in 1891 after several of his sheep strayed onto the main line and were killed by a train. The railway company sent the carcases to a local butcher and gave the farmer a cheque for six shillings (£44). As usual Mr Preston put the case for the LNWR and denied that the gate was poorly maintained. The jury disagreed and awarded Gratton eleven times what the company had sent him.[40]

Fire was a regular community hazard in the days of coal and steam when combined with the presence of combustible materials on and near the railway. The original station at Conwy was almost destroyed in 1858:

About 2 o'clock last Saturday morning Mr Hughes, stationmaster, at Conway [*sic*] ... was awakened, nearly suffocated by smoke, and soon found that the place was all in flames. All the family were immediately aroused, and but narrowly escaped, as they had not a rag on except their night dresses when they arrived at the Erskine Arms Hotel. An alarm was given through the town, and a great number of people were immediately on the spot. The nearest water available was that at the tank that supplies the engines, some distance from the place. The men worked nobly, and between 4 and 5 o'clock mastered the destructive element, not, however, before all the roof, the upper rooms, and furniture were almost totally destroyed. The office on the ground floor was saved. As usual in our small towns, no fire engine could be had.[41]

Old Colwyn station had a narrow escape in 1898 after the 2.45 p.m. express passed. Staff at Colwyn Bay noticed a fire close to the line and contacted the signal box nearby. Foreman platelayer Aldis, and his crew found a waggon of hay and an empty return truck were on fire and had ignited the sleepers. They managed

75. *In June 1979, the destruction of old Conway [sic] station is almost complete – with just one doorway remaining – as 47450 heads west with a substantial passenger train. In 1858 the stationmaster and his family fled to the Erskine Hotel, seen in the background, to escape a serious fire. The more recent destruction was more permanent with only platforms and basic shelters returning for the 1987 reopening.* **(Photo: John Hobbs)**

to contain the fire before it reached the station buildings.[42] Four years later the same station suffered again when a passing train caused a fire in a haystack in an adjoining field. It then spread to the station and set fire to the creosoted railings on the down platform. Unlike Conwy in 1858, there was a fire brigade available in 1902 that contained the blaze.[43] The inflammable nature of wood treatments was demonstrated spectacularly in 1905 at Nant Hall as the widening work on the line progressed:

> Great excitement was caused in Prestatyn on Thursday morning by the statement that a goods train had taken fire, and many scores of persons wended their way down to the railway line to satiate their curiosity. It appears that at about nine o'clock a goods train was proceeding from Talacre to Prestatyn,

when Fireman Walter Jones was alarmed at noticing a column of smoke issuing from one of the trucks … Investigation showed that a truck containing several hundred sleepers was on fire. A messenger was despatched to the station and a break-down gang soon appeared on the scene. … The sleepers were for use in relaying the metals at Prestatyn station and had only recently been pickled so that they were soaked with tar and resin. The fire is thought to have been caused by sparks from the engine.[44]

Further up the line in 1910 one farmer appreciated the input of the LNWR in lieu of the fire brigade when at 3.45 a.m. at Bodlondeb Farm near Holywell station a haystack caught fire. Stationmaster J.O. Hughes attended with the LNWR's fire engine and a crew of railway workers to put out the fire before it spread.[45] Two years later schoolboys returning from Ireland to Stonyhurst College near Preston caused the destruction of a carriage between Mochdre and Colwyn Bay when they set fire to 'antiseptic material' from the train's lavatory. Several boys were burned and two fell from the train as they escaped the blaze, though fortunately none was killed.[46] The damage caused was extensive but there is no evidence of any police action against these miscreants from wealthy families. Compare that with many of the punishments handed out by the courts to local people for much less serious crimes noted earlier.

The peculiar susceptibility of this portion of line to fire was emphasised when Llandulas (*sic*) station was burnt down in October 1913. The notion that the 'mail must get through' can never have been clearer:

Several trains were delayed by the fire, but the Irish boat express, dashed through the blazing station on the way from London to Holyhead. It is believed that one of the express compartments was damaged. Fire brigades from Llandudno, Colwyn Bay, Rhyl, and Abergele were engaged on the conflagration, but they could only prevent the spread of the fire to the buildings on the opposite platform. Serious damage was done.[47]

Before the arrival of motorised road transport, the railway was the best mechanism to market goods and the farms themselves. That was demonstrated in 1917 when hard-pressed farmers, struggling to provide for a nation under the strain of shipping losses to German submarines, rising prices and labour shortages, held the 'Gaerwen Junction Smithfield' close to the eponymous station that was accessed by farmers across the island and buyers of produce from much further afield – as the local paper noted: 'Dealers attended from all parts resulting in an entire

76. Llandulas (sic) Station opened in 1889, proved popular with tourists but was little used out of season. It was almost destroyed by fire in 1913, restored as seen in this picture from around 1935 and finally closed in 1952. The site of the viaduct destroyed in 1879 is just beyond the station. (Photo: John Alsop Collection)

clearance at satisfactory prices.' In the same issue it was reported that the nearby farm of Myfyrian Isa was sold, and again the railway was vital in the process:

> The yard presented quite a busy appearance all the morning and the arrival of the mid-day train brought two well-known buyers from Birmingham and about a dozen large Cheshire milk sellers and dealers, in addition to buyers from Prestatyn, Denbigh, Mold, Rhyl, Colwyn Bay, and Llandudno … Mr MacKenzie, in a few well-chosen remarks, informed the company that the reason this sale had been called was because it was Mr Roberts' decision to alter his system of farming owing to the expense of feeding stuffs and the labour necessary to keep a winter dairy.[48]

Those farmers who did not have good access to the railway were clearly at a disadvantage. One example was Llangaffo which is close to the line, but not to a station, and was a lively agricultural district in Anglesey that relied on its supplies

Above: 77. *Fire was a recurrent feature of the line – quite often on the stretch from Abergele to Colwyn Bay. In 1912, schoolboys returning to Stonyhurst college from Ireland set fire to this carriage and caused the train to stop at Colwyn Bay. Station staff are pictured in the aftermath of the blaze.* **(Photo: John Alsop Collection)**

Below: 78. *Gaerwen station was a focus for the farming community in Anglesey for many years so that a 'Gaerwen Junction Smithfield' was held in 1917 that brought together traders from far and wide. It is the only CHR station lost on the Anglesey mainland having been closed in 1966 and never reopened.* **(Photo: John Alsop Collection)**

GAERWEN STATION

via the Tal y Foel ferry from Caernarfon and road transport to the farms. The issue was raised several times with the LNWR, especially when the company provided a station at Mochdre in 1889 – which the Llangaffo farmers regarded as a much smaller place with no need for a station. As we have seen, the Mochdre station appeared not long after the 1887 tithe riots and was probably for the benefit of the police rather than the farmers. The Llangaffo farmers never got their station.[49]

The status of the railway was not only measured in terms of traffic but also in the attention paid to it by the communities through which it passed. At Valley in 1862, farmers marked the retirement of stationmaster Coles by meeting at a local hotel to open a subscription on his behalf because:

> For a number of years … he has given the greatest satisfaction to the inhabitants of Valley and the surrounding neighbourhood, in having on all occasions shown civility and attention to them; and also … properly discharged his duties to his employers.[50]

As late as 1935, the retirement of signalman Walter Jones after forty-four years' service on the line (thirty-seven in the same signal box at Llandudno Junction) merited a few lines in the Liverpool papers.[51]

Retirement was a happy occasion, but some popular figures on the line did not reach that stage and died in service. In the days before pensions and social benefits, the death of a such a person was dealt with jointly by community and employer. In the case of R. Williams of Ty Croes in 1886 a farmer and the vicar organised a collection which was then circulated locally and at stations along the line. In this way nearly £60 (£8,000) was raised for Mr Williams' pregnant widow and their three young children: half locally and the rest from other stations. She received £15 (£2,000) for immediate expenses and the rest put in trust for the children. The LNWR then offered Mrs Williams a post in the café at Bangor.[52]

But there was near celebrity status for David Parry, the stationmaster at Rhyl in the heyday of the CHR. His appointment in June 1888 was covered in the local paper and he was in charge of employees at an event in November 1891 when fifty staff were treated by Mr Pratt of nearby Brynllithrig Hall to supper (and a three-hour bar extension) at Costigan's Refreshment Rooms. Sadly, David Parry lasted less than a year as he died from influenza during a pandemic in August 1892, though his demise attracted great attention. There was an extensive account in the local paper that gave some insight into a career with the LNWR in north Wales. David Parry had a basic education but passed his entry examination for the LNWR with credit. He proved to be a diligent and enterprising employee who furthered the interests of the railway and moved from Padeswood to Flint and then Rhyl, which was a major post on the line. Throughout his career, 'his tact and other qualities, together with his kindness of heart and thorough honesty of character, made him much respected. His end came unexpectedly in the midst of his career'. His funeral was one of the largest seen in Mold for many years with a large contingent joining the funeral train at Flint, on which there were already many mourners from Rhyl. Many of the stationmasters from the line were present with Mr Parry's family, and the coffin was carried on the shoulders of four railway porters in full uniform. Mourners totalled about 400.[53]

The generosity of the wider public towards station staff continued, and as late as 1902 local people contributed to an outing for the Rhyl team which, as the local paper commented, 'speaks volumes of the popularity of the staff with the residents of the town'.[54] By 1913 there was some concern that the promised slot machines for platform tickets were still not available on Rhyl station. That was part of a wider problem so that officials of Rhyl Urban District Council decided to: 'interview the railway company as to granting concessions to tradespeople having business on the station, and to ask also for extra booking facilities owing to the congested state of the station during the holiday season'.[55] In Rhyl, as in other towns along the line, the railway station was at the very centre of the local community.

As we noted in the case of Richard Preston, the LNWR solicitor, the company had a close relationship with the Church of England which was evident on several occasions. In 1852 Queen Victoria was feted at Saltney Junction by the local vicar on her return from a visit to the Britannia Tubular Bridge:

> The indefatigable Rector of St Mary's chose this day to mark the event of roofing in of the Saltney Church School by assembling the children of the parish in the school to witness the passing of Her Majesty [in the royal train]. The church stands so nearly on the confines of England and Wales that one standard on the west of the building was raised on Welsh ground [and] another to the east on English ground.[56]

The railway was more directly involved in the strange case of Reverend William Anwyl Roberts Rector of Llanddyfnan in Anglesey who had been reported to Church authorities by station staff at Bangor for drunkenness on railway property. Evidence was given by George Jackson, police officer; Hugh Griffiths, booking clerk; Eleanor Ward, buffet attendant; Miss King, buffet manager; Mr Jones, stationmaster; Thomas Griffiths, signalman; and David Hughes, the guard of the train that Reverend Roberts took to Llandudno Junction. All of them were employed at Bangor, and all agreed that the poor clergyman had been helplessly drunk. The senior churchmen on the panel were happy to take the word of these railway employees and referred their colleague to a higher authority. He was still at work at Llanddyfnan in 1886 so the sanction cannot have been too severe.[57] A rather more senior churchman featured on the line in 1896 when the coffin of Edward White Benson, Archbishop of Canterbury, was dispatched from Sandycroft to Canterbury after he died during a service at Hawarden Church while visiting William Gladstone, four times prime minister, at Hawarden.[58]

When Gladstone's turn came to enter eternity in May 1898, his coffin was carried with great ceremony from Hawarden to Broughton Hall station on the Mold line that joined the CHR one mile away at Saltney Ferry (Mold Junction). The three-coach special train was hauled to London by *Gladstone*, a London Brighton & South Coast Railway Stroudley 'B' class 0-4-2 No 214, painted black for the occasion. This was perhaps the most significant train journey in the history of the line, albeit only covering three and three quarters of a mile of the eighty-five miles between Chester and Holyhead.

All the way from Broughton Hall to Chester crowds of people, old and young, were seen at short intervals by the roadside and on the railway embankments. In many places, little children of the labouring classes were assembled in scores and hundreds. It seemed as if their parents had brought them out in order that they might say in after years that they had seen Mr Gladstone's funeral train pass by. … Rough navvies and coalheavers, smeared with the grime and dust of their daily toil, desisted for a moment from their task and stood cap in hand as the train sped by. The engine drivers of the trains lying stationary in railway sidings saluted. Everywhere little knots and gangs of men could be descried, clustered together, with their foremen in front of them, in momentary homage to the memory of the great Englishman. At eight o'clock the train crossed over the Dee and slowed down as it passed through Chester. Here there was a very remarkable demonstration. Thousands of people lined the city walls … heads were silently and sadly uncovered. The platforms of Chester station were thronged with citizens, and here there were the same indications of personal sorrow and of national bereavement.[59]

Frederick Temple, the ageing successor as archbishop to the unfortunate Benson, officiated at Gladstone's state funeral, and also had occasion to use the CHR in

October 1901 – a time when stations could not always be described as suitable for people with disabilities. He had an interesting exchange with the stationmaster at Colwyn Bay where the archbishop had been attending a church gathering. Temple left the event a little late, causing the train to be held at the station where it was obstructing the busy schedule and troubling the staff:

> Perhaps the Archbishop observed signs of their state of mind. Owing to his advanced years, the ascent of the steps leading to the up platform was expected to be a difficult task for the Primate, so Mr Vaughan [stationmaster] promptly advanced, as the Primate placed his foot on the first step, and asked, 'Is there anything I can do to assist your Grace?' Laying his hand on Mr Vaughan's arm, the aged Primate replied in significant tones, 'Yes, there is one way – patience.' This remark caused good-humoured laughter, in which the Archbishop heartily joined.[60]

By the end of the following year Temple had joined Benson and Gladstone.

Those three learned men would no doubt have appreciated the philosophical approach to misfortune exhibited by an elderly man named Edward Williams who lived in Llanfairfechan and whose job it was to collect the mail from the station and distribute it. In December 1864, the inhabitants suddenly noted that the mail had been interrupted but the reason only became clear when the postmaster at Bangor received a telegram from Douglas in the Isle of Man. This told him that Edward Williams had arrived there by ship the previous evening. Slowly the story was put together when a man who had travelled with Williams on the train from Llanfairfechan to Conwy recounted that the old man had told him that he intended sail his boat back home in time to meet the mail train at the station and then deal with the post at his usual time. The trip went terribly wrong and he drifted miles to the middle of the Irish Sea as he recounted:

> I have no faith in leaving that which is one's duty in life and health to do till the very last moment of one's life. I really thought that my duty in such an emergency was to use all my efforts to save myself, and having done my duty towards myself, to leave all the rest to God. ... I thought of my friends at Bangor and Llanfairfechan – what would become of the letters and what in the world would they think had become of me? I had no idea what time it was; and though I had not tasted a morsel of anything to eat or drink since five o'clock on Friday morning, at Bangor, strange to say, I did not feel the want of anything. [I was eventually taken on board a passing ship] and a medical

man happening to be on board, ordered me to be placed in a warm bed, which was immediately done, and restoratives were applied.[61]

The railway station was the centre of small rural communities in north Wales and although trains marked an intrusion of the modern into places that had seen little change in centuries there were occasions when the old and the new ways combined. Such a case was Bodorgan Station at the centre of the estates of the Meyrick family. The station served as a venue for a ceremony that had echoes of the feudal nature of society from which Wales was slowly emerging with the help of railways. For it was here in 1882 that Sir George Meyrick held his annual rents event in January where the: 'tenants were joyously entertained at dinner … in course of which speeches were made indicating the sincere feeling of respect that exists between the tenants and their worthy landlord, who has returned them ten per cent of their annual rent'.[62]

79. Bodorgan station sits amid glorious farmland but attracts little use these days – around ten passengers a day on average. In 1882 it was at the centre of this agricultural area as Sir George Meyrick held his annual rents event at the station. In February 2020, 158839 bound for Birmingham has paused at Bodorgan but the London–Holyhead express rushes through. **(Photo: Phil Lloyd Collection)**

Workers in other industries close to the line also benefited from the occasional generosity of those who profited from their labour. So, the employees at the Llanerch-y-Mor lead works enjoyed a trip to Llandudno by rail in 1876 on which: 'the weather was delightfully fine, the excursion was a very pleasant one [and] through the liberality of their employer, Adam Eyton … had their tickets provided for them.'[63] On at least one occasion the entertainment came to the community, albeit unintentionally. The train carrying James Welch and his 'New Clown' theatre company stalled on a hill two miles short of Bangor in 1903. The event was captured by a Nottingham newspaper:

> The guard started back down the line with a red flag to meet the Irish Mail. Meanwhile Welch and his company alighted and became the centre of considerable interest for the Welsh peasants, who were attracted there in large numbers. Some of the onlookers provided the artists with milk, biscuits, and other light refreshments from the neighbouring farmhouses. After the lapse of an hour the Irish Mail arrived and slowly pushed the special train into Bangor, where a fresh engine was procured.[64]

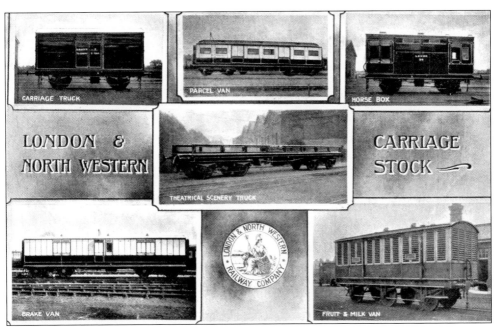

80. *The variety of freight rolling stock on the LNWR is illustrated in this postcard. It seems likely that a 'theatrical scenery truck' would have been part of the train that stalled near Llandegai in 1903, leaving the locals to entertain the 'New Clown' theatre company until a following train shunted them to Bangor.* **(Photo: Phil Lloyd Collection)**

But perhaps the ultimate statement of railway power in north Wales is the creation of a railway town. If there is an equivalent to Crewe in the region it is probably Llandudno Junction which was not on a map before the railway arrived and still retains its historical railway connections north, south, east and west. As the name suggests, the town is a creation of the railway. But how did this name come about? In 1901 a correspondent to the local paper explained, and offered a strong view about adopting the name:

> Sir, it being understood that the residents in the district adjacent to the above-named station are about to be asked to decide by ballot whether the name of this now extensive district shall be fixed as above or have the addition of 'Penrhos.' I should like to urge my fellow voters to vote for the additional name on the following grounds. The advocates of '*Llandudno Junction*' will not be deprived of their favourite name. Welshmen who love their own language, and do not like to see the ancient poetic placenames of their country gradually giving way to English and semi-English names will be gratified. English visitors are attracted to Wales not only by its natural charms, but also to a great degree by its romantic and historical interest. To call a beautiful district a '*Junction*' does not add to this charm. Penrhos is an appropriate and poetic local name. A '*Junction*' is a part of the railway and has no significance beyond that. That these few remarks may influence all to vote for Penrhos is the earnest wish of A DWELLER IN THE DISTRICT.[65]

Whether such a ballot was held is unknown, but the power of the railway to determine the name of this town and the shape of much of the region is clear enough even today after many years of the dominance of the motor car and lorry.

Rapid Decline, Slow Recovery and New Threats

All decisions affecting our regional railways and rural services are taken from outside our borders. There is a case for considering the future of Welsh railways in a Welsh context.[1]

Car ownership was building before the Second World War, bus and coach travel often offered a cheaper alternative to rail and people increasingly wanted to avoid the crowds that gathered at venues served by rail. After the war, petrol rationing prevented an immediate resurgence of car ownership but the general availability of fuel in 1950, a growth in living standards and a worn-out rail system contributed to a weakening of the hold that rail travel had on holidaymakers.

After 1955 the decline set in – slowly at first – so that by the time of the Beeching Report in 1963 there was enough justification in the opinion of government to hasten the decline further with draconian cuts. From the 1920s railways gradually moved away from the foreground of life in north Wales as interest turned to the need for better roads and facilities for the increasing numbers of cars and buses. For the historian that means there is less evidence of the daily detail of the operation of the lines in newspapers and Parliament, with just occasional mentions such as the 1920 diversion of holiday trains through the 'considerable detour' via Denbigh after a truck was derailed at Connah's Quay.[2] It is therefore more difficult to track what was happening unless it was something serious that involved multiple fatalities or serious storm damage. Whereas the death of a hare on the line warranted a newspaper report in 1848, the death of a railway worker might be worth barely a few lines after 1918. The chapter on holiday traffic covered the period up to Beeching so this chapter charts the decline after that report as the Chester and Holyhead Railway (CHR) retreated from the mainstream of life in north Wales and became secondary to the motor car and the ever-growing A55.

In the aftermath of Beeching, British Railways decided that it required fewer stations and a better image. So, in January 1965 a corporate blue replaced such variations as the green of the Southern Region, the maroon on other regions and the chocolate and cream of Pullman cars. In the spirit of the sixties, Dr Beeching unveiled this new look at the Design Centre in London, where the now familiar double arrow symbol was also introduced, and British Railways became British Rail.

In north Wales, the battle between road and rail took a more direct form in January 1965 when a Crosville bus demolished a level crossing gate at Llandudno Junction causing significant delays to trains, although the bus suffered only minor damage. More damage was caused to services on 14 February 1966 when many stations along the CHR closed as the Beeching changes began to bite. In April 1966, the British Railways Board advertised the sale of railway station houses and buildings, fishing rights, houses and cottages in north Wales.

It was not long before another aspect of rail modernisation took effect: the demise of steam. In July 1967 there were regular reports of steam haulage on the CHR but by February 1968 it was mostly English Electric Type 4s and Sulzer

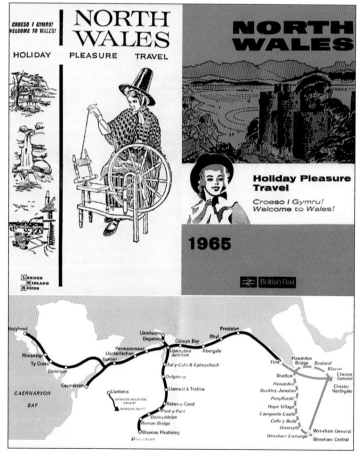

81. *The 1963 London Midland Region holiday brochure echoes the 1950s, while the post-Beeching shift to a corporate British Rail style and logo is evident in the 1965 offering. The map from the 1968 leaflet (no longer a brochure) shows that behind the style change the CHR reached its lowest ebb with just twelve stations between Chester and Holyhead.* **(Photo: Phil Lloyd Collection)**

Type 2s with an occasional Brush Type 2 on the Holyhead–London service. Steam appeared on special trains featuring engines such as the *Flying Scotsman* which made its first trip on the line in 1966 – early signs of the nostalgia that helped keep the line going through its most difficult years. The end of steam took with it a way of life for the army of workers that had kept the engines running. While writing this account I spoke to one of the few survivors from engine shed 6G at Llandudno Junction. Derek Williams worked at the shed from the late fifties until redundancy in 1966 as modernisation proceeded. He recalled a large staff group at the shed at its busiest and that there was a thriving culture and camaraderie that was lost when the shed closed. He has worked hard to ensure that they are 'gone but not forgotten'.[3]

These changes to the CHR were focused by an event in 1970 that threatened the future of the line in Anglesey and potentially its entire existence. The destruction of the Britannia Tubular Bridge occurred during the 23/24 May just a few months over 120 years since it had been opened to traffic with such fanfare in March 1850. Accounts suggest that the fire occurred when youths who had been hoping

82. *Change is in the air at Llandudno Junction in August 1966 as class 8F 2-8-0 48253 takes water with under a year left before it was scrapped. Life is much easier for the crew of the diesel multiple unit at Platform 4.* (**Photo: Geoff Smith, Online Transport Archive**)

83. *The weather is glorious, but the signs of decay are apparent at Llandudno Junction shed in February 1978 as 24035 prepares to run light engine to Chester. In 2020 this site was a cinema complex.* (**Photo: David Plimmer**)

to attend a party were frustrated and decided instead to go and look inside the tube of the bridge. They crossed a stile onto the railway and ventured into the tube, lighting a piece of paper to see their way. It ignited tar on the line and the fire spread quickly aided by the draft created by the wind in the tube. There was little that the local fire service could do to stop the conflagration, especially as there was no water supply to deal with this known fire risk. It was also noted that a guard who had been posted on the bridge to prevent trespass had been withdrawn – a symptom of the extensive cost-cutting that beset the railways at this time.

It was difficult for the authorities to claim that the risk to the bridge was unknown as there had been an incident in June 1946 that could have inflicted damage at the 1970 level. The crew of the Irish Mail entered the tube and became aware of dense smoke and flame. They made an instant decision to run through the conflagration and emerged safely with their seventy passengers. The second portion of the train with Driver O.E. Owen of Holyhead in charge attempted a similar feat but encountered dense smoke that caused fireman Vincent Evans to pass out. Owen reversed the train slowly to Llanfair P G where 200 passengers were put on buses to resume their journey within the hour. Meanwhile local fire services battled the blaze and by the late afternoon had it under control at the price of blocking both lines. Despite this near-catastrophe the next evening's mail train from Holyhead to Manchester was the first train through the tunnel – albeit fifty-five minutes late at Bangor at 9.20 p.m.[4] One can only marvel at the brilliant response from workers and public with years of practice in dealing with the disasters and traumas of war; and wonder how long the recovery of the service would have taken in modern times?

It was perhaps fortunate that the 1970 disaster occurred as a general election was due. A new Conservative government was elected under Edward Heath which could ill-afford to start its term by closing a major railway line. In an era when politicians seemed committed to shedding as much of the rail network as possible, the risk must have been very great. As it was, there was a clear statement of intent in Parliament from the British Railways Board before the election, backed by the outgoing administration, which added to the pressure on the new government:

> As a result of the provisional engineering assessments made during the last 10 days the Railways Board have now informed the Minister of Transport that the Britannia Bridge over the Menai Straits may well take up to one year to reconstruct at a cost of up to £2 million [£31m]. The Board intend to go ahead with the reconstruction as a matter of urgency subject to a more detailed engineering assessment. Constant readings are being taken to record any change in the movement of the bridge, but while immediate repairs are being made to maintain stability, British Railways have advised the appropriate authorities that vessels should not pass under the bridge until further notice. Although the risk of collapse is considered remote, stability may be affected by extremes of temperature or extremely high winds. When restored, the bridge will be re-opened with a single line only, but additional signalling will enable the traffic requirements to be adequately met. In the meantime, passenger services on the Holyhead–Dun Laoghaire route will continue to operate from Heysham, with connecting boat train services. Car ferry services from Holyhead are not affected and will run as advertised. Detailed provision to handle all freight services, including containers, is still being finalised.

The irony of the situation was not lost on Cledwyn Hughes MP who noted that this happened so soon after total diesel operation on the line, as he told the House of Commons: 'It is remarkable that it should have gone on fire after more than a century's use by steam engines of various kinds'.[5] Perhaps the only positive result for rail services from the fire was the re-opening of Llanfair P G station which became the southern terminus of the railway on Anglesey.

The failure of the bridge hastened the shift from rail to road. As the statement above made clear, car and freight continued by road to Holyhead or was shifted to Heysham. That frustrated British Rail's plans to develop its terminal facilities at Holyhead while road carriers took advantage to steal business from the railways. And there was more trouble ahead for rail. A major limitation on road transport was the comparatively flimsy road from Bangor to Holyhead, dependent as it was on Telford's beautiful but restrictive suspension bridge over the Menai Straits, so some road freight traffic was diverted to Caernarfon. But as the plans for reinstating the Britannia Bridge developed, it became clear that the railway would literally be relegated below the road – running on a single track beneath a road deck that would in due course become part of a massive investment in the road structure of north Wales.

It was not long before the plans began to emerge and by June 1971 there was a scheme in place to upgrade the A55 from Chester to Bangor.[6] Progress was slow and the debate was reminiscent of the old arguments about rail routes through north Wales in 1830s and 1840s. Colwyn Bay was a pinch point, just as it had been when the LNWR wanted to increase from two tracks to four as part of the scheme in the late 1890s. The danger of splitting the town from its beach was an evident

84. *'Some fine morning the tube might break down', said Dublin MP John Reynolds in 1850. The blaze that destroyed the Britannia Tubular Bridge in May 1970 may be regarded as the moment when the CHR finally lost its position as a major connection between Britain and Ireland. This is the most dramatic photograph ever taken on the line, matching the enormity of the event.* (Photo: PA Images/Alamy Photo Stock)

85. In September 1977, 47533 crosses the Britannia Bridge – no longer a tubular bridge – with an up service to London. The space that could have accommodated a second track has since been used for water and gas pipelines. (Photo: David Plimmer)

one and sadly – as anyone visiting the town can see today – one that became a reality. That is also true along many other stretches of the coastline where the road from Abergele to Holyhead (which it reached in 2001) dominates the railway, the coast and countryside in an ugly and intrusive fashion under the name of the 'North Wales Expressway'. Further increases in its size cannot be ruled out.[7]

That investment in the roads was inversely matched in the decline of government support for railways, and particularly the north Wales coast railway. The gap was partly filled by the local authorities in the region. Shotton Low Level station was re-opened in 1972 while in June 1981 Gwynedd and Clwyd county councils met with British Rail officials and agreed a series of improvements in train frequency

86. 47448 works the 15:05 Bangor-Scarborough in August 1983, arriving at Colwyn Bay on the original track alignment, as work on the dominant A55 goes on all around. (Photo: David Plimmer)

and speed and negotiated the reopening of Valley station on Anglesey; there was even talk of electrification, though that seemed an unlikely outcome. Anthony Meyer, MP for Clwyd North-West summarised the position during a debate in 1983. He appreciated the work of British Rail in the region and found most trains to London clean, fast and punctual. He also noted that the region still had many visitors by rail who were having to contend with a reduced service that limited the number of passengers, which in turn led to a further reduction in services. Meyer considered that was not helped by the loss of catering services on trains and the deterioration in rolling stock – particularly the bone-shaking diesel multiple units – so that it would probably have been impossible to consume a drink even if one had been available. He had clearly given up on any serious investment in the north

87. *There has been a slow fightback from the Beeching cuts along the CHR. Shotton, Conwy, Llanfair P G and Valley have so far turned the tide. The opening of Valley was celebrated by carrying a special postcard on the first train but now looks little different from the photograph of the station in its LNWR prime, though it was an unstaffed request stop in 2021.* (Photos: Phil Lloyd Collection; Valley station: John Alsop Collection)

Wales main line, and so did not follow up the earlier call for electrification, which he thought would be a poor investment and a blight on the landscape – though it could surely be no worse than the appalling visual damage done by the A55.[8]

A low point for railways in the UK came in 1983 with the commissioning of the Serpell Report, which appeared to have the potential to be a second Beeching Report. It included in three of its six options the possibility that the CHR would be closed and with it the connection from Chester to Crewe. Opponents argued that the line should be kept open and electrified rather than being replaced by a bus service.[9] Although Margaret Thatcher was no supporter of railways, she was alert to the political realities and the report went no further. But by 1988 there was still some doubt about the future of the CHR which was only resolved when British Rail confirmed its commitment to the line. Ieuan Wyn Jones, MP for Anglesey, pressed the government about the state of the station at Holyhead, where the old LNWR hotel that closed in 1955 had been demolished but the site remained undeveloped despite a 1979 promise to spend £4m (£20m) – reduced to £2.5m ten years later (£6m). His generally forward-looking plan was somewhat undermined by a call to resume the use of steam engines on the line, which had been prevented by the lack of a turntable at Holyhead, though he noted that this had been corrected by the creation of a triangular track arrangement near Valley that enabled engines to turn.

In his response, the government minister confirmed the secure future of the CHR, noting that British Rail had cut fares on the route for a trial period and was intent on marketing the line effectively. He was less optimistic about the electrification of the line (then discussed quite often) which he regarded as a matter for British Rail.[10] The Single European Act of 1986 that paved the way for the single market renewed the case for improvements on the line to Holyhead. In the 1840s it had been argued that the line would create a more integrated UK; 150 years later the focus apparently was integrating the European Union and its single market. In practice this was achieved more by an increase in lorries on the ferries between the UK and Ireland, helped by the conversion of the former tubular bridge over the Menai Straits to road and rail use in 1980 and building a dual carriageway on most of the A55 from Chester to Bangor.

In its heyday the CHR had attracted the most powerful engines and top quality rolling stock, but by the end of the 1980s the line was served by cheaper options such as class 150s ('Sprinters'), class 142s ('Pacers') and class 156s ('Super Sprinters'), although it retained larger services that called for more powerful locomotives such as class 40s, 47s and 56s – the last-named used to assist in the 'Judas' duties of removing debris from the A55 Conwy tunnel to create yet more traffic that would continue to weaken the position of the railway in north Wales. Those duties had one good outcome in the reinstatement of the former Conway (*sic*) Station in June 1987. It was appropriately renamed in the Welsh language format of Conwy, but without the magnificent station buildings that had been demolished after closure in 1966. The railway was notably marginalised by the A55 between Llandudno Junction and Colwyn Bay, burying the site of the world's first railway water troughs at Mochdre under tarmac in the process. The CHR rendered Telford's London to Holyhead road obsolete within three decades of its completion in 1826: the revenge of the road took a bit longer, but by the end of the 1980s it was complete. The claims made for the new road may not have matched the benefits that Sir Robert Peel had seen for the CHR in the 1840s, but one ministerial statement in 1987 made clear the extensive scope of the project:

> The capital programme that I have described is only part of what is being done to improve the economic infrastructure of north Wales. A road programme larger than ever before is improving the access to the English motorway system, the routes north and south and, above all, westwards along the A55 where the new dual carriageway between Chester and Bangor is now two thirds completed and journey times have been dramatically reduced in the last year. Work has started on the Conwy crossing and the Penmaenbach tunnel. This new A55 dual carriageway will bring the whole north Wales coastal strip, Gwynedd and Anglesey, within easy driving distance of Manchester airport and the heart of industrial Britain.[11]

The decline of passenger traffic was apparent through the loss of stations and service while the decline of freight was less clear to the public but equally severe. The loss of all rail traffic to Holyhead in 1970 weakened its position as a railway port and five years later cattle traffic – one of the staples of the line – was lost, for reasons that echoed the logic of the Beeching Report on passenger services, as the minister made clear in Parliament:

> The decision by British Rail to close the cattle ferry was taken in the light of hard economic facts. For some years now the level of cattle traffic passing through Holyhead has declined significantly. In seven years, the level dropped by almost a half. Compared with 143,000 head which passed through in 1967, only 73,000 were imported to Holyhead in 1974. Based on traffic in the first 10 months of this year, the effect of the decline was that the service was losing some £650,000 [£5.5m] a year.[12]

Nonetheless, a variety of freight traffic remained on the line – much of it recorded by David Sallery on his excellent website to which much of what follows is owed. The foremost reason for establishing the CHR with government support in the 1840s was to speed the mail to and from Ireland. That traffic lasted until 23 May 1994 when the last travelling post office traversed the line. The Irish Mail continued as a named train until June 2002 when it was dropped by Virgin Trains as part of a general policy. Coal was a regular freight from the various Flintshire mines of which Point of Ayr was the last to close in 1996. Petroleum coke that was landed at Immingham dock was another long-standing freight that began in 1971 to serve the aluminium works near Holyhead. That traffic lasted until January 2008, the year before the plant closed. There was a regular roadstone traffic from Penmaenmawr until 1993 that was associated with major projects such as remodelling Manchester Piccadilly in 1988. There were up to four trains a day to various destinations until 2000 when a virtual quarry was established at Crewe. This was supplied by one block train a day from Penmaenmawr. The supply of ballast from there to Crewe finished in 2004.

Mostyn had lost its station in 1966 but traffic to and from the docks by rail continued. That traffic included moving sulphur to Amlwch that had been imported from France (ended in 1988) and a regular acetic acid train from Hull between 1991 and 2009. Steel arriving by rail from

88. *Point of Ayr – the colliery here originally used ships to transport its coal, but rail eventually replaced it. By 2020 only the footbridge remained as a testament to many hard years of mining. The impressive Inter-City 125 was on its way to Holyhead in August 1996 – confounding critics who thought the line was being run down and would not attract such high-quality trains.* **(Photo: David Sallery, Penmorfa.com)**

Redcar was sent from Mostyn to Northern Ireland between 1998 and 2002. The CHR also had its share of the British Rail Speedlink service – a general freight service that lasted from 1977 to 1991. The Freightliner container trains also served Holyhead with four trains a day in each direction with up to twenty-five wagons before the economic imperative ended that service in 1991. The railway undermined itself by its contribution to the construction of the A55. A long siding and discharge point were constructed at Llandudno Junction. Fly ash from Fiddlers Ferry power station was brought in and used as the base for the A55 from Mochdre to the Conwy tunnel. There were also sidings built at Conwy Morfa to supply the A55 construction.

The line contributed to industry in north Wales for many years. This included explosives from Maentwrog Road until around 1988 from Cookes in Penrhyndeudraeth. The new goods yard at Llandudno Junction, built to replace Colwyn Bay, which was swallowed by the A55, handled household coal and fuel oil. Bangor had two cement silos built to supply Dinorwic pumped storage power station, the cement came from Penyffordd on the Wrexham to Bidston line. Bangor also loaded bricks made in Caernarfon from 1966 until the brickworks closed in 2008. Courtaulds in Greenfield had trainloads of fuel oil and chemicals until the mid-1980s, while Crumps Wagon Repairs in Connah's Quay received a lot of wagons for scrap, overhaul and rebuilding.

Plenty of aluminium was transported from Holyhead over the years – much of it to Austria – until the plant closed in 2009. Elsewhere in Anglesey, Associated Octel was an important customer of the railway from the opening of its Amlwch plant in the early 1950s until 1993. There was a daily Ellesmere Port–Amlwch train and return freight which conveyed ethylene dibromide and liquid chlorine.

This general freight traffic ended in October 2011 with a trainload of empty bogie bolster wagons from the Anglesey aluminium works to Tees Yard. The last freight service on the line carried flasks of nuclear waste from Trawsfynydd and Wylfa power stations to Sellafield in Cumbria and ended in 2019. The flasks from the two locations were brought together at Llandudno Junction.[13] There are hopes that freight may return in the form of container traffic, slate waste, roadstone and domestic waste recycling but at the time of writing these hopes have not been realised.

Into the 1990s the threats to passenger services on the line continued, notably through the privatisation of the railways that was proposed from the beginning of 1993 by John Major's Conservative government. Meanwhile services on the CHR were managed by Regional Railways and Wales continued to be regarded as an extension of England, consistent with a statement from Professor William

Gruffydd in Parliament ahead of rail nationalisation after the Second World War: 'Every railway in Wales has been built to take Englishmen to Wales, and Welshmen to England. It has been built for the sake of London.'[14] By the time of privatisation this had changed – but only to the extent that London was replaced by Manchester, Birmingham and Swindon according to one MP who noted that:

> All decisions affecting our regional railways and rural services are taken from outside our borders. There is a case for considering the future of Welsh railways in a Welsh context. As the Welsh Office is now assuming greater responsibility for administrative affairs and public finance in Wales, the future of our rail services should be considered from a Welsh perspective.[15]

That request was ignored, but significant changes did follow privatisation and the dire warnings that the move would destroy much of the rail network in vulnerable regions such as north Wales were not realised. In practice the railways did rather well, though whether this was a product of privatisation or of an underlying change in the public attitude is not clear. Ministers gave early reassurance about the future of the CHR and its regular service to London, and the line benefited from changes elsewhere on the system that caused the reallocation of locomotives and rolling stock. Class 37 locomotives were beneficial, and the line also saw the arrival of the ultra-modern Inter-City 125s on the London and Holyhead route. It was not electrification, but it could not be called neglect either. The split between ownership of the infrastructure and the operation of the services was introduced so that the track passed to Railtrack, a private company, and the routes were divided into franchises. The CHR was covered by North Western Trains, and the London–Holyhead service was allocated to Virgin Trains, with the former becoming First North Western.

The arrival of the Labour government of 1997 heralded changes that finally shifted the balance of power towards Wales. The first step was the referendum that produced a wafer-thin majority in favour of a Welsh Assembly, although one that had limited powers. Those powers did not include running railways, so that the 2003 franchise award to Arriva Trains Wales was not a complete shift to a national railway for the country. It was also limited because it assumed that there would be no growth in traffic during the fifteen-year term despite the evidence of a steep rise in demand for rail transport from around 1995. Arriva inherited an ageing stock of trains but managed to increase passenger numbers and satisfaction and ran a lot more trains than had been anticipated. It also exceeded its requirements by partially adopting the Welsh language requirements even though it did not apply to them as a private body.

Overcrowding seemed to be the main problem faced by the company in Wales. On the CHR this manifested itself at holiday times and exceptional circumstances such as when a ferry failed to connect with the Virgin West Coast train at Holyhead, leaving the passengers to crowd a two- or three-coach unit. The company faced much criticism that should properly have been directed at the government agencies overseeing the arrangement from London. Initially that was the UK government, but from 2006 there was an increasing role for the Welsh government which acquired greater powers over rail arrangements. It was the Welsh government that undertook the process to create a replacement for Arriva when the franchise ended in 2018. For the CHR, the most important element of this increased role for the Welsh government was the certainty over the line's future. As we have seen, the question mark that remained from the implementation of the Beeching proposals was a serious threat when the Serpell report was published and when privatisation loomed. Once the railways in Wales became the responsibility of the Welsh government it was never an option to close a major line in north Wales. The problem for that government was the impossibility of integrating the country through the transport infrastructure. The whole system of roads and rail was built on its connection to England; in the north that meant to Liverpool and Manchester, and to a lesser extent, Birmingham and London. Creating a connection between the north and the Welsh capital in Cardiff remains a challenge. It has been partially resolved by the daily 'Gerald of Wales' train; a rare locomotive-hauled train on the Welsh network (before 2020) that makes a return trip between Cardiff and Holyhead during the week and provides an enhanced level of service. The only quicker alternative is the small plane that flies from Valley to Cardiff and back during the week. There has been some interest from the Welsh government in the idea of opening a station at the airport to improve connectivity within Wales still further. The connection to Ireland is still relevant but the numbers using the train are relatively small, the station is now a bus ride away from the ferries and foot passengers are last on and last off at both ends of the sea crossing. Trains do not necessarily connect with ferries and in the absence of the mail traffic on the line there is no longer any pressing reason for them to do so.

The first year of operation of the new Transport for Wales rail system was a challenging one with a decline in passenger numbers and many complaints about overcrowding on the commuter routes and the poor quality of the trains. But there is an ambitious plan for more and bigger trains, better stations and cheaper tickets, and work on the stations is apparent at places like Rhyl. There is also a scheme

89. *The countryside becomes rockier between Ty Croes and Holyhead so that agriculture features rather less in the landscape; 37089 has just passed Valley heading south in July 1999 and is close to the site of the RAF station and small civilian airport. Ideas have been floated to create a railway station to serve the airport.* **(Photo: David Sallery, Penmorfa.com)**

for an entity called the North Wales Metro that will provide more and better connections around the Deeside area, but given there is only a fragment of the rail system in north Wales compared to the position in the early 1950s, the scope for a comprehensive network is limited. Some small changes could make a big difference. Shotton has potential as a transport hub if a more integrated station is created. Additionally, the long gap between Flint and Prestatyn would benefit from reopening one of the closed stations on that stretch, with the old Holywell Junction being perhaps the best option.

The clientele of the railway has gone through many changes. For the first seventy-five years of the CHR almost all significant travel to and from and within north Wales was by train, with coastal shipping and horse-drawn vehicles some way behind. Even the early days of the motor car did not make massive inroads on that

90. *Rhyl station had been in decline for some time, but the Welsh government made improvements to stations a priority and the work is evident as an Avanti West Coast Voyager arrives in January 2020. The redundant Rhyl No. 2-signal box (left) seems unlikely to be included in the improvements.* (**Photo: Phil Lloyd Collection**)

position. As we have seen, all that began to change, apart a brief interruption during the Second World War, after which the role of railway travel and freight carriage shrank. The recent rise in use by passengers probably has a number of elements: leisure travel by older citizens with time, money and senior rail cards is clearly part of it; students at Bangor University give a welcome cosmopolitan feel to the line; there is a slight increase in the use of the line for holidays, but more particularly in connection with the Wales Coastal Path, much of which can be accessed by rail from Chester to Bangor, and with a little more effort between Bangor and Holyhead. Anyone travelling on the line from Friday afternoon to Sunday evening cannot fail to notice the increase in city-break travelling. For the future, the opening of the Halton Curve may tend to increase commuter traffic from Liverpool, adding to that already undertaken from Chester, Manchester and all points between.

At the time of writing, some of the stations have been given a welcome facelift, notably Rhyl, Llandudno Junction, Bangor and Colwyn Bay. Rail was an issue at the December 2019 general election and whichever party won seemed likely to provide a cash boost. That hope quickly vanished with the sudden onset of the coronavirus from February 2020 and the instruction to people not to travel on public transport. How long it will last, and how long it will take the public to regain their willingness to travel on trains alongside others is a question that must remain unanswered at this time. The early response was to block off some seats with signs and to require face coverings on services which then needed additional enforcement on trains and stations. One outcome of the pandemic was the collapse of the franchise arrangement because of the loss of revenue, which led the Welsh government to nationalise rail services in Autumn 2020. Thus, an objective of the Welsh nationalist movement at the end of the nineteenth century was achieved, albeit in strange and rather unpromising circumstances.

91. *The redundant but preserved Prestatyn signal box is just visible in August 2020 amid the greenery as 158837 for Manchester approaches the station with Snowdonia as a backdrop. Note the social distancing markers behind the line on the platform, placed there during the COVID-19 pandemic.* **(Photo: Phil Lloyd Collection)**

At the beginning of the chapter, we noted future threats to the CHR's fragile recovery. To understand the greatest threat, we must return to the origins of the line and the way that George Stephenson underestimated the problems of building a railway from Chester to Holyhead. These were noted in Chapter 1, as were the problems subsequently encountered from the design and route of the railway. We have seen how those weaknesses have impacted upon the operation of the railway – for example in the loss of a goods train to the sea near Penmaenmawr in 1899. Such events result from the problem of the railway being constructed along a coastline that is backed by hills and so vulnerable from the twin impact of the tide and the run-off of water from the mountains – identified by Charles Vignoles in the 1830s. In fact, the line is at risk for much of its length: from Chester to Point of Ayr it is at sea level and liable to flooding; from there to Prestatyn it takes a more inland route but soon after Rhyl it is exposed again to the moods of the sea. Even as it rises to enter the Penmaenrhos tunnel it is vulnerable from the streams that it crosses that can quickly become torrents. From Colwyn Bay to Conwy the line is more secure but then extremely exposed as it emerges from Penmaenbach tunnel and proceeds to Llanfairfechan. Back in 1850 the route was still preferable to sailing from Liverpool to Dublin, particularly in winter – as noted in 1863:

> During one week of the recent stormy weather there arrived at Holyhead by the railway cattle boats: – 3,700 head of horned cattle, 2,500 head of sheep, 1,603 head of pigs, while during the same period not 50 head of either were received in Liverpool from Dublin. The difference between 6 and 13 hours in the passage of cattle has settled the question in favour of Holyhead, except in the finest weather.[16]

These weather risks were well known and influenced the decision to route Telford's road via Shrewsbury and Corwen rather than through Chester and along the coast. Politicians had their own reasons for taking the risk of the coastal route, mostly related to the power of landowners, financiers and industrialists. Once work began the reality of the task became apparent as this report in October 1846 makes clear:

> During the last week, the succession of heavy gales which occurred without intermission for some days much retarded the operations on this line; and on the night of Thursday an extensive breach was made by the sea in the solid wall now in the course of construction under the Penmaen Mawr [*sic*] mountain. The waves ran very high, and completely washed over the [...] whole course, effecting large openings. This portion of the works is much

92. In August 1879 LNWR shareholders heard of the 'disaster' at Llanddulas where the line was 'washed away by a kind of avalanche and thrown into the sea'. Brilliant engineering work by Francis Webb at Crewe had the line running in just four weeks and ended the embarrassment of the Irish Mail being carried over the Great Western system. (Photo: Phil Lloyd Collection)

exposed to the assaults of the sea, and peculiarly liable to injury. Robert Stephenson, the engineer, and several other gentlemen inspected the damage on the following day and directed measures for the repair to be undertaken. The works on the railway between Conway and the Menai Bridge, when completed, will embrace a number of difficult and formidable obstacles than can be found, for similar distance, on any other line.[17]

The easiest part of the line to construct had been that from Chester to Talacre as it was on level ground with little tunnelling or bridging work once the line cleared Chester and its river – but there was a price to pay for this simplicity of construction. The severity of the weather in March 1853 caused the line to be reduced to a single track between Rhyl and Queensferry and in several places the line was completely washed away. The effect on the engines and carriages arriving at Chester was remarked on by the local paper as, 'encrusted with a coating of salt caused by the evaporation of sea water, and appeared as if they had been enveloped in a frosty snow storm'.[18] Six years later the storms that sank the *Royal Charter* and its cargo of gold bullion off the coast of Anglesey also wrecked the railway line to the east and west of Penmaenmawr and on the stretch from Rhyl to Flint that had been destroyed in 1853.[19] An early version of rail replacement buses was used to convey passengers around the breaches to the west of Penmaenmawr.[20]

The areas away from the mountains of Snowdonia do not tend to experience the extremes of cold of the upland areas, but occasionally it does happen. In 1867 the wind direction allowed for a heavy fall of snow on the line for nearly eight miles under cover of the Penmaenmawr and Llanfairfechan mountains and hills. The drifts varied from nine to fifteen feet deep despite the efforts of 400 'navvies' who had been employed to clear the line. One train came to a stand near to William Gladstone's villa and the local paper picked up the story of the stranded passengers at Llanfairfechan who:

> Sought shelter from the pelting snow and strong cold northern wind directly blowing from the sea, at the station, which is but a small building. Our correspondent was informed that the passengers had been brought to a state of hunger and thirst which was a pity to behold. What refreshments there were at hand were readily given. 'I would,' said a guard, 'have given a shilling for a glass of water, but it could not be obtained, as the pump was frozen.' The neighbouring inhabitants rendered what assistance they could to relieve the passengers. For twelve to twenty hours, they had to shelter there, while the hundreds of navvies were clearing the line.[21]

These days they would have been even more exposed as Llanfairfechan boasts nothing grander than a bus shelter on each platform.

Only five years elapsed before the same area experienced the impact of a storm just a short time after extensive repair work. Current practice would be to suspend services in the face of such storms, but in 1872 extreme weather had been battering the coast for some hours and two trains had still passed the site just before the sea damaged three-quarters of a mile of the line with one of the breaches being thirty-five yards wide and twenty feet deep. Fortunately, the block-working system stopped the Irish Mail from Holyhead in good time.[22] Snow was clearly a problem on this part of the line as it was just north of mountains that are over 3,000 feet high. Unsurprisingly, there were similar problems in 1881 and 1886 that required work gangs to clear snow, though not on the scale of 1867. Across the Menai Straits in Anglesey, snow was rarely a serious issue but in 1886 a severe snowstorm at Holyhead required two engines to move the 11.20 am Irish Mail

LLANFAIRFECHAN STATION.

93. Llanfairfechan appears to be a well-presented station with a full range of facilities for passengers. In 1867 it was rather different when passengers stranded in a blizzard could not even get a drink of water. The main station building gave way to the A55 in 1987 and was replaced with accommodation that would certainly not suffice in a snowstorm. (Photo: John Alsop Collection)

train away from the pier – at the cost of derailing carriages and the travelling post office. Once it was ready to leave, three engines were attached but only managed to travel a short distance from the station before returning. The train did not get away until 1.39 p.m.[23]

These events were overshadowed by perhaps the largest impact on the line by the weather. It occurred eleven years after the Abergele rail disaster of 1868 and about 200 yards further towards Holyhead. It was here that Vignoles' predictions about the vulnerability of the coastal route were borne out in full. The Dulas river is normally little more than a stream but in August 1879 there was heavy rain in the upland area of Denbighshire, and this gradually created a torrent that swept away a house next to the river estuary and piled rubble up against the pillars of the Llanddulas railway viaduct, thereby increasing the pressure on it. Even so, trains were permitted to cross the bridge as a gang of men below struggled to remove the debris and enable the water to pass freely into the sea; all to no avail. The middle of the bridge collapsed first, and the rest followed. The impact on the CHR was dramatic, as the chairman, Richard Moon, made clear to shareholders:

During the last ten days we have probably sustained greater disaster than has ever been sustained by the company before – bridges have been washed away, culverts broken down, … one large viaduct that has stood for forty years [at Llanddulas] washed away by a kind of avalanche and thrown into the sea.[24]

To add insult to injury, a large section of the line through mid-Wales that George Stephenson had condemned as impossible in 1839 was used for traffic to Holyhead as a notice issued by George Findlay made clear:[25]

London and North Western Railway

CHESTER AND HOLYHEAD DISTRICT

TO STATION AGENTS, BOOKING CLERKS, GOODS CLERKS, AND OTHERS CONCERNED.

In consequence of the Viaduct at Llandulas having been partially destroyed by the recent heavy Storms the regular Passenger Service West of Abergele will be suspended for the present. Passengers and Parcels will however continue to be booked through as usual, arrangements having been made for transferring passengers with their luggage from one train to another at Llandulas by means of Horses and Carriages or otherwise.

GOODS TRAFFIC

Arrangements have been made for Goods Traffic between Ireland and the Chester and Holyhead District West of Llandulas, to be worked temporarily in both directions over the Cambrian and Great Western Lines, *via* Afonwen, Dolgelly, Ruabon, and Chester.

CATTLE TRAFFIC

For the present, the Cattle Traffic will be Booked Through from Ireland by the City of Dublin Steam Packet Company's Boats via Liverpool.

G Findlay: Chief Traffic Manager's Office

Euston Station, August 18th, 1879.

Unfortunately for Charles Vignoles, surveyor of the lines to Porth Dinllaen, he had died in 1875 and did not live to see his apt criticism of the CHR route justified. It was estimated that the repair of the viaduct would take two months but the chief mechanical engineer Francis Webb and his workers at Crewe manufactured a replacement so quickly that the service was back to normal after just four weeks. LNWR pride in this achievement was such that a postcard was produced to mark its success.

On Anglesey the risk is from strong winds from the west and south-west, as was demonstrated in November 1887 when experienced engine drivers claimed there occurred the most ferocious gale they had ever experienced. The daytime up Irish Mail was close to two hours late at Chester having left an hour and a half late from Holyhead. The extra lost time was caused by signals and telegraph wires being blown down along the route, especially between Llanfairfechan and Aber. Telegraphs were received at Chester indicating that the sea had washed away the line across the Stanley Embankment that links mainland Anglesey with Holy Island. In fact, the line was flooded right up to Valley station rather than being destroyed. Work parties were sent from Chester and Bangor and a temporary arrangement put in place between Valley and Holyhead, but remarkably the down Irish Mail got through before the floods arrived and a full service was returned within twenty-four hours, another testament to the resilience and ingenuity of railway officials and workers.[26]

In 1945 Rhosneigr station was cut off from the town by a tremendous storm that flooded the golf course and meant that children bound for school in Holyhead had to be taken to the station by lorry.[27] I was able to confirm the impact of such storms on this portion of the line during January 2020 when catching a train from Ty Croes and meeting another passenger who pointed to a cone placed on the platform and commented, 'There was a shelter there last week!' The area had been subjected to Storms Brendan, Ciara and Dennis in the space of a week or two.

In 1901 there was a brief account of the line under the title of 'A Thrilling Railway Route' which confirmed the predictions of the 1846 account we noted earlier:

> Of all the railway lines round our coast that which hugs the shore in North Wales has the most thrilling. Extending as it does from Chester to Holyhead, the road over which the traveller to Ireland passes [means the traveller] will have plenty to think about, particularly on a rough night, when there is a wind from the sea that you could almost lean against. To keep [the sea] at bay strong defence walls have been built at certain points; but when a gale is accompanied by a high tide there is always the possibility that it may force its way on to the metals. For this reason, some sections are patrolled night and day in times of storm. Each of the platelayers is given charge of one mile of the permanent way, and over this 'beat' is constantly passing in readiness to give the alarm immediately he discovers that the sea has succeeded in making an inroad on his territory.[28]

94. *Ty Croes is one of the original stations on the CHR, but these days is a request stop with relatively few passengers. It features a fine 1872 signal box, level crossing and a rather basic shelter on the up platform as a down express approaches in June 1987. The shelter was swept away by storms early in 2020.* (**Photo: Phil Lloyd Collection**)

95. *The return of steam has provided valuable traffic and excellent photo opportunities on the CHR such as this shot of 60163 **Tornado** – the first newly built main line steam locomotive in the UK since **Evening Star** in 1960 – passing the golf course adjacent to Rhosneigr station in April 2013 with snow still visible on the mountains of Snowdonia. In December 1945, this whole area was flooded.* (**Photo: John Martin Davies/Alamy Stock Photo**)

The article went on to discuss the drama of the Penmaenbach tragedy of 1899 described in Chapter 4 as evidence of the continued battle between the line and the weather as the end of the century approached.

Work on the line adjoining the Dee estuary near Mostyn provided an indirect benefit in 1870 when dense fog, another weather hazard on that stretch of line, caused a collision. The driver of the 6.15 a.m. down parliamentary train missed the signal before Mostyn which was set at danger because a goods train was emerging from the siding. The collision caused at least one serious injury and blocked the line for several hours. The report noted that because of persistent weather damage to the sea wall there were many labourers at work repairing it, before revealing the prevailing logic of railway accidents at the time by commenting: 'Who was the cause of the accident has not yet transpired.' In 1870 it was still 'who?' rather than 'what?', even after the Abergele crash of 1868 at which poor management was clearly a factor.[29]

In October 1903, 'the rainstorm in the Chester district was the severest in living memory' and the line was washed away at Pentre near Flint.[30] Less than a year later,

96. *Mostyn station was the scene of a collision in 1870 when fog from the adjoining Dee estuary caused the driver of a passenger train to miss the signal and hit a freight train. Fortunately, there were many workers present repairing the sea wall who helped recover the wreck. The station closed in 1966 but its impressive main building remains as a private dwelling.* **(Photo: John Alsop Collection)**

Mostyn featured once again when the newly-widened stretch of line was destroyed, despite the fact that it had been raised by two or three feet to reduce the risk of incursion by the sea. The LNWR engineers returned to the site and added large boulders to reinforce the sea wall.[31] This incident, as with many others, was widely reported in Ireland since any interruption of the CHR threatened personal and postal communication between Ireland and mainland Britain – equivalent to an internet outage in present times. Irish reports of the 1904 storms made clear that the impact on the CHR extended beyond Mostyn and had been felt as far west as Llanfairfechan. Those reports also explained that there had been a dispute between the LNWR and some landowners arising from the negotiations over the widening of the line, and that the LNWR had abandoned its sea defence plans as a result. However, 'for months past they [the LNWR] have expected what would befall them, and their engineers have been busily forming a pitched slope to their line from Holywell station to Llanerch-y-Mor, which will, it is hoped, be a sufficient defence when the sea reaches it'.[32] There was to be no complete solution to the problems experienced

97. *A Transport for Wales class 175 speeds through Llanerch y Mor in September 2020 where the* **Duke of Lancaster** *ferry has been beached since 1979. Although primarily used on the Heysham – Belfast route, the ship was briefly a relief vessel between Holyhead and Dun Laoghaire. Floods overwhelmed the line here in 1904 – a threat that clearly remains.* (**Photo: Phil Lloyd Collection**)

in this area. In 1990 the line was flooded at Towyn and Mostyn where the track had to be replaced and protected by sandbags until a new sea wall could be built.[33]

Further down the line at Foryd, extensive sea defences were built because of the risk of flooding from the combined effect of the tide and Clwyd river. This moved rather than the solved the problem, as the report of an alarming incident in 1910 demonstrated. Close to the estuary there was a goods line from the harbour that passed under the main line through a cutting and then joined the Vale of Clwyd line. This cutting was flooded at high tide, putting at risk the lives of people in the nearby railway cottages, and LNWR workers had to access the upper storeys of these houses by boat and ladder in order to rescue residents from the 'highest and roughest tide seen in Rhyl for 20 years'.[34]

Work gangs had more success when the sea struck in 1943 in the same area as high seas and strong winds combined to engulf the promenade and golf links in Rhyl and threatened the railway line – where only sustained hard work succeeded in holding back the flood.[35] At the end of the war, when the railway might have hoped for a traffic boom, the line was wrecked by a massive storm in September 1945. The sea washed away the railway embankment at Towyn, near Abergele, and

98. Ffynnongroyw – the 1990 floods caused immense damage along the north Wales coast and wrecked the CHR here. This picture shows the temporary arrangements to protect the new track from the sea with sandbags. The storm was thought to be a 'once in a century' occurrence but climate change has revised that assessment. (Photo: David Sallery, Penmorfa.com)

99. *This picture from 1990 is from the same location as the 1939 photograph of Kinmel Bay (see photo 57). The four tracks, the halt and the siding have gone: caravans cover the whole field. The extensive flooding occurred after the sea wall collapsed during severe weather and high tides.* (**Alamy Photo Stock**)

flooded the line and six holiday camps between Kinmel Bay and Abergele. The track was blocked between Rhyl and Abergele and for a time traffic was worked on a single line.[36]

No amount of engineering could tackle some of the problems with the weather. At Aber, which as we have seen was particularly vulnerable to extreme cold, the 'wrong kind of snow' was at work in 1905. It did not form the drifts that the area had experienced in 1867 and 1872, but after an express train stopped because of two fallen telegraph poles the snow penetrated the brake system and froze it solid so that the train could not move once the line was cleared. The driver of the London-bound train used his exhauster to defrost the vacuum cylinders, but the brake blocks remained firmly frozen to the wheels and the train could not move.[37]

It was the strength of the wind rather than the temperature at work in February 1907 when a double-headed boat express from London could not refill tanks from the troughs at Prestatyn because the gale blew the water out as faster than it was pumped in. As a result, the train had to stop for fifteen minutes at Rhyl to fill the tenders. That was a minor inconvenience compared to that of the 2.55 p.m. from Chester that was brought to a dead stop by the wind and between blasts proceeded at little more than two miles per hour to its destination.[38] It was a similar story at Aber in November 1952 when the mail trains and an early morning newspaper train were held by trees blown across the line. Fortunately, patrols spotted the danger in time to halt traffic and worked through the night, but could not prevent the 6.30 a.m. from Bangor to London leaving six hours late.

The weather seemed to be the best explanation for why a couple died on the line about a mile to the east of Rhyl station in 1931. William Roberts, a newspaper reporter from Abergele, and Sarah Griffiths of Blaenau Ffestiniog were found dead on the track after a report from the driver of the 8.06 p.m. slow train from Chester. Around the time of the tragedy there was an extreme gale combined with a hailstorm and the initial theory was that the couple had taken a short cut into Rhyl along the track from where a path crosses the line near Plas Newydd.[39] However, at the inquest two days later it emerged that the couple had known each other for some time and, although married, were in a relationship. Sarah's husband suggested that he and his wife had moved to Blaenau Ffestiniog to break the relationship and she assured him she was not meeting Roberts. They had visited friends in Abergele over Christmas, and she had seen him off on the train at Rhyl a short time before her death. The coroner thought that the fact that they were facing the engine when hit might suggest that this was a suicide pact but the lack of any note to relatives was an odd omission. The jury returned an open verdict.[40]

Most recently, the Mostyn stretch of the line was flooded and great damage done to the sea wall in December 2013 causing a break in service until the 16 December: the impact of the storms in the first quarter of 2020 have been noted. By then the context of the debate about such events had become global rather than regional under the heading of 'climate change'. It is clear from the accounts in this chapter that severe weather events have been a regular feature consistent with the closeness of the CHR to the sea. But some changes are clear, most notably the absence of the instances of severe cold such as those recorded at Aber and discussed earlier. In place of such events the line at Aber was closed in August 2020 because the volume of water coming off the mountains during Storm Francis was so great that it flooded the line.

There was some disruption to services during the prolonged freezes in 1947 and two men from the same Greenfield street were killed on snow clearing duties near Flint in January. Lawrence Wight and John Owen Williams, both of Gas Row, Greenfield, died when they were hit by the Llandudno to Manchester express.[41] Troops were used to clear snowdrifts as late as March 1947 and there were similar problems in the 1962/1963 winter.[42] But the trend towards warmer average temperatures is clear. The impact of these changes is a subject of intense debate though the general direction – towards warmer temperatures and rising sea levels – seems beyond doubt. And it is from this cause that the threat in the title of this chapter becomes clearer. The Climate Central mapping of north Wales for 2050 suggests that the CHR may be celebrating its bicentenary occasionally under water. There could be only a stretch of line from the west of Abergele to Mochdre, another few miles of track from Bangor to Gaerwen, and a last stretch from Bodorgan to Ty Croes still visible at high tide during an extreme climate event.

100. *At Ffynnongroyw in August 2020, the Birmingham-bound 158830 is on time despite torrential rain from Storm Francis that caused widespread damage in north Wales and closed the CHR at Aber. The sea defences near Mostyn survived (left) – but for how much longer?* **(Photo: Phil Lloyd Collection)**

Climate Central's map shows areas 'below the projected high tide line, at risk of at least annual coastal flooding, or at risk of at least once-a-decade coastal flooding' but adds that its maps 'can't account for coastal defences, such as seawalls or levees, that exist now or might be built in the future to protect certain areas'.[43]

By contrast, much of the alternative route suggested by Vignoles that terminated at Porth Dinllaen will survive the rising sea levels. So, the argument between Stephenson and Vignoles that we explored in the opening chapter might finally be resolved in favour of the Irishman. But whether his line to Porth Dinllaen is ever built as the rail and sea link to Ireland in the wake of climate change is beyond the

101. *The scale of works on the tubular bridges tended to overshadow other features of the CHR, but Anglesey provided challenges of its own such as crossing Malltraeth with this elegant viaduct, seen here with a down Avanti West Coast Voyager in February 2020. How the structure will cope with rising sea levels only time will tell.* **(Photo: Phil Lloyd Collection)**

scope of this book to determine, and for its future readers to discover. But to close let us consider the wise reflections of a commentator on the extreme weather that affected the line in 1886:

> The storm shows the weak spots in our general social organisation no less than in our private physical ones, and the miles of telegraph-poles on the ground serve to remind us how very dependent we are upon fine weather and the permanence of familiar conditions.[44]

The Chester and Holyhead Railway: An Overview

I have explored many themes in this book: the political, economic and social impact of the railway, its accident record, its role in warfare, its status as a holiday line, the threats to its existence from the 1960s until the arrival of a degree of self-government in Wales, the impact of the weather on its operation and the coming existential threat from climate change. As I was finishing the book one unexpected factor was added: the impact of the COVID-19 pandemic, though that affects railways in general rather than the CHR specifically. In the course of my studies, I was intrigued by the involvement of a range of managers, employees, politicians, businesspeople, passengers and bystanders who appeared, sometimes very briefly, in the long story of the CHR – a story that has included joy, sadness, crisis, comedy, anger, sadness, conflict, bravery, mystery, criminality, fire, water, wind and waves; almost all imaginable aspects of life – not excluding death. I have examined every mile of the line, walked and photographed those parts accessible by public road or footpath and obtained at least one piece of information from most years that the line has operated.

But these studies did not entirely explain why the line is unique on the British railway network. True, it must be the only line to engage five politicians who had been, were, or would become prime ministers: Sir Robert Peel, without whom the line would probably never have been built; the Duke of Wellington, who guided the legislation through the Lords and made a personal visit to the line; Lord John Russell, who hoped to use it to govern Ireland directly from London; William Gladstone, who supported it at the Board of Trade in the 1840s, used it often but was critical of its monopolistic status in north Wales; and David Lloyd George, who gained status in north Wales from his frequent criticism of the LNWR in the 1890s. The line was reckoned by some to be the most lucrative on the LNWR network, which itself constituted the largest industrial corporation in the world for the whole of its existence. It was the technological centre of the most important political debate of the nineteenth century – Britain's relationship with Ireland. It was quintessentially an English railway that operated initially in an Irish context, and then increasingly as a vital feature that shaped the landscape and society of north Wales. The engagement of politicians demonstrates that it was not only an English railway, but also a *political* railway – and one with a claim to being the first imperial railway in the world because of its role in governing Ireland. While writing the book I happened to read Tolstoy's *Anna Karenina* and unexpectedly found there an excellent explanation of the impact of political railways on an essentially agricultural environment – for Russia read north Wales:

> [Vronsky] maintained that the poverty of Russia arises not merely from the anomalous distribution of landed property and misdirected reforms, but that what had contributed of late years to this result was the civilization from without abnormally grafted upon Russia, especially facilities of communication, such as railways, leading to centralization in towns, the development of luxury, and the consequent development of manufactures, credit and its accompaniment of speculation – all to the detriment of agriculture. It seemed to him that in a normal development of wealth in a state all these phenomena would arise only when a considerable amount of [labour] had been put into agriculture, when it had come under regular, or at least definite, conditions; that the wealth of a country ought to increase proportionally, and especially in such a way that other sources of wealth should not outstrip agriculture; that in harmony with a certain stage of agriculture there should be means of communication corresponding to it, and that in our unsettled condition of the land, railways, called into being *by political and not by economic needs* [my emphasis], were premature.[1]

I think that the CHR may be said to have been 'premature' and to have been 'abnormally grafted' onto the landscape of north Wales to achieve a purpose that had nothing to do with north Wales. Once there, it was inevitable that this enormous investment in the most up-to-date technology would impact on its host communities and on individuals within them, and change the region for ever. These changes are the ones examined in this book – political, economic, social, cultural, environmental and personal.

These changes were reinforced when internal combustion and personal transport replaced steam and mass travel and transport. There has been a further imposition on the landscape in the form of the A55 that follows the CHR closely from Abergele westwards and now dominates the crossing to Anglesey. In the era before radio, TV and the internet, the CHR also served as the principal form of information technology in north Wales and that too has disappeared. So how is the CHR relevant in north Wales today?

The CHR does not represent the past, the present or the future – rather it represents a sense of both *continuity* and *identity*. The world has changed in so many ways, so many things have happened, do happen, and will happen, but the reassuring pulse of the railway continues to be predictable and reliable and to connect north Wales solidly to the wider world. It may no longer fulfil the extensive duties of its first hundred years, but it remains a vital link for tourism, commuting and routine travel. But railways – not only the CHR – may represent something more than their mere usefulness; they offer a sense of place, connectedness and continuity amid rapid change. Since devolution of power to the Welsh Assembly the railway has become vital to support national identity, even though its route means that it cannot avoid being more connected to London, Manchester and Birmingham than to Cardiff. It is difficult to avoid the conclusion that the alternative route to Porth Dinllaen that crossed the centre of Wales would have been more relevant to its modern politics – but that case was lost in 1846.

The Porth Dinllaen route may also have been more resilient to the dramatic changes being wrought by climate change. The harsh truth is that the CHR

102. *The first of two photographs that show how dramatically the fortunes of the CHR have changed. In this picture a double-headed express emerges from the Britannia Tubular Bridge in November 1904 when the line was a vital link between London and Dublin.* (Photo: John Alsop Collection)

103. The modern status of the CHR is encapsulated by this picture in which the former Britannia Tubular Bridge – the symbol of its power – is reduced to a single line of railway beneath a road deck that has shrouded the iconic lions. A class 175 for Manchester glides across the straits almost unnoticed beneath the traffic in August 2018 as the Arriva Trains Wales franchise nears its end. (Photo: Phil Lloyd Collection)

may not even exist in its current form by the time of its bicentenary, because it is likely to be increasingly disrupted by rising sea levels and severe weather. Many thought that science was capable of conquering every problem when the CHR was being built – and achievements such as the Britannia Tubular Bridge reinforced that notion from the 1850s onwards. But perhaps, as water, wind and heat increasingly threaten the line, as has happened several times this century, we – or those who come after us – may have to think again.

Appendix 1

Stations on the CHR with
Opening and Closing Dates

Station	Opened	Closed	Reopened	Closed	Notes
Chester	1840	1848	1848		CHR used joint station 1849
Aber	1848	1960			
Abergele and Pensarn	1848				
Bangor	1848				
Conwy	1848	1966	1987		Name changed from Conway 1987
Flint	1848				
Holyhead	1848				
Holywell Junction	1848	1966			'Junction' added 1912
Llanfair PG	1848	1966	1970	1972	Open 1973
Mostyn	1848	1966			
Prestatyn	1848				Re-sited west 1897
Queensferry	1848	1966			
Rhyl	1848				
Ty Croes	1848				
Bagillt	1849	1966			Re-sited 1871
Bodorgan	1849				

Station	Opened	Closed	Reopened	Closed	Notes
Colwyn Bay	1849				Originally Colwyn
Gaerwen	1849	1966			
Penmaenmawr	1849				
Valley	1849	1966	1982		
Britannia Bridge	1851	1858			Replaced by Menai Bridge
Holyhead Admiralty Pier	1851	1925			
Llandudno Junction	1858				Re-sited 1897
Menai Bridge	1858	1966			Replaced Britannia Bridge station
Llanfairfechan	1860				Buildings demolished for A55
Llysfaen	1862	1931			Changed from 'Llandulas' in 1889
Connah's Quay	1870	1966			
Old Colwyn	1884	1952			'Old' added in 1885
Sandycroft	1884	1961			
Foryd	1885	1917	1919	1931	Foryd on Clwyd line opened 1858 closed 1885
Llandulas [sic]	1889	1952			English spelling used
Mochdre and Pabo	1889	1917	1919	1931	
Conway Morfa	1894	1929			Station for army volunteers
Talacre	1903	1966			Was to be called 'Morfa Crossing'
Rhosneigr	1907	1917	1919		
Shotton	1907	1966	1972		
Kinmel Bay Halt	1938	1939			On the site of Foryd

The author acknowledges Michael Quick's *Railway Passenger Stations in Great Britain: A Chronology*, Fifth Edition, Version 5.02, September 2020, accessed at https://rchs.org.uk/railway-passenger-stations-in-great-britain-a-chronology/ on 11 February 2021 to check these details. Any errors are the author's alone. Dates do not include temporary closures of Conwy, Valley and Llanfair PG during the COVID pandemic.

Appendix 2

Each Mile of the CHR Linked to Years, Incidents and Photographs (stations are in bold, the other names for each mile have been created by the author)

Mile	Station or place	Distance	Gap	Photo	Event	Person	Year
0	**Chester**	0	0	3, 47	Death of the CHR solicitor	Richard Preston	1891
1	Northgate			26	Detention of trespasser	Earl of Kingston	1860
2	Dee			9	Collapse of bridge		1847
3	Saltney				Widening of cutting		1903
4	Mold Junction	3.75	3.75	15, 65	Fatal collision	Joseph Burrows	1867
5	Broughton			36	Fatal Fall	Elias Jones	1908
6	**Sandycroft**	5.75	2	17	Despatch of deceased archbishop to London	Edward White Benson	1896
7	Mancot				Two coal pits created	Lord Mostyn	1869
8	**Queensferry**	7.25	1.5	48	Police act on suspected attack on Gladstone	Inspector Aplin	1883
9	**Shotton**	8.25	1	22	Fatality	George Terry	1911
10	**Connah's Quay**	9.25	1	16	Train fire	Robert Stephenson	1965

Mile	Station or place	Distance	Gap	Photo	Event	Person	Year
11	Kelsterton				Flooding		1853
12	Oakenholt				Flooding		1903
13	**Flint**	12.25	3	41,54	Near miss	Owen Roberts	1913
14	Coleshill				Flooding		1859
15	**Bagillt**	14.25	2	52	Celebration of the Relief of Mafeking		1900
16	Bagillt Bank			64	Bird strike	J.A. Walker	1910
17	**Holywell Junction**	16.75	2.5	63	Depot for widening scheme		1899
18	Llanerch y Mor			97	Flooding		1904
19	Glan y Don				Animal strike	Farmer Evans	1889
20	**Mostyn**	20	3.25	96	Death of four lineside workers		1922
21	Ffynnongroyw			98, 100	Obstruction placed on the line	John Hughes	1881
22	Tanlan Hall			88	Fatality	Leon Gabriel	1887
23	**Talacre**	23	3	68	Collision		1904
24	Tyn y Morfa			39	Animal fatality		1896
25	Gronant				Child fatality		1885
26	Nant Hall				Train fire		1905
27	**Prestatyn**	26.25	3.25	73, 91	Fatality	Matthew M'Garry	1901
28	Towyn isaf				Fall	James Aulds	1875
29	Rhyl East			67	Double fatality	Sarah Griffiths	1931
30	**Rhyl**	30	3.75	62, 90	Non-stop service from London		1908
31	Foryd			10	Flooding		1910

Mile	Station or place	Distance	Gap	Photo	Event	Person	Year
32	**Kinmel Bay**	31	1	57, 99	Final closure of station		1939
33	Towyn				Animal strike	Farmer Kerfoot	1855
34	Belgrano				Fatality	George Wright	1893
35	**Abergele & Pensarn**	34.25	3.25	31, 51	Boer War celebration	Francis Dent	1900
36	Gwrych Castle			30	Largest rail crash on the line	Driver Arthur Thompson	1868
37	**Llanddulas**	36.75	2.5	76, 92	Viaduct washed away	Francis Webb	1879
38	**Llysfaen**	37.75	1	25, 29	Construction fatality	Martin Halloran	1847
39	**Old Colwyn**	38.75	1	37, 53	Fire at the station	Platelayer Aldis	1898
40	**Colwyn Bay**	40.25	1.5	58, 70, 77, 86	Train fire		1912
41	Llandrillo				Redirection of the track		1986
42	Bryneuryn				Installation of world's first railway water troughs		1860
43	**Mochdre & Pabo**	42.25	2	49	Station opened		1889
44	Pabo			40	Death of former line superintendent	Ephraim Wood	1915
45	**Llandudno J**	44.75	2.5	59, 60, 61, 82, 83	Fatality	Robert Brereton	1884
46	**Conwy**	45.5	0.75	7, 11, 12, 35, 66, 75	Construction of the CHR commenced		1845
47	Conwy Morfa			50	Station created for an army camp		1894
48	Penmaenbach			33	Fatality	Edward Evans	1899

Mile	Station or place	Distance	Gap	Photo	Event	Person	Year
49	Dwygyfylchi				Serious injury	Henry Evans	1846
50	**Penmaenmawr**	50	4.5	8, 21, 34	Fatal collision	John Williams	1950
51	Viaduct			5, 32	Maintenance fatality	Herbert Lees	1895
52	Gerazim				Fatal fall	Edgar Swan	1940
53	**Llanfairfechan**	52.75	2.75	93	Snow		1867
54	Madryn			14	Installation of water troughs		1871
55	**Aber**	54.75	2	38	Gales		1952
56	Wig			19	Fatality	Catherine Williams	1848
57	Glan y Mor				Fatal fall	John Parry Jones	1908
58	Tal y Bont			80	Stalled train		1903
59	Llandegai			4	Fatal fall	Michael Kelly	1905
60	**Bangor**	60	5.25	6, 20, 55, 72	Robbery	Alfred Wilson	1869
61	**Menai Bridge**	61.25	1.25	28	Non-fatal collision		1865
62	**Britannia Bridge**			13, 18, 84, 85, 102, 103	Fire		1970
63	Column			27	Fatal derailment		1861
64	**Llanfair PG**	63.5	2.25	42	Military parade		1892
65	Llanddaniel X				Fatal collision		1965
66	**Gaerwen**	66.25	2.75	78	Fatal injury to soldier		1916
67	Myfyrian				Farmer's market		1917
68	Penyrorsedd				Fall from train	Lennard Lucas RN	1898
69	Llangaffo				Campaign for a station		1890

Mile	Station or place	Distance	Gap	Photo	Event	Person	Year
70	Trosyrafon				Collieries open near line		1851
71	Malltraeth			101	Construction fatality	William Lewis	1847
72	Tunnels			24	Construction fatality	James Morris	1847
73	**Bodorgan**	72.75	6.5	71, 79	Landlord and tenants meeting	Sir George Meyrick	1882
74	Ty Mawr				Fatal fall from a bridge	Owen Thomas	1891
75	Rhospadrig				Fatality	William Roberts	1875
76	**Ty Croes**	75.25	2.5	94	Prosecution	Owen Owen	1887
77	**Rhosneigr**	77	1.75	69	Flooding		1945
78	Trewan Sands X			95	LNWR opposes dynamite factory		1897
79	Airfield			89	Proposal for a new station		2019
80	Llanfihangel yn Nhowyn				Prosecution	John Owen	1902
81	**Valley**	81	4	87	Dinner given for retired employee	Stationmaster Coles	1862
82	Stanley Bank			74	Flooding		1887
83	Penrhos				Collision		1872
84	Trefignath				Platelayer fatality	John Hughes	1885
85	**Holyhead**	84.5	3.5	23, 43, 46, 56	New station opened	Prince of Wales	1880
86	**Admiralty Pier/ Breakwater**			1, 44, 45	Station closed		1925

Endnotes

Chapter 1

1. 'Public meeting – Holyhead Harbour', *North Wales Chronicle*, 16 February 1836.
2. *Extracts from the Minutes of Evidence given before the Committee of the Lords on the London and Birmingham Railway Bill*, London, 1832, 33, 64 and 36.
3. Henry Fairbairn, 'Project for Land Communication with Ireland', *The United Service Journal and Naval and Military Magazine*, 1832, Part 1 (London: Henry Coulburn and Richard Bentley) 209–213.
4. 'The London and Birmingham Railway', *The Cambrian Quarterly Magazine and Celtic Repertory*, Vol 4, No. 16, 1 October, 1832, 423–432.
5. 'Ffestiniog Railway', *North Wales Chronicle*, 14 August 1832.
6. Report of the Select Committee on Private Business, House of Commons, 17 July 1840.
7. 'Direct communication between London and Dublin', *North Wales Chronicle*, 2 February 1836.
8. 'Public Meeting – Holyhead Harbour', *North Wales Chronicle*, 16 February 1836.
9. St George's Harbour and Railway Company, *Report and Evidence before the Select Committee on Harbours Refuges and Shipwrecks* (London: Effingham Wilson 1836).
10. Ibid., 52.
11. Parliamentary Papers, House of Commons and Command, Volume 50, Session 31 January–17 July 1837,151.
12. 1837–38 (654) Railroad Commission, Ireland. Treasury minute, dated 3 November 1836, respecting the Railroad Commission for Ireland.
13. George Smyth, *Railways and Public Works in Ireland, Observations upon the Report of the Irish Railway Commissioners with a Review of Failures which have already occurred under the different Government Boards and Commissions connected with Public Works in Ireland*. (London: Henry Cooper, 1839), 22–23.

14. 'Dublin and London: Direct Communication through Wales', *Chester Chronicle*, 25 March 1836.

15. Second report of the commissioners appointed to consider and recommend a general system of railways for Ireland 1837–38, 42 (145) XXXV 449, Appendix A, No. 3.

16. Second report of the commissioners, Appendix A, 44.

17. House of Commons Debate (henceforth HC Deb) 1 March 1839 volume (henceforth vol.) 45, chapter (henceforth c.) 1077.

18. 'Letter from Mr O'Connell', *Freeman's Journal*, 11 March 1839.

19. 'Chester and Holyhead Railway', *Chester Chronicle*, 2 November 1838.

20. 'Ffestiniog Railway', *North Wales Chronicle*, 14 August 1832.

21. 'Report of George Stephenson Esq upon the proposed railway communication with Ireland', *Freeman's Journal*, 15 January 1839.

22. 'Railway communications with Ireland', *Chester Chronicle*, 4 January 1839.

23. Smiles, Samuel, *The Lives of George Stephenson and of his son Robert* (New York: 1868, 441).

24. John Herapath, *The Railway Magazine and Steam Navigation Journal*, Volume 6, (London: James Wyld, 1839), 345.

25. Editorial, *Chester Chronicle*, 18 January 1839.

26. 'Communication between London and Dublin', *Chester Chronicle*, 11 January 1839.

27. 'Railway Communication between London & Dublin', *Chester Chronicle*, 25 January 1839.

28. 'Copy of Mr Vignoles observations on Mr Stephenson's report to the Chester and Crewe Railway directors', *Freeman's Journal*, 19 January 1839.

29. 'Chester and Holyhead Railway', *Chester Chronicle*, 8 February 1839.

30. 'The Irish railway question', *Chester Chronicle*, 15 March 1839 (italics in the original).

31. House of Commons Debate 12 August 1839, Vol. 50 chapters [henceforth cc] 213–214.

32. 'London and Dublin direct communication', *Chester Chronicle*, 22 May 1840, 3.

33. Ibid.

34. HC Deb 23 June 1840 vol. 55 cc 12–18.

35. HC Deb 23 June 1840 vol. 55 c. 18.

36. Ibid.

37. 'Anglo-Hibernian Railways', *Chester Chronicle*, 21 August 1840.

38. 'Worcester and Port Dynllaen Railway', *Worcestershire Chronicle*, 9 September 1840.

39. 'Direct London and Dublin Communication', *Chester Chronicle*, 4 December 1840.

40. 'Chamber of Commerce', *Freeman's Journal*, 3 March 1841.

41. 'London and Dublin direct Communication', *Chester Chronicle*, 19 February 1841.

42. 'Letters to the Editor', *North Wales Chronicle*, 25 January 1842.

43. 'Communication between London and Dublin', *North Wales Chronicle*, 22 March 1842.

44. 'Communication between England and Ireland', *North Wales Chronicle*, 21 June 1842.

45. *Report from the Select Committee on Post Office Communication with Ireland*, together with the minutes of evidence, appendix and index ii 1842 (373) IX.343.

46. 'Communication between London and Dublin', *Freeman's Journal*, 21 March 1843.

47. HC Deb 9 May 1843 vol. 69 cc 23–5.

48. HC Deb 10 May 1843 vol. 69 c. 101.

49. HC Deb 12 May 1843 vol. 69 cc 246–247.

50. 'Editorial', *The Times*, 9 October 1843.

51. 'Report of J. Walker, Civil Engineer, To Sir John Barrow, Secretary to the Admiralty', *Morning Post*, 25 October 1843.

52. 'Ireland, from our Correspondent, Dublin', *Morning Post,* 20 December 1843.

53. 'Conviction of the Irish Conspirators', *Morning Post,* 12 February 1844.

54. Philip Lloyd, *The Chester and Holyhead Railway and its political impact on North Wales and British policy towards Ireland, 1835–1900,* unpublished PhD thesis, University of York, 2017, 131–134.

55. HC Deb 23 February 1844 vol. 73 c. 254.

56. 'Harbours of Refuge – Holyhead and Porth-Dynllaen (from the *Railway Gazette*)', *Cork Examiner*, 19 February 1845.

57. 'Trent Valley Railway', *Staffordshire Advertiser*, 8 May 1847.

58. Chester and Holyhead railway. Copy of Mr Rendel's report to the Admiralty on Chester and Holyhead railway, 12, 1844 (262) XLV. 545

59. Holyhead harbour of refuge. Copy of a letter from Sir Love Parry, in the year 1844, in reference to a proposed harbour of refuge at Holyhead, with a copy of the plan annexed thereto,1. 1846 (380) XLV.521.

60. House of Lords (henceforth HL Deb) 10 June 1844 vol. 75 cc 415–419.

61. 'Chester and Holyhead Railway', *Chester Chronicle*, 6 September 1844.

Chapter 2

1. Editorial, *The Times,* 7 March 1850.
2. Philip Lloyd, *The Chester and Holyhead Railway and its political impact on North Wales and British policy towards Ireland, 1835–1900,* unpublished PhD thesis, University of York, 2017, 113–114.
3. (Part I.) Minutes of evidence taken before the Select Committee on the Oxford, Worcester, and Wolverhampton Railway, and Oxford and Rugby Railway, Bills. (Group F.) 516, **1845** (360) (360-II) XI.1,583. The date of Walker's evidence was 31 May 1845, 2.
4. 'Railway Committees', *Worcester Journal*, 5 June 1845.
5. 'Oxford, Worcester and Wolverhampton Railway – Half-Yearly Meeting', *Worcestershire Chronicle*, 4 March 1846.
6. 'Railway Notabilia', *Worcestershire Chronicle,* 3 June 1846.
7. Holyhead harbour, correspondence, minutes, between Her Majesty's government and the Chester and Holyhead Railway Company, respecting the carrying Her Majesty's mails, and the construction of a packet and refuge harbour at Holyhead; 19, 1847 (339) LXI.77.
8. Ibid., 41.
9. Report from the Select Committee on Holyhead Harbour, 1847.
10. The Railway Commissioners replaced the Railway Department in 1846.
11. Third report from the Select Committee on Railway Bills,11-12, 1847–1848 (287) XVI.269
12. 'House of Commons – Tuesday, May 23' *Freeman's Journal,* 25 May 1848.
13. Ibid, 1.
14. Ship Owners Association, *Reasons against conceding to the Chester and Holyhead Railway Company power to become a steam ship company with limited liability.* (London: Hume Tracts, 1846), 7.
15. 'Another 'Kirwan' movement – incitement to tumult', *Freeman's Journal,* 25 May 1848.
16. 'Justice to Ireland – the Chester and Holyhead Monopoly', *Cork Examiner,* 26 May 1848.
17. 'Electric telegraph', *Chester Chronicle,*16 May 1845.
18. 'Telegraphic Communication between Holyhead and Liverpool', *Dublin Evening Mail,* 20 December 1850.
19. 'Completion of the submarine telegraph between Ireland and England', *Freeman's Journal*, 2 June 1852.
20. 'The Chester and Holyhead Railway', *Monmouthshire Merlin,* 15 March 1845.
21. 'The Chester and Holyhead Railway', *Pembrokeshire Herald,* 30 May 1845.

22. 'Railway accidents', *North Wales Chronicle*, 20 January 1846.
23. 'The truck system', *Morning Post*, 3 February 1846.
24. 'Strike on the railway', *North Wales Chronicle,* 24 March 1846.
25. 'Welsh Labour on Welsh Railways' *North Wales Chronicle*, 17 June 1845.
26. 'Wales – riot on the Chester and Holyhead Railway', *Freeman's Journal*, 30 May 1846.
27. 'Railway accident at Chester: conclusion of the inquest', *North Wales Chronicle,* 22 June 1847.
28. 'The Chester and Holyhead Railway', *Pembrokeshire Herald*, 16 May 1845.
29. 'Chester and Holyhead Railway – Rhyl', *Carnarvon and Denbigh Herald*, 16 October 1847.
30. 'The Conway iron tubular railway bridge', *The Principality*, 14 March 1848.
31. 'Conway', *North Wales Chronicle*, 30 November 1847.
32. 'Bangor railway works', *Carnarvon and Denbigh Herald*, 17 June 1848.
33. 'Accident to Mr Robert Stephenson the engineer', *The Principality*, 8 September 1848.
34. 'Concert extraordinary', *North Wales Chronicle*, 22 May 1849.
35. 'Tubular bridge over the Menai Straits', *Manchester Times,* 23 June 1849.
36. 'The Britannia bridge', *Glasgow Herald*, 17 August 1849.
37. 'Accident at the Britannia bridge', *London Daily News,* 20 August 1849.
38. *North Wales Chronicle*, 11 September 1849.
39. 'The Britannia tubular bridge', *Oxford Journal*, 6 October 1849.
40. 'The tubular bridge', *Ipswich Journal*, 13 October 1849.
41. 'Curious christening', *Liverpool Mercury*, 16 October 1849.
42. 'Britannia bridge – Menai Straits', *Northern Star and Leeds General Advertiser*, 8 December 1849.
43. 'The Queen's Speech – The Chester and Holyhead Railway', *Freeman's Journal*, 6 February 1850.
44. Editorial, *The Times,* 7 March 1850.
45. HC Deb 08 March 1850 vol. 109 c. 535.
46. HC Deb 17 May 1850 vol. 111 c. 176.
47. HC Deb 17 May 1850 vol. 111 c. 216.
48. HC Deb 10 June 1850 vol. 111 c. 1029.
49. 'Parliamentary Intelligence, House of Lords, 27 June 1850' *The Times,* 28 June 1850.
50. HC Deb 12 August 1850 vol. 113 c. 1037.

51. Anonymous, *A letter addressed to the shareholders in the Chester and Holyhead Railway Company and the London and North Western Railway Company on the doings of directors in the case of the Chester and Holyhead Railway, and the Mold Railway. By a Shareholder*, (London: Effingham Wilson n.d.), 17.

52. Ibid.

53. Philip Lloyd, *The Chester and Holyhead Railway and its political impact on North Wales and British policy towards Ireland, 1835–1900,* unpublished PhD thesis, University of York, 2017, 131–134.

54. HC Deb 26 April 1853 vol. 126 c. 553

55. Report from the Select Committee on Communication between London and Dublin; together with the proceedings of the committee, minutes of evidence, appendix, and index, 2, **1852–1853** (747) XXIV.611

56. Ibid. 171.

57. Post Office (Irish mails) 'Returns of the hours at which the Irish day mails, leaving Euston Station at 7:30 a.m., since 1st October last, were due at Kingstown harbour; and, of the exact times of the arrival of the packets at Kingstown harbour, and the occasions when any of the night mail trains left Dublin without the English mails, etc.', 1861 (388) XXXV.7

Chapter 3

1. 'Talk about Wales and the Welsh; by an Old Mountaineer', *North Wales Chronicle*, 26 December 1863.

2. 'Chester and Holyhead Railway', *Carnarvon and Denbigh Herald*, 30 September 1848.

3. 'Opening of the Conway and Llanrwst Railway', *Liverpool Daily Post*, 17 June 1863.

4. HC Deb 15 August 1850 vol. 113 c. 1078.

5. Charles Wye Williams, *Remarks on the proposed asylum harbour at Holyhead: and the monopoly contemplated by the Chester and Holyhead Railway Company, in a letter addressed to Lord Viscount Sandon* (Liverpool: 1847)

6. 'Chester and Holyhead Railway' *Dublin Evening Mail*, 28 August 1850.

7. Ibid.

8. Edward Parry, *The Railway Companion from Chester to Holyhead*, (Chester: Thomas Catherall,1848), 12.

9. 'Chester and Holyhead Railway meeting', *North Wales Chronicle*, 22 March 1851.
10. 'Anglesey Coal Company', *North Wales Chronicle*, 29 March 1851.
11. 'Chester and Holyhead Railway', *Carnarvon and Denbigh Herald*, 22 March 1851.
12. 'Chester and Holyhead', *Chester Chronicle*, 4 September 1852.
13. 'Mining operations in north Wales', *Aberystwyth Times*, 30 January 1869.
14. 'The station at Connah's Quay', *Cheshire Observer*, 30 April 1870.
15. 'Commercial and Markets', *Liverpool Mercury*, 1 March 1884.
16. 'Navy outbreak', *North Wales Chronicle*, 26 May 1846.
17. 'The Queen's visit to North Wales', *The Welshman*, 22 October 1852.
18. 'Britannia bridge. Inauguration of tube the first', *North Wales Chronicle*, 26 June 1849.
19. 'The Duke of Wellington in Wales', *London Standard*, 27 August 1851.
20. 'Fatal railway accident', *North Wales Chronicle*, 11 July 1848.
21. 'Narrow escape', *North Wales Chronicle*, 30 October 1849.
22. 'Time, tide and train wait for no man', *North Wales Chronicle*, 13 January 1855.
23. 'Hare trapped', *North Wales Chronicle*, 5 September 1848.
24. 'Greenwich Time *v.* Bangor Time' *North Wales Chronicle*, 9 May 1848.
25. '[LNWR]: Diminution of local trains', *North Wales Chronicle*, 8 November 1862.
26. 'Talk about Wales and the Welsh; by an Old Mountaineer', *North Wales Chronicle*, 26 December 1863.
27. 'The Bangor railway station – Influential Meeting', *North Wales Chronicle*, 6 February 1869.
28. Ibid.
29. 'Fatal accident at Bangor railway station', *North Wales Chronicle*, 24 April 1869.
30. 'Assessment of the railways', *North Wales Chronicle*, 15 July 1871.
31. 'Railway rating', *North Wales Chronicle*, 27 January 1872.
32. 'Honour to whom honour is due', *North Wales Chronicle*, 24 February 1872.
33. 'The Chronicle', *North Wales Chronicle*, 20 January 1846.
34. 'Proposed carriage drive round the Great Orme's Head', *North Wales Chronicle*, 9 December 1871.
35. 'Bangor Local Board', *North Wales Chronicle*, 9 March 1878.
36. 'Local bills', *North Wales Chronicle*, 1 June 1878.

37. 'Rates and fares on the Chester and Holyhead Railway', *Carnarvon and Denbigh Herald*, 10 May 1879.

38. Ibid. (my italics).

39. 'Parliamentary intelligence', *The Times*, 22 July 1879.

40. 'Pointsmen', *North Wales Chronicle*, 27 May 1871.

41. 'Holyhead – the strike', *North Wales Chronicle*, 3 July 1875.

42. 'Chester and Holyhead Railway Servants' Friendly Society', *Liverpool Mercury*, 25 January 1877.

43. 'Railway dinner at Bangor', *North Wales Chronicle,* 25 January 1879.

44. 'Anglesey Chair Eisteddfod', *North Wales Chronicle*, 5 August 1876.

45. 'Mr Gladstone's visit to Ireland', *Manchester Courier and Lancashire General Advertiser*, 20 October 1877.

46. 'Mr Gladstone's visit to Wales', *North Wales Chronicle,* 7 October 1882, 6.

47. 'Mr Gladstone and the new Railway', *The Times*, 22 October 1892.

48. 'Mr Preston on the [LNWR]', *Rhyl Advertiser*, 22 January 1881.

49. 'The late Holyhead accident', *North Wales Chronicle*, 24 February 1883, 5.

50. '[LNWR]: annual dinner of the officers of the Chester and Holyhead district', *Cheshire Observer*, 10 February 1883.

51. 'The Holyhead disturbances', *Freeman's Journal*, 20 August 1885.

52. 'Disaffection among railway servants', *Manchester Courier and Lancashire General Advertiser*, 22 August 1885.

53. 'The Holyhead disturbances – more attacks on Englishmen', *Freeman's Journal*, 25 August 1885.

54. 'Obstructing railway servants', *Carnarvon and Denbigh Herald,* 21 August 1885.

55. 'Proposed new railway to Rhyl – Public Meeting', *Rhyl Advertiser*, 25 June 1887.

56. 'Mr Michael Davitt in Wales', *Cambrian News*, 19 February 1886.

57. 'The Employers' Liability Bill', *Carnarvon and Denbigh Herald*, 2 February 1894.

58. 'The [LNWR] and their Welsh employees', *North Wales Chronicle,* 3 November 1894.

59. 'Conway Board of Guardians', *The Weekly News and Visitors Chronicle*, 23 November 1894.

60. 'Anglesey County Council and the railway employees', *Carnarvon and Denbigh Herald*, 22 February 1895.

61. 'Mr Lloyd George's candidature', *North Wales Express*, 12 July 1895.

62. 'Carnarvon district borough election', *The Weekly News and Visitors' Chronicle*, 26 July 1895.
63. HC Deb 28 May 1900 vol. 83 cc 1457–1476.
64. 'Carnarvonshire County Council: the Lleyn light railway', *Carnarvon and Denbigh Herald*, 3 August 1900.
65. 'A railway under Carnarvon castle', *Llangollen Advertiser, Denbighshire, Merionethshire, and North Wales Journal*, 15 July 1870.

Chapter 4

1. Text of a Gregorian chant featured on the memorial at Abergele church to the victims of the nearby rail crash of August 1868.
2. F.G.P. Neison, 'Analytical View of Railway Accidents', *Journal of the Statistical Society of London* Vol. 16, No. 4 (December 1853), pp. 289–337. This summary and analysis are taken from 'Analytical View of Railway Accidents', *North Wales Chronicle*, 22 October 1853.
3. 'Mr Gladstone to the railway servants', *The Star,* 29 March 1877.
4. 'Another fearful mining accident, near Holywell – sixteen lives lost', *North Wales Chronicle*, 15 February 1862.
5. 'Frightful accident at Llandudno Junction', *North Wales Chronicle,* 24 May 1884.
6. 'Fatal Accident', *North Wales Express*, 10 July 1885.
7. 'Mostyn', *The Principality*, 18 August 1848.
8. 'Dinner to Mr Cropper, late of the Chester and Holyhead Railway, *North Wales Chronicle*, 6 May 1854.
9. 'Accident at Penmaenbach tunnel', *North Wales Chronicle*, 18 August 1846.
10. 'Inquest', *North Wales Chronicle*, 7 September 1847.
11. 'Penmaenbach', *North Wales Chronicle*, 27 October 1846.
12. 'Fatal accident', *North Wales Chronicle*, 1 June 1847.
13. 'Fatal accident', *North Wales Chronicle*, 22 June 1847.
14. 'Shocking Accidents', *North Wales Chronicle*, 10 August 1847.
15. 'Dreadful accident', *North Wales Chronicle*, 26 December 1848.
16. 'Accident', *North Wales Chronicle*, 18 February 1854.
17. 'Collision on the Chester and Holyhead Railway', *Wrexham Advertiser*, 7 October 1854.
18. 'The late accident on board the *Eblana* steamer at Holyhead', *North Wales Chronicle*, 21 December 1850.

19. 'Fatal accident to a railway porter', *North Wales Chronicle*, 26 June 1858.
20. 'Another railway catatrophe', *Pembrokeshire Herald and General Advertiser,* 18 January 1861.
21. 'Railway collision at Menai Bridge', *North Wales Chronicle*, 13 May 1865.
22. 'The appalling railway disaster: medical examination of the remains', *Lloyds Weekly Newspaper,* 30 August 1868, 7.
23. 'Chester and Holyhead Railway meeting', *North Wales Chronicle*, 18 September 1851.
24. 'The Blackburn passengers', *Blackburn Standard*, 26 August 1868.
25. 'In a railway smash', *Tyrone Constitution,* 7 April 1905.
26. 'Death of Owain Alaw', *Rhyl Record and Advertiser,* 3 February 1883, 3. He was listed among the dead as: 'Mr W H Owen, of Dublin. Organist', see 'The appalling railway disaster', *Lloyd's Weekly Newspaper*, 30 August 1868.
27. The late railway accident at Holywell', *North Wales Chronicle*, 10 October 1868.
28. 'Railway accident near Abergele', *Wrexham Advertiser*, 24 July 1869.
29. 'Alarming railway accident', *North Wales Chronicle,* 27 July 1872.
30. 'Fatal accident near Llanfairfechan', *North Wales Chronicle*, 10 August 1895.
31. 'Serious accident on the Chester and Holyhead Railway', *North Wales Chronicle*, 23 November 1872.
32. 'An appeal', *North Wales Chronicle*, 21 January 1899.
33. 'Wales and the border', *Wrexham Advertiser*, 7 April 1900.
34. 'The north Wales train tragedy', *Gloucester Citizen*, 8 September 1922.
35. 'Extraordinary railway adventure: perilous condition of Holyhead man', *Carnarvon and Denbigh Herald and North and South Wales Independent,* 5 November 1886.
36. 'Prestatyn', *North Wales Times,* 16 March 1901.
37. 'The Prestatyn railway fatality: the mystery unsolved', *Carnarvon and Denbigh Herald*, 22 March 1901.
38. 'The Anglesea [*sic*] railway mystery', *North Wales Times*, 2 April 1898.
39. 'Madman in the train', *South Wales Daily News*, 7 August 1903.
40. 'Wife's message cost her life', *Liverpool Echo,* 30 May 1942.
41. 'Mysterious death on the London and North Western Railway', *North Wales Chronicle*, 6 July 1878.
42. 'Tunnel tragedy at Bangor', *Carnarvon and Denbigh Herald*, 8 September 1905.

43. 'Wigan collier's shocking death', *Bolton Evening News*, 17 December 1906.

44. 'Prestatyn', *Flintshire Mining Journal*, 12 July 1888.

45. 'Railway fatality', *Cheshire Observer*, 22 August 1908.

46. 'Shocking accident to a child', *Flintshire Observer Mining Journal,* 12 March 1885.

47. 'Fatal accident on the railway', *Wrexham Advertiser,* 8 May 1875.

48. 'Shocking death of a railway fitter', *North Wales Chronicle,* 30 September 1893.

49. 'The railway mystery: identification of the deceased', *Flintshire Observer and Mining Journal*, 29 September 1887.

50. 'Rhyl', *Rhyl Record and Advertiser*, 21 January 1899.

51. 'Men and Matters', *Dundee Courier*, 30 January 1911.

52. 'Nurse's tragic death', *Framlingham Weekly News*, 9 March 1912.

53. 'Tragic railway accident', *Welsh Coast Pioneer,* 20 June 1907.

54. 'A scare', *Wrexham and Denbighshire Advertiser*, 24 August 1895.

55. 'Shocking railway fatality', *Welsh Coast Pioneer*, 30 July 1908.

56. 'Three horses killed', *North Wales Chronicle*, 3 February 1855.

57. 'Prestatyn', *Rhyl Journal,* 3 October 1896.

58. 'Greenfield', *Rhyl Record and Advertiser*, 6 July 1889.

59. 'A midnight flight', *Nottingham Evening Post*, 19 September 1910.

60. 'Valley: Petty Sessions', *North Wales Express*, 12 September 1902.

61. 'Fatal accident', *Flintshire Observer Mining Journal*, 11 December 1874.

62. 'Narrow escape of the Irish Mail train', *Freeman's Journal*, 3 July 1883.

63. HC Deb 9 July 1883 vol. 281 cc 771.

64. 'Porter averts tragedy at Flint station', *Flintshire Observer and Mining Journal*, 10 April 1913.

65. 'A lady rewarded for gallantry', *Flintshire Mining Journal*, 31 July 1890.

66. 'Mochdre', *North Wales Chronicle*, 11 December 1903.

67. 'Killed on railway', *Liverpool Echo*, 11 February 1936.

68. 'Anglesey crossing railway accident', *North Wales Chronicle*, 23 August 1918.

69. 'Report on a fire that occurred in a diesel multiple unit near Connah's Quay station, 29 August 1965', *Ministry of Transport, Railway Accident*, HMSO 22 April 1966.

70. 'Report on the collision that occurred on 4th September 1965 at Holyhead', *Ministry of Transport, Railway Accident*, HMSO, 7 February 1966.

71. 'The Provinces', *London Evening Standard*, 22 October 1904.

72. HC Deb 23 March 1990 vol. 169 c. 1352.

Chapter 5

1. HC Deb 19 April 1898 vol. 56 c. 400.
2. 'House of Commons – Tuesday, May 23', *Freeman's Journal*, 25 May 1848.
3. 'Chester and Holyhead Railway: communication with Ireland', *Freeman's Journal*, 2 September 1844.
4. 'Chester and Holyhead Railway', *North Wales Chronicle*, 3 May 1851.
5. 'The Holyhead harbour works', *North Wales Chronicle*, 9 October 1851.
6. 'Distressing incident on the Holyhead railway', *Athlone Sentinel*, 5 March 1851.
7. 'Serious disturbances amongst the labourers at the great Holyhead breakwater works', *North Wales Chronicle*, 17 May 1851.
8. 'The late accident at Holyhead', *North Wales Chronicle*, 18 March 1851.
9. 'Holyhead harbour works', *North Wales Chronicle,* 2 September 1854.
10. 'Holyhead old harbour', *North Wales Chronicle*, 20 August 1864.
11. 'Opening of the new harbour and breakwater', *Flintshire Observer and Mining Journal*, 22 August 1873.
12. 'The new Holyhead harbour', *Freeman's Journal*, 17 June 1880.
13. 'The royal visit to Holyhead', *Freeman's Journal*, 18 June 1880.
14. Ibid.
15. Ibid. (my emphasis).
16. 'The proposed visit of the Prince of Wales to Rhyl', *Rhyl Advertiser*, 19 June 1880.
17. 'A trial of speed', *Freeman's Journal*, 29 March 1883.
18. HC Deb 19 April 1898 vol. 56 c. 400.
19. 'Fog bell', *Carnarvon and Denbigh Herald*, 31 January 1857.
20. 'Launch', *North Wales Chronicle,* 29 September 1860.
21. 'Perilous escape', *Illustrated Usk Observer and Raglan Herald*, 25 April 1863.
22. 'Shipping disasters', *Liverpool Mercury*, 24 June 1873.
23. 'A fatal accident on a Holyhead steamer', *North Wales Chronicle,* 18 September 1875.
24. 'The fatal collision in Holyhead harbour', *North Wales Chronicle*, 9 October 1875.
25. 'Launch', *Llangollen Advertiser,* 19 October 1877.
26. 'Drowned', *Llangollen Advertiser,* 14 December 1877.
27. 'Fearful collision with a Dublin & Holyhead steamer', *Liverpool Mercury*, 1 November 1883.

28. 'Collision off Holyhead', *Western Mail*, 20 January 1885.
29. 'Two steamers ashore at Holyhead', *Aberdeen Press and Journal,* 17 January 1887.
30. 'Run down in broad daylight', *Cardiff Times*, 16 July 1887.
31. 'Steamer on Holyhead breakwater', *Leeds Mercury*, 9 January 1888.
32. 'Presentation to a captain', *North Wales Express*, 16 November 1888.
33. 'Holyhead steamers in collision', *Carnarvon and Denbigh Herald*, 20 September 1889.
34. 'The Violet', *Carnarvon and Denbigh Herald*, 28 November 1890.
35. 'Collision and fatal accident', *Carnarvon and Denbigh Herald*, 7 August 1891.
36. '*Violet* in collision', 'Retirement of Admiral Dent', *Carnarvon and Denbigh Herald*, 25 November 1892.
37. 'Fares on L and N W steamers', *Carnarvon and Denbigh Herald*, 14 February 1896.
38. 'A new steamer for the railway company', *Carnarvon and Denbigh Herald*, 13 August 1897.
39. 'A new railway steamer', *Carnarvon and Denbigh Herald*, 9 November 1900.
40. 'A new Holyhead steamer', *North Wales Express,* 20 October 1899.
41. Ibid.
42. 'Holyhead steamers in collision', *Welsh Coast Pioneer*, 29 June 1900.
43. 'Mishap to a Holyhead steamer', *Welsh Coast Pioneer*, 20 June 1907.
44. 'Holyhead steamer in collision', *Carnarvon and Denbigh Herald,* 3 January 1908.
45. 'The Holyhead collision', *North Wales Express*, 11 September 1908.
46. Postcard in the author's collection.
47. 'Steamer ashore', *Carnarvon and Denbigh Herald,* 24 September 1909.
48. 'NWR [*sic*] steamer in collision', *Carnarvon and Denbigh Herald*, 25 March 1910.
49. 'Holyhead steamers and their wireless apparatus', *North Wales Chronicle*, 28 June 1914.
50. '*Lusitania*: landing survivors at Holyhead', *North Wales Chronicle*, 14 May 1915.
51. 'Frightful disaster in Irish channel', *Cambrian Daily Leader*, 4 November 1916.
52. 'Irish boat collision', *Abergavenny Chronicle*, 22 March 1918.
53. 'Collision in the channel', *Manchester Evening News*, 1 April 1918.
54. '500 lives lost on the *Leinster*', *Huddersfield Daily Examiner*, 11 October 1918.

55. 'Echo of the *Leinster* disaster: the company's position', *Irish Independent*, 22 May 1919.
56. 'Four new LNWR steamers', *Irish Independent,* 20 November 1919.
57. 'Gale in the channel: steamer in peril at Holyhead', *Western Mail*, 16 January 1922.
58. 'Holyhead harbour: sheltered passage from train to mail packets', *Western Mail*, 2 March 1925.
59. 'Irish mail steamer gunned: officer dead', *Daily Record,* 20 December 1940.

Chapter 6

1. 'The Volunteers in North Wales', *Staffordshire Advertiser*, 19 May 1883.
2. 'The army', *Morning Post*, 16 May 1836.
3. 'Conveyance of military by railway', *Glasgow Herald*, 7 March 1845.
4. 'Steam navigation – rapid passage', *London Evening Standard*, 9 May 1848.
5. 'The Fenian convicts passing', *North Wales Chronicle*, 20 January 1866.
6. 'The late gale', *Kings County Chronicle*, 12 December 1866.
7. 'Fenian attempt upon Chester', *Chester Chronicle*, 16 February 1867.
8. 'Fenian alarm at Holyhead', *Greenock Advertiser*, 16 November 1867.
9. 'Fenian railway outrages', *Burnley Advertiser*, 2 January 1869.
10. 'The "Fenian shot" at a railway train', *Glasgow Evening Citizen*, 24 December 1867.
11. 'The Fenian scare', *Whitby Gazette,* 19 February 1881.
12. 'Fenian alarm at Holyhead', *Northern Whig*, 11 April 1883.
13. 'Fenians and Mr Gladstone: extraordinary precautions at Hawarden', *Monmouthshire Merlin*, 21 December 1883.
14. 'Discovery of dynamite at Flint station', *South Wales Echo*, 26 August 1887.
15. 'The anti-tithe disturbances in Wales', *North Wales Chronicle*, 3 September 1887.
16. 'The volunteers in North Wales', *Staffordshire Advertiser*, 19 May 1883.
17. 'Volunteer camps in North Wales', *Montgomeryshire Express*, 4 August 1891.
18. 'Volunteers in camps', *Liverpool Mercury*, 6 June 1892.
19. 'Railway accident in North Wales', Cardiff Times, 6 August 1892.
20. 'Army, militia and volunteers', *Wrexham Advertiser*, 26 May 1894.
21. 'Morfa station', *Carnarvon and Denbigh Herald*, 10 May 1901.
22. 'March of the Welch Fusiliers through North Wales', *North Wales Chronicle*, 10 September 1892.

23. 'Bagillt', *Flintshire Observer Mining Journal and General Advertiser,* 24 May 1900.
24. 'Lord Dundonald's welcome home', *North Wales Chronicle*, 8 December 1900.
25. 'Coventry cadets camp', *Coventry Evening Telegraph*, 31 July 1914.
26. 'Railway roll of honour: Chester and Holyhead district', *North Wales Chronicle*, 15 March 1915.
27. *London Gazette*, 22 February 1916, pp. 1946–1947.
28. 'Fallen North Wales railwaymen', *North Wales Chronicle*, 23 May 1919.
29. 'Fallen North Wales railwaymen: memorial service', *North Wales Chronicle* 23 May 1919.
30. 'Roll of Honour', *North Wales Chronicle*, 15 November 1918.
31. 'Fatal railway accident near Gaerwen', *North Wales Chronicle*, 15 December 1916.
32. 'Railway company and the employment of women', *North Wales Chronicle*, 11 April 1919.
33. 'The prisoners' arrival at Holyhead', *Irish Independent,* 4 May 1916.
34. 'Man with a revolver', *Dublin Evening Telegraph*, 12 February 1923.
35. 'North Wales round about', *Liverpool Echo*, 23 June 1939.
36. 'The Welsh coast air tragedy', *Liverpool Echo*, 18 September 1937.
37. 'Funerals of *Thetis* victims', *Western Daily Press*, 6 September 1939.
38. 'North Wales welcomes the BEF', *Liverpool Evening Express*, 31 May 1940.
39. 'The "invasion" of North Wales', *Chester Chronicle*, 15 September 1945.
40. 'Train load of civil servants', *Liverpool Daily Post*, 8 December 1945.
41. 'North Wales train tragedy', *Liverpool Echo*, 4 June 1940.
42. HC Deb 19 July 1991 vol. 195 cc 728–734.

Chapter 7

1. Wording from British Railways tourist brochures for north Wales.
2. 'The Blanketeers', *The North Wales Chronicle and Advertiser for the Principality*, 9 September 1830.
3. The *Sun* (London), 18 March 1801.
4. 'North Wales packet', *Chester Courant*, 15 December 1829.
5. 'The Spirit of Opposition', *North Wales Chronicle*, 16 June 1840.
6. 'Excursions in the Principality', *Chester Chronicle*, 14 September 1850.
7. *Sun* (London), 12 June 1851.

8. 'Scenes in North Wales', *North Wales Chronicle*, 22 August 1857.
9. 'Chester and Holyhead Railway meeting', *North Wales Chronicle*, 22 March 1851.
10. *Sun* (London), 5 June 1852,
11. 'Tourists in North Wales', *Express* (London) 1 September 1857.
12. 'New watering place, Llandudno, North Wales', *North Wales Chronicle*, 29 August 1857.
13. 'Scenes in North Wales', *North Wales Chronicle*, 22 August 1857.
14. 'The Mechanics Institution trip to North Wales', *Wigan Observer and District Advertiser*, 25 June 1859.
15. 'The tourist season in North Wales', *London Daily News*, 19 October 1864.
16. 'North and south Wales and the Wye', *Liverpool Mail*, 11 August 1866.
17. Proposed carriage drive round the Great Orme's head', *North Wales Chronicle*. 9 December 1871.
18. Editorial, *North Wales Chronicle,* 21 August 1880.
19. *Denbighshire Free Press*, 26th August 1882.
20. *North Wales Chronicle*, 7 October 1882.
21. 'Bank Holiday', *Manchester Courier and Lancashire General Advertiser*, 5 August 1890.
22. 'North Wales and railway extension', *Carnarvon and Denbigh Herald*, 21 April 1893.
23. 'Welsh and Border News', *Wrexham Advertiser*, 25 June 1892.
24. 'Widening the Holyhead line', *Cheshire Observer,* 16 May 1896.
25. 'The [LNWR] extension in North Wales', *North Wales Express*, 20 November 1896.
26. 'The [LNWR] Report', *Manchester Evening News*, 8 February 1897.
27. 'Railway development in North Wales', *Cheshire Observer*, 18 February 1899.
28. Ibid.
29. 'New railway bridge', *Flintshire Observer,* 11th May 1899.
30. 'The widening of the Chester and Holyhead Railway', *North Wales Chronicle*, 22 December 1900.
31. 'Chester & Holyhead Line: improvements in progress', *Cheshire Observer,* 5 September 1903.
32. '[LNWR] Meeting', *Staffordshire Advertiser*, 20 February 1904.
33. 'Bagillt: extension of the station and railway', *Flintshire Observer and Mining Journal*, 13 June 1907.
34. 'The railway station', *Welsh Coast Pioneer*, 5 October 1900, 7.
35. Advertisement, *Field*, 4 August 1900.

36. 'Rhyl and weekend rail tickets', *The Welsh Coast Pioneer*, 15 January 1904.
37. 'The new Talacre Arms Prestatyn', *North Wales Times*, 18 April 1903.
38. 'The Season 1906 in North Wales', *Liverpool Daily Post*, 11 September 1906.
39. 'Proposed explosives factory', *North Wales Chronicle*, 13 March 1897.
40. 'The Welsh Tourist Racer: First Long Non-Stop Run', *Carnarvon and Denbigh Herald*, 3 July 1908.
41. 'Eastertide railway traffic', *The Weekly News and Visitors Chronicle for Colwyn Bay*, *5 April 1907, 13.*
42. 'North Wales for tourists', *Newry Reporter*, 24 April 1909.
43. 'North Wales as a holiday resort', *Coventry Herald,* Friday 18 June 1909.
44. 'Advertising of North Wales: the Colwyn Bay Conference', *North Wales Chronicle*, 2 October 1909.
45. *The Referee*, 1 May 1910.
46. 'Rash young promenaders', *Sheffield Daily Telegraph*, 15 April 1914.
47. 'L&NW Railway', *Birmingham Mail*, 28 July 1914.
48. 'Rhyl 'Full Up', *Manchester Evening News*, 2 August 1915.
49. 'Welsh News: Whitsun on the coast', *Liverpool Daily Post*, 13 June 1916.
50. 'Railway returns as to traffic: some extraordinary figures', *Coventry Evening Telegraph*, 10 August 1917.
51. 'Bank Holiday at Chester: record motor traffic'. *Cheshire Observer*, 29 May 1920.
52. 'Competing with the railway in north Wales', *Western Mail,* 12 September 1921.
53. 'North Wales as a winter holiday', *Reading Observer,* 10 November 1922.
54. 'Britain's enterprising railways', *Buckingham Advertiser and Free Press*, 4 August 1923.
55. 'North Wales Advertising Board's experience', *Western Mail*, 7 October 1924.
56. 'Popular north Wales', *Western Mail*, 6 November 1925.
57. 'Whitsuntide in North Staffs', *Staffordshire Advertiser* 29 May 1926.
58. 'Changed railway policy', *Staffordshire Sentinel,* 31 July 1926.
59. 'Excursions to North Wales', *Burnley Express*, 14 May 1927.
60. 'The Year in North Wales', *Western Mail*, 2 January 1928.
61. HC Deb 28 February 1928 vol. 214 cc 301–359.
62. 'Bus firm bought', *The Scotsman*, 5 August 1929.
63. 'Railway speed-up', *Western Gazette*, 12 July 1929.
64. 'Free lantern lectures', *Lichfield Gazette*, 16 August 1929.
65. 'Rail and road: coordination of North Wales services' *Western Mail,* 30 April 1930.

66. 'Wireless for the weekend', *Liverpool Echo*, 12 June 1937.
67. 'LMS holiday caravans', *Clitheroe Advertiser and Times, 4* March 1938.
68. 'North Wales holiday camp', *Belfast Evening Telegraph*, 21 December 1938.
69. 'Car value in use', *Gloucester Citizen*, 27 February 1932.
70. 'Interesting rail statistic', *Staffordshire Sentinel*, 6 August 1936.
71. 'North Wales traffic', *Liverpool Daily Post*, 30 May 1939.
72. 'In North Wales' *Liverpool Daily Post*, 15 April 1941.
73. 'Rush to North Wales', *Liverpool Daily Post*, 26 July 1943.
74. 'North Wales loads', *Liverpool Echo*, 5 August 1944.
75. 'Blackpool 1,500,000 led the LMS rush', *Manchester Evening News,* 4 October 1945.
76. HC Deb 05 May 1947 vol. 437 cc 36–171.
77. HC Deb 24 November 1949 vol. 470 c. 604.
78. British Railways Board, *The Reshaping of British Railways*, (London: HMSO 1963), 14.
79. HC Deb 29 April 1963 vol. 676 cc 722–846.
80. HC Deb 27 July 1966 vol. 732 c. 308.

Chapter 8

1. 'Bodorgan', *North Wales Chronicle*, 6 May 1853.
2. 'North Wales circuit', *North Wales Chronicle*, 8 August 1848.
3. 'The Chronicle', *North Wales Chronicle*, 27 March 1849.
4. 'Caution to travellers', *North Wales Chronicle*, 25 September 1849.
5. 'Cigar instead of a ticket', *Liverpool Echo*, 25 October 1932.
6. Chester and Holyhead Railway, *Rules and regulations for the conduct of traffic*, London, 1853, 48.
7. 'Brutal and inhuman conduct of railway servant', *North Wales Chronicle,* 20 July 1850.
8. 'Felonious wounding', *Wrexham Advertiser*, 6 August 1859.
9. 'Flintshire Assizes', *North Wales Chronicle*, 29 October 1853.
10. 'Boys charging with placing obstructions on the railway line', *The Rhyl Advertiser,* 26 November 1881.
11. 'Chester', *Wrexham and Denbighshire Advertiser*, 15 September 1860.
12. 'The Railway outrage', *Flintshire Observer Mining Journal*, 9 July 1875.
13. 'Startling incident on the railway', *Denbighshire Free Press*, 23 November 1889.

14. 'Curious railway outrage', *Worcestershire Chronicle*, 9 December 1876.
15. 'Scene in a train', *Liverpool Echo*, 23 August 1937.
16. 'Temperance among railwaymen', *Flintshire Observer Mining Journal*, 18 September 1884.
17. 'The new railway temperance hall', *North Wales Chronicle*, 11 February 1893.
18. 'LNWR Temperance Union Shield', *North Wales Weekly News*, 29 April 1910.
19. 'Extensive robbery of jewellery at Bangor' *North Wales Chronicle,* 31 July 1869.
20. 'Attempted fraud upon the [LNWR]', *North Wales Chronicle,* 31 July 1869.
21. 'Latest report', *Evening Express*, 8 January 1909.
22. 'Allen v the Chester and Holyhead Railway Company', *North Wales Chronicle*, 21 February 1857.
23. 'Manslaughter', *North Wales Chronicle*, 30 March 1867.
24. 'The alleged outrage in a railway carriage', *Wrexham Guardian*, 23 March 1878.
25. 'Disgraceful conduct to ladies', *Denbighshire Free Press*, 12 December 1896.
26. 'Valley Petty Sessions', *Carnarvon and Denbigh Herald*, 8 March 1887.
27. 'Bodorgan: A railway porter killed', *Carnarvon and Denbigh Herald*, 13 November 1891.
28. 'Important Inquest on the body of a passenger', *North Wales Chronicle*, 26 September 1868.
29. 'Death of the Chester Registrar', *Cheshire Observer*, 3 October 1891.
30. Ibid.
31. 'Greenfield station, Holywell' *North Wales Chronicle*, 5 October 1850.
32. 'Talhaiarn and the Denbigh Eisteddfod', *North Wales Chronicle*, 8 September 1860.
33. 'The National Eisteddfod', *North Wales Chronicle,* 5 September 1863.
34. 'The Eisteddfod', *Wrexham Advertiser*, 30 August 1873, 6.
35. 'Chester and Holyhead Railway', *Llangollen Advertiser*, 1 October 1869.
36. 'Connah's Quay', *Llangollen Advertiser,* 21 August 1891.
37. 'The Chronicle', *North Wales Chronicle*, 29 December 1900.
38. 'Bodorgan', *North Wales Chronicle,* 6 May 1853.
39. 'Anglesey Agricultural Society Show', *North Wales Chronicle*, 8 August 1890.
40. 'The railway company and the farmer', *North Wales Chronicle,* 21 March 1891.
41. 'Conway railway station destroyed by fire', *Cardiff and Merthyr Guardian,* 27 November 1858.
42. 'Old Colwyn: fire at the station', *Carnarvon and Denbigh Herald*, 25 November 1898.

43. 'Old Colwyn', *Carnarvon and Denbigh Herald*, 18 July 1902.
44. 'Goods train afire: hundreds of sleepers burned', *Rhyl Record and Advertiser,* 25 February 1905.
45. 'Fire at Bodlondeb Farm', *Flintshire Observer Mining Journal*, 3 March 1910.
46. 'Colwyn Bay train fire', *Liverpool Echo*, 18 September 1912.
47. 'Fire at a North-Western station', *Derby Daily Telegraph,* 29 October 1913.
48. 'Gaerwen Junction Smithfield', 'Anglesey Farm Stock Sale', *North Wales Chronicle*, 28 September 1917.
49. Untitled, *North Wales Chronicle*, 15 February 1890.
50. 'The Valley', *North Wales Chronicle*, 13 May 1862.
51. '44 years on the railway', *Liverpool Echo*, 25 January 1935.
52. 'Ty Croes', *North Wales Chronicle*, 9 October 1886.
53. 'Death of Rhyl stationmaster', *Wrexham Advertiser*, 27 August 1892.
54. 'Railwaymen's outing', *Rhyl Record*, 27 September 1902.
55. 'Requests to railway company', *Flintshire Observer and Mining Journal*, 15 May 1913.
56. 'Conway', *London Illustrated News,* 23 October 1852.
57. 'The charge against an Anglesey clergyman', *North Wales Chronicle*, 19 July 1879.
58. 'Death of the Primate at Hawarden Church', *Lloyd's Weekly Newspaper*, 18 October 1896.
59. 'Mr Gladstone: the last journey', *Westmorland Gazette*, 28 May 1898.
60. 'Colwyn Bay', *Rhyl Journal* 26 October 1901.
61. 'Perilous adventure of Post Office messenger', *North Wales Chronicle*, 10 December 1864.
62. 'Llanerchymedd', *North Wales Chronicle*, 4th February 1882.
63. 'Excursion', *Flintshire Observer and Mining Journal,* 4 August 1876.
64. 'Curious accident to a theatrical company', *Nottingham Evening Post*, 25 May 1903.
65. 'Llandudno Junction', *The Weekly News and Visitors' Chronicle,* 14 June 1901.

Chapter 9

1. HC Deb 29 October 1992 vol. 212 cc 1160–233.
2. 'North Wales breakdown', *Liverpool Echo*, 11 August 1920, 8.
3. Williams, D.R. *Men of 7A6G Loco Shed Llandudno Junction: 'gone but not forgotten'* (Gwasg Carreg Gwalch: Llanrwst, 2007).

4. 'Train runs through flames', *Yorkshire Post and Leeds Intelligencer*, 14 June 1946.
5. HC Deb 24 July 1970 vol. 804 cc 1023–1039.
6. HC Deb 10 June 1971 vol. 818 cc 1251–1368.
7. See for example HC Deb 21 March 1974 vol. 870 cc 1377–1464.
8. HC Deb 01 July 1985 vol. 82 cc 159–166.
9. HC Deb 03 February 1983 vol. 36 cc 43–-510.
10. HC Deb 28 April 1988 vol. 132 cc 622–628.
11. HC Deb 02 March 1987 vol. 111 cc 600–679.
12. HC Deb 02 December 1975 vol. 901 c. 1655.
13. David Sallery, www.penmorfa.com.
14. HC Deb 28 October 1946 vol. 428 c. 376.
15. HC Deb 29 October 1992 vol. 212 cc 1160–1233.
16. 'Holyhead as a harbour for transit', *North Wales Chronicle*, 3 January 1863.
17. 'The Chester and Holyhead Railway: damage to the sea wall', *Saunders Newsletter*, 30 October 1846.
18. 'The late storm', *North Wales Chronicle*, 11 March 1853.
19. 'Accident on the Chester and Holyhead Railway', *Huddersfield Chronicle*, 29 October 1859.
20. 'The late fearful storm', *North Wales Chronicle*, 29 October 1859.
21. 'Destructive gale and snowstorm', *North Wales Chronicle*, 12 January 1867.
22. 'Serious accident on the Chester and Holyhead Railway', *North Wales Chronicle*, 23 November 1872.
23. 'Severe snowstorm', *North Wales Express*, 5 March 1886.
24. 'London and North Western Railway', *London Daily News*, 25 August 1879.
25. See *Journal of the Railway and Canal Historical Society*, Vol. 29 Pt. 1 No. 135, March 1987.
26. 'The Gale in North Wales: The [CHR] submerged', *South Wales Daily News*, 2 November 1887, 3.
27. 'Mountainous seas on Welsh coast', *Liverpool Post*, 19 December 1945.
28. 'A Thrilling Railway Route', *Northants Evening Telegraph*, 25 May 1901.
29. 'Serious collision on the [CHR]', *Flintshire Mining Journal*, 7 October 1870.
30. 'Storms and Floods', *Wellington Journal*, 31 October 1903.
31. 'Collapse of the Dee embankment: inrush of the sea', *Gloucestershire Echo*, 26 September 1904.
32. Railway line threatened: sea encroachments in Flintshire', *Irish Independent*, 27 September 1904.
33. David Sallery, www.penmorfa.com.

34. 'Floods in North Wales', *Lichfield Mercury*, 25 November 1910.
35. 'North Wales flooding', *Liverpool Daily Post*, 17 April 1943.
36. 'Heavy seas leave a trail of havoc in North Wales', *Yorkshire Post*, 25 September 1945.
37. 'The Welsh railway block', *Liverpool Echo*,18 January 1905.
38. 'Express brought to a standstill', *Coventry Evening Telegraph*, 21 February 1907.
39. 'North Wales mystery', *Liverpool Echo*, 29 December 1931.
40. 'Couple who met in secret', *Dundee Evening Telegraph*, 31 December 1931.
41. 'Snow clearers killed', *Liverpool Echo*, 6 January 1947.
42. 'Troops and prisoners of war digging out trains buried by blizzard', *Liverpool Echo*, 6 March 1947.
43. Peter Girard, Director of Communications at Climate Central in an email to the author, 5 August 2020.
44. 'The Storm', *Western Mail,* 29 December 1886.

Chapter 10

1. Leo Tolstoy, *Anna Karenina,* Project Gutenberg, 1998, Part 5, Ch. 15.

Bibliography and Further Reading

Much of the information on incidents and issues was collected from newspapers, many of which are available on the National Library of Wales, Llyfrgell Genedlaethol Cymru website and the British Newspaper Archive of the British Library. The notes show the newspapers referred to in the text.

1. Government Reports

Communication with Ireland. Copy of report on Holyhead and Port Dynllayn harbours, by Captain Back and Captain Fair, to the Lords Commissioners of the Admiralty. Copy of report of James Walker, Esq., civil engineer, to the Lords Commissioners of the Admiralty. **1844** (43) (633) XLV. 509.

Copy of Mr. Rendel's Report to the Admiralty on Chester and Holyhead Railway Report to Admiralty on Chester and Holyhead Railway. **1844** (262) XLV.545.

Extracts from the Minutes of Evidence given before the Committee of the Lords on the London and Birmingham Railway Bill, London, 1832.

Holyhead Harbour. Copy of Treasury Minute Relative to the Formation of a Harbour at Holyhead; Treasury Minute, April 1846, Relative to Formation of Harbour at Holyhead, and Agreements with Chester and Holyhead Railway Company to Contribute Towards Harbour.

Holyhead Harbour, &C. Correspondence, Minutes, &C. Between Her Majesty's Government and the Chester and Holyhead Railway Company, Respecting the Carrying Her Majesty's Mails, and the Construction of a Packet and Refuge Harbour at Holyhead; Correspondence, Minutes and Agreements with Chester and Holyhead Railway Company Respecting Construction of Packet Harbour at Holyhead. **1847** (339) LXI.77.

Holyhead and Portdynllaen Harbours. Menai Bridge. Copy of Letters of Instructions to the Naval Officers and Civil Engineers Appointed in 1843, to Report on the Harbours of Holyhead and Portdynllaen. Copy of Report of Mr. Provis on the Menai Bridge. Letters of Instructions to Naval Officers and Civil Engineers on Harbours of Holyhead and Port Dynllaen as Packet Stations between London and Dublin, and as Harbours of Refuge, 1843; Report on Menai Bridge, 1843–1844. **1844** (214) XLV.503.

Report from the Select Committee on Post Office Communication with Ireland; together with the minutes of evidence, appendix and index ii **1842** (373) IX.343.

The Reshaping of British Railways, British Railways Board, HMSO, London, 1963.

2. Older Secondary Sources

Parry, Edward, *The Railway Companion from Chester to Holyhead.* Chester: Thomas Catherall,1848.

St George's Harbour and Railway Company, George's Harbour and Railway, *Report and Evidence before the Select Committee.* London: Effingham Wilson, 1836.

Ship Owners Association, *Reasons against conceding to the Chester and Holyhead Railway Company power to become a steam ship company with limited liability,* London: Hume Tracts, 1846.

Smiles, Samuel, *The Lives of George Stephenson and of his son Robert.* New York, 1868.

Steele, Wilfred L., *The History of the London and North Western Railway.* London: Railway and Travel Monthly, 1914.

3. Secondary Sources

Baughan, Peter, *A Regional History of the Railways of Great Britain, Volume 11, North and Mid Wales.* Newton Abbot: David & Charles, 1980.

————. *The Chester & Holyhead Railway: Volume 1, The Main line up to 1880.* Newton Abbot: David and Charles, 1972.

Connolly, J. (ed.), *The Oxford Companion to Irish History.* Oxford: Oxford University Press, 1999.

Davies, John., *A History of Wales.* London: Penguin Books, 1993.

Dodd, A.H., *History of Caernarvonshire, 1284–1900.* Wrexham: Bridge Books, 1990.

————. *The Industrial Revolution in North Wales.* Cardiff: University of Wales Press, 1951

Dunn, John Maxwell, *The Chester & Holyhead Railway*. South Godstone, Surrey: Oakwood Press, 1948.

Ellis-Williams, M., *Packet to Ireland*. Caernarfon: Gwynedd Archives Service, 1984.

Gourvish, T.R., *Mark Huish and the London & North Western Railway: A Study of Management*. Leicester: Leicester University Press, 1972.

Grigg, John. *Lloyd George: The Young Lloyd George.* London: Penguin, 1997.

Hughes, David Lloyd, *Holyhead: The Story of a Port*, ed. Dorothy Mary Williams. Holyhead (Anglesey): D.L. Hughes & D. M. Williams, 1967.

Jenkins, Geraint H., *The Foundations of Modern Wales; Wales 1642–1780*. Oxford: New York: Clarendon Press, 1987.

———. *The Welsh Language and Its Social Domains, 1801–1911*. Cardiff: University of Wales Press, 2000.

Jones, Ivor Wynne, *Shipwrecks of North Wales,* Newton Abbot: David and Charles, 1973.

Lloyd, Philip, *The Chester and Holyhead Railway and its political impact on North Wales and British policy towards Ireland, 1835–1900,* unpublished PhD thesis, University of York, 2017, http://etheses.whiterose.ac.uk/19201/.

———. '"The Great Railway Problem": Politics, Railways and Nationalism in North Wales, 1870–1900', *Welsh History Review*, Volume 29, Number 1, June 2018, pp. 73–98 (26).

Morgan, Kenneth O. *Rebirth of a Nation; Wales, 1880–1980*. Oxford: Oxford University Press, 1982.

———. *Wales in British Politics 1868–1922*. Cardiff: University of Wales Press, 1991.

Quartermaine, Jamie, *Thomas Telford's Holyhead Road; The A5 in North Wales*. Ed. Barrie Stuart Trinder, R.C. Turner, Jo Bell, Edward Holland, Archaeology Council for British Monuments, Welsh Historic and North Oxford Archaeology. York: Council for British Archaeology, 2003.

Quick, Michael, *Railway passenger stations in Great Britain: a chronology*. Electronic version, https://rchs.org.uk/railway-passenger-stations-in-great-britain-a-chronology/.

Reed, M.C. (ed.) *Railways in the Victorian Economy: Studies in Finance and Economic Growth*. Newton Abbot: David & Charles, 1969.

———. *The London & North Western Railway; A History*. Penryn: Atlantic Transport, 1996.

Rolt, L.T.C., *George and Robert Stephenson; The Railway Revolution*. London: Penguin, 1988.

————. *Red for Danger*. London: Pan Books, 1966.

Simmons, Jack. *The Railway in England and Wales, 1830–1914, Vol. 1: The Railway in Town and Country*. Leicester: Leicester University Press, 1978.

————. *The Victorian Railway*. London: Thames & Hudson, 1991.

Simmons, Jack, and Gordon Biddle, *The Oxford Companion to British Railway History from 1603 to the 1990s*. Oxford: Oxford University Press, 1997.

Vignoles, Keith H., *Charles Blacker Vignoles; Romantic Engineer*. Cambridge: Cambridge University Press, 1982.

Williams, D.R., *Men of 7A6G Loco shed Llandudno Junction: 'gone but not forgotten'*. Gwasg Carreg Gwalch, Llanrwst, 2007.

Williams, G. Haulfryn. *Rheilffyrdd Yng Ngwynedd. Railways in Gwynedd*, Caernarfon: Gwynedd Archives Service, 1979.

4. Websites

The history of the CHR and its current operation are well covered in excellent websites such as the following.

North Wales coast railway: Rheilffordd arfordir gogledd Cymru www.nwrail.org.uk

2D53 Main line railways of north Wales 2D53@plimmer.plus.com

'Railways of north Wales: 25 years of evolution' is on the *Penmorfa* site, David@penmorfa.com

Detailed coverage of the history of the Llandudno Junction shed 6G at www.6g.nwrail.org.uk/

Useful information is also held among others by these sites.

Climate Central, https://www.climatecentral.org/

London and North Western Railway Society, https://www.lnwrs.org.uk

Railway and Canal Historical Society, https://rchs.org.uk/

Index

Items in bold are stations or relate to the information contained in Appendix 2 on pages 237-41.

A55, North Wales Expressway, 204, 206, 208-212, 220, 232, 236
causes redirection of the railway, 206 [Photo 86]
Aber (incl. station) 62, 64, 169, 172, 181, 227-29 **[Photo 38]**
water troughs, 51 **[Photo 14]**
wind damage, 227
Abergele and Pensarn (incl. station), 30, 81, 133, 180-83, 226-28, 235 **[Photos 31, 51]**
rail crash of 1868, 84-90
Accidents and Incidents:
Collisions,
Abergele, 84-8
Chester, 81 [Photo 26]
Conwy, 44
Holywell, 87
Llandegai, 181
Menai Bridge, 82
Mostyn, 224
Penmaenmawr, 93 (1950), **[Photo 34]**, 131 (1891)
Penmaenrhos, 88
Valley (Penrhos), 89
Civilians hit by train,
Llanddaniel, 105
Llandudno Junction, 104

Penmaenrhos, 99
Point of Ayr, 98
Rhyl East, 228 **[Photo 67]**
Shotton, 98
Wig, 61
Derailment,
Connah's Quay, 200
Holyhead, 220
Llanfair PG, 82 [Photo 27]
Penmaenbach, 90-1 [Photo 33]
Talacre, 106
Employees hit by train,
Abergele, 98
Glan y Mor, 100
Greenfield, 228
Llandudno Junction, 78
Mostyn, 92-3
Rhyl, 92
Ty Croes, 183
Employee incidents,
crew asleep, 102 [Photo 40]
Fall from a train,
Bodorgan, 95
Gerazim, 144
Glan y Mor, 99 [Photo 38]
Llandegai, 96
Penmaenrhos, 81
Penyrorsedd (nr. Gaerwen), 94

Prestatyn, 178
Sandycroft, 97
Talybont, 97
Towyn, 94
Passenger incidents,
    Conwy, 95 [Photo 35]
    Gaerwen, 138
Railway deaths statistics, 77-8
Stalled train, 81, 88-9, 102, 197
Admiralty Pier, (incl. station), 109,
    [Photo 1]
    closure of station, 121
Agriculture:
    cattle traffic, 57, 117, 185, 209, 217
    farmers' markets, 190
    importance of the railway to, 190-92
Airplanes and airfields, 140, 142, 170,
    213 **[Photo 89]**
Alcohol, 179-80
Animals on the line, 63, 102, 187
    at Glan y Don, 100
    at Tyn y Morfa, 101 [Photo 39]
Aplin, Inspector (Flintshire
    Constabulary), 126-7
Archer, Henry, 14, 16, 19, 32
Arriva Trains Wales, 212-213
Aulds, James, 178

Bagillt, (incl. station), 103, 133, 158,
    172 [Photos 52, 64]
Bangor (incl. station), 16, 26, 62-64,
    68, 75 [Photos 20, 55, 72]
    and the armed forces, 1914-18,
    135-37
    Bishop of, 30 **[Photo 6]**
    jewellery robbery, 179-180
Beaufort, Admiral Sir Francis, 18,
Beeching Report, 172-74, 199-200

Binger, J. O., 180-81,
Birkenhead, 50-51, 115-117, 140, 148
Birmingham, 13, 32-4, 149, 159,
    190, 213
Bodorgan, (incl. station), 79, 95, 186,
    196 [Photo 71, 79]
Borderlands line, 68
Brereton, Robert, 78
Britannia Bridge station, 61
Britannia Tubular Bridge:
    construction of, 45 **[Photo 13]**
    concert in, 45
    "Curious Christening" at, 47
    fire of 1946, 202-203
    fire of 1970, 122, 172 [Photo 84]
    hydraulic press explosion, 46
    impact on local people, 60 **[Photo 18]**
    memorial to those who died in its
        construction, 81
    political significance of opening, 48
        [Photo 102]
    rebuilding, 204 **[Photos 85, 103]**
    security, 126
    testing of, 47
    tourism to, 147, 185,
    working conditions at, 46
British Railways (incl British Rail),
    122, 199-200, 203-211
Bulkeley, Sir Richard, 16, 24, 64
Burrows, Driver Joseph, 181

Caernarfon, 14, 26, 33, 66, 72, 75
Chandos, Marquis of, 110
Charges and fares on the railway, 66,
    72, 186
Chartism, 27
Chester (incl. station), 21-25, 38-40,
    81, 142, 2 [Photos 3, 47]

Chester and Crewe Railway, 20, 142
Chester and Holyhead Railway:
   absorbed into LNWR, 77
   Act of Parliament, 30
   builds hotel, 148
   construction begins, 37
   dissolved, 66
   mineral traffic, 57
   police force, 176
   power to operate steamships, 36, 55,
     112, 122
City of Dublin Steam Packet Company,
   36, 52, 112-15, 120, 193-94
Clergy and the railway, 30, 109, 137,
   194-95
   Benson, Edward, (Archbishop of
     Canterbury), 194
   Williams, Rev William Venables,
     65-6, 73
Coal mines opened near the line, 57
   Point of Ayr, 210 **[Photo 88]**
Colwyn Bay (incl. station), 142-43,
   153, 162, 195, 204 [Photo 58]
   Train fire, 189 [Photo 77]
Communication cord use, 94-5, 178
Connah's Quay (incl. station), 58-9,
   106, 199, 211 [Photo 16]
Construction of the railway, 37-47
Conwy (Conway) (incl. station),
   63, 65-6, 73-5, 158, 187, 209-211
   [Photo 75]
   1900 improvements, 158-59
     [Photo 66]
   accident involving Robert
     Stephenson, **44 [Photo 12]**
   Construction of CHR begins at, 37
     [Photo 7]
   creation of shellfish industry, 56-7

   tubular bridge, 42, 95, **[Photos 11,**
     35, 59]
Conwy Morfa army volunteers'
   station, 130-31, 211 [Photo 50]
Corn Laws, 34
COVID-19, 231 **[Photo 91]**
Creed, Robert, 29
Crime on the railway, 174-80
   disorder, 178-179
   fare dodging, 176
   fraud, 180
   items placed on the line, 177
   manslaughter, 69, 181
   murder, 127, 176, 178
   private prosecution, 87
   sexual offending, 181-82
   theft, 179-180

Dalhousie, Earl, 30
Damages sought against the railway,
   180-81, 187
Dee Bridge collapse,
   39-40 [Photo 9]
Demise of steam, 200
Dent, Charles, 116, 183
   Francis, 133-35 [Photo 51]
Drummond, Thomas, 18-20
Dublin, 13-22, 24-29, 34-37, 139-40,
   144, 186
   impact of railway on communication
     with, 47-53
Dublin and Kingstown
   Railway, 19, 24
Dundas, Charles, 25
Dundonald, Lord, 133
Dun Laoghaire (Kingstown), 18, 49,
   120, 121, 123, 203
Dwygyfylchi, 38

Earl of Kingston, 177-78
Edward, Prince of Wales, 103, 111-12
Eisteddfod, 67, 87, 185
Electric Telegraph, 36, 48-9, 53, 178
Electrification, 158, 206-208, 21
Evans, Henry, 38

Fairbairn, Henry, 13
Fatalities on the line, 62, 78-9, 85-6,
    89-90, 94-7
Ffestiniog Railway, 14-15
Ffynnongroyw, 177, 226, 229 **[Photos
    98, 100]**
Fire, 84, 105, 173, 187-191, 201-203
First World War, 134-35
    casualties, 135
    memorial, 137
    memorial service, 137
**Flint, (incl. station), 102, 127, 172,
    193, 224, 228 [Photos 41, 54]**
**Foryd, (incl. station), 140, 187
    flooding, 226
    Clwyd bridge, 41 [Photo 10]**
Freight, 14, 57, 203, 209-212, 215
    [Photos 51, 59]

Gabriel, Leon, 98
**Gaerwen, (incl. station), 172, 189,
    228 [Photo 78]**
Gauge Commission, 34
George's Harbour Railway, 16-18, 24
Gerazim, 144
Giles, Francis, 20-21, 26, 30
Gladstone, William Ewart, 68, 72, 112,
    151, 194, 231
Graham, Sir James, 26
Grand Junction Railway, 13, 17, 20,
    26, 34

Great Western Railway, 32, 34-5, 51,
    54-5, 76, 98
Greenwich Mean Time, 63
Griffiths, Sarah, 228
Gronant, fatality of child, 97
Gwrych Castle, 133
    the CHR near, 86 **[Photo 30]**

Harrison, Frederick, 71
Hibbert, Leonora, 109-11
Holoran, Martin, 79
**Holyhead, (incl. station), 15-21,
    24-8, 35-6, 70, 160, 183, 203-205,
    208-209**
    advantage over Liverpool, 217
    **breakwater, 17, 28, 109, 115, 121
        [Photo 44]**
    disorder at, 81
    fatal accident at the station, 105
    freight at, 211,
    Great Eastern at, 114
    harbour, 16-18, 25, 28-9, 35-6, 49, 55,
        109-112, 183 **[Photos 23, 46, 56]**
    impact of war on, 137-40
    new station opened, 111
    **railway hotel, 107, 109, 111
        [Photo 43]**
    railway policy for, 71
**Holywell and Junction, 78, 87, 99,
    172, 185-86, 225 [Photo 63]**
    **Depot for track widening scheme,
        155**
**Hughes, John,
    Ffynnongroyw, 177
    Trefignath, 78**

Industrial Relations, 67, 71-4
    strikes, 38, 67, 136, 166, 171

Influenza, 136, 192

Inquests, 39-40, 68, 90, 93-95, 114, 228

Ireland:

    Act of Union, 12, 27, 87

    Easter Rising, 1916, 139

    Fenians, 124-126 [Photos 47, 48]

    Great Famine, 36, 51

    independence negotiations, 139

    Irish Railway Commission, 19-21,
      24, 25-7, 30

    Irish Republican Brotherhood, 126

    Lord Lieutenant of Ireland,
      48-51, 87

    rebellion of 1848, 51

Irish Mail, 63, 92-5, 106, 125-26,
  209, 222,

Jocelyn, Lord, 27

Jones,

    Elias, 97 [Photo 36]

    John Parry, 99-100

Kelly, Michael, 96

Kerfoot, farmer, 100

Kinmel Bay, (incl Kinmel Bay Halt),
  227 [Photos 57, 99]

    Final closure, 140

Labouchere, Henry, 25, 36

Ladysmith, Relief of, 133, 135

Landowners in north Wales, 24-5, 65,
  76, 186, 217, 225

    Meyrick, Sir George, 196
    [Photo 79]

Lees, Herbert, 89 [Photo 32]

Lichfield House Compact, 18

Liverpool, 13-18, 34-5, 170, 213,
  215, 217

Liverpool and Manchester Railway, 13,
  111, 123, 145

Llanddulas (Llandulas) (incl.
  station), 84, 172, 189, 218
  [Photo 76]

    Viaduct collapse at, 220-21
    [Photo 92]

Llandegai, 22, 96, 181 **[Photo 4]**

Llandudno, 16-17, 66, 147, 151, 155,
  160-62

Llandudno Junction, 102, 104, 142,
  173, 192 **[Photos 61, 82]**

    engine shed, 201 **[Photos 82, 83]**

    original station, 152-53 **[Photo 60]**

Llanerch y Mor, 79, 197,

    Flooding at, 225 [Photo 97]

Llanfairfechan, (incl. station),
  64, 144, 172, 195, 217-22, 225
  [Photo 93]

    snowstorm of 1867 at, 219

Llanfair PG, (incl. station), 105, 132,
  172, 203-204 **[Photo 42]**

Llangaffo, 190-1

Lloyd George, David, 72-4, 137,
  153, 231

Llysfaen, (incl. station), 79, 84,
  [Photo 29]

Local government and the railway, 66,
  75, 131, 142, 193,

Locomotive and train types, 194, 208,
  212 **[Photo 70, 71]**

    at the end of steam, 200

    diesel multiple unit, 105, 206
    [Photos 72, 82]

    "Gerald of Wales", 213
    [Photo 47]

    Precursor class, 162

    Problem class, 163

London and Birmingham Railway, 13-14, 24, 29, 34
London and North Western Railway:
Act of Parliament, 34,
David Lloyd George campaign against, 72-3
largest industrial corporation in the world, 54-5
local courts and, 69, 95
management style, 85
payment of local rates, 65
relationship with landowners, 63-4
London and North Western Railway Ships:
Admiral Moorsom, 113, 115
Anglia, 117-18, 121, 135-37, 140
Banshee, 115-16
Cambria, 114-119, 121-22 **[Photo 45]**
Connemara, 118-20
Duchess of Sutherland, 114
Earl Spencer, 95, 114-15
Edith, 114-16
Eleanor, 115, 118
Galtee More, 119
Greenore, 114, 116-19
Hibernia, 117, 121, 135, 139
Holyhead, 115
Irene, 116
Isabella, 115-116
Lily, 112-113, 115-16
Rathmore, 120
Shamrock, 115
Slieve Bloom, 120
South Stack, 117
Telegraph, 114
Violet, 115-16
London and South Western Railway, 35

London Midland and Scottish Railway, 121-22, 141-42, 166-70
Lucas, Lennard RN, 94-5

Mail contract, 16, 34, 112-13
Malltraeth, 230 **[Photo 101]**
Manchester, 45, 47, 71, 149, 159, 186
Manchester, Sheffield and Lincolnshire Railway, 153
Mancot, 57
Melbourne, Lord, 17
Menai Bridge, (incl. station), 82, 113, 172 **[Photo 28]**
Menai Straits, 21-4, 30-2, 45-7, 147-48, 203-204
Menai Suspension Bridge, 21-4, 204
M'Garry, Matthew, 94
Mochdre, (incl Mochdre and Pabo station), 51, 104, 128, 192 **[Photo 49]**
siting of water troughs nearby, 208
Mold, 30, 155, 180, 185, 193-94
Mold Junction, 57, 181 **[Photos 15, 65]**
Moorsom, Constantine, 109, 113
Morpeth, Lord, 20
Morris, James, 79 [Photo 24]
Mostyn, (incl. station), 125, 146, 172, 210-11, 224-26, 228 **[Photo 96]**
Motor traffic increase, 165-68, 172, 199

Nant Hall train fire, 188
Nantlle Railway, 14
Nationalisation, 170-2, 212
'New Clown' Theatre Company, 197 [Photo 80]
Non-stop running, 161

North Staffordshire Railway, 99, 167
  [Photo 37]
North Wales in the Second World War,
  142-44, 169

O'Connell, Daniel, 16-20, 25, 28, 30,
  51, 66
Old Colwyn, (incl. station), 99, 134,
  172, 187 **[Photo 53]**
  Fire, 187-88
Oxford, Worcester and Wolverhampton
  Railway, 32, 34

Passenger profiles, 85, 95, 147, 215
Peace Train, 144
Peel, Sir Robert:
  opposes the Irish Railway
    Commission, 20
  votes against the first CHR
    proposal, 25
  includes the CHR in his Irish
    policy, 27-30
  the end of his government in
    1846, 31-3
  supports CHR's right to operate
    steamships, 35-6
  his death weakens the CHR, 56
  his criterion for CHR success, 118
Penmaenbach, 79, 93, 131, 140, 209,
  217, 224
  derailment at, 90-1 **[Photo 33]**
Penmaenmawr, (incl. station),
  21-24, 38, 93, 130-131, 210, 219
  [Photo 21]
  crash of 1950, 93 [Photo 34]
  riot at, 39 [Photo 8]
Penmaenrhos, 88, 99, 102, 217
  [Photo 25]

Pennant family, 57, 63, 179
Pen-y-Clip, 23, 89, 180 **[Photos 5, 32]**
Peto, Samuel Morton, 56-7, 85
Poor Law Union, 64-7, 73,
Porth Dinllaen (incl. variations in
  spelling) 15-20, 28-30, 32-4, 51,
  57, 75-6, 108, 153, 221, 229, 233
  [Photo 2]
Porthmadog, 14, 72
Preston, Richard Montague (solicitor),
  66, 68, 174, 178
  death of, 183-84
Prestatyn, (incl. station), 106,
  153, 172, 178, 188-89, 207
  [Photos 73, 91]

Queensferry, (incl. station), 57,
  126-27, 158, 172, 218 **[Photo 48]**

Railway Commissioners, 35
Reform Act 1867, 64, 67, 93
Relief of Mafeking, 133
Reopening stations, 140, 208, 214
  [Photo 87]
Return of steam, 202, 208 [Photo 95]
Rhosneigr, (incl. station), 161-62, 222
  [Photo 69]
Rhyl, (incl. station), 41, 98, 130, 154,
  192, 227-28 **[Photo 62, 90]**
Riot, 39, 109, 128
River Clwyd, 40, 154, 226
River Dee, 38-9, 75, 155, 158,
  194, 224
RMS *Trent* incident, 128
Roads:
  congestion, 172
  deaths, 107
  strategy for north Wales, 209

Roberts, Owen, 103-104 [Photo 41]
Robertson, Henry, 40
Rockliffe Hall, 99
Royal Navy ships, 95, 109, 125,
   136, 140
Royal Train, 60, 92, 193

Saltney, 39, 57, 155,
Sandycroft, (incl. station), 58, 97,
   155, 172, 178, 194, [Photo 17]
Serpell Report, 207, 213
Shotton, (incl. station), 68, 98, 135,
   172, 205, 214 [Photo 22]
Shrewsbury, 12, 15, 30, 32, 174, 217
Shrewsbury and Chester Railway, 40
Spring Rice, Thomas, 17, 19
Stalbridge, Lord, 73-4, 90
Stanley Embankment, 89, 176,
   [Photo 74]
   Flooding, 222
Stanley, W. O., 63, 175
Stephenson,
   George, 14, 21-4, 41, 51, 217, 221
   Robert, 42-4, 47, 81, 218
   Robert, (driver), 105

Talacre, (incl. station), 106, 140, 145,
   160, 172, 188 [Photo 68]
Tamworth, 29, 34
Telford, Thomas, 12, 22, 24, 47, 172,
   174, 204
Terry, George, 98
Thomas, Owen, 183
Thompson, Driver Arthur, 87
Tithe War, 128
Tolstoy, 232
Tourism, 145-189:
   brochures, 166 **[Photo 81]**

camping coaches, 169
coach tours, 151
decline in use of rail for, 167-68,
   172, 199
films, 164
package holidays, 159 **[Photo 67]**
post-war boom, 199-200
Prestatyn holiday camp, 169
price cutting, 166
purchase of bus companies, 168
statistics, 160
ticketing complexity, 148

Track widening, 104, 153, 158, 188, 225
   at Bagillt, 158 **[Photo 64]**
   at Saltney, 155 [Photo 65]

Transport for Wales, 213
Trent Valley Railway, 34, 29
Trewan Sands, 161 [Photo 95]
Truck system, 37-8
Tunnels:
   Bangor, 31 **[Photo 6]**
   Bodorgan, 79 **[Photo 24]**
   Conwy, 37 **[Photo 7]**
   Llandegai, 22, 96 **[Photo 4]**
   Northgate, 38, 81 **[Photo 26]**
   Penmaenrhos, 88, 99 **[Photo 25]**
Ty Croes, (incl. station), 182-83, 192,
   222, 228 [Photo 94]
Tyn y Morfa, 100 [Photo 39]

Valley, (incl. station), 101, 126, 172,
   192, 206-208, 222 **[Photo 87]**
   possible new station for the
     airport, 213
Vignoles, Charles, 19-21, 24, 32, 217,
   220-21, 229

Virgin Trains, 209, 212-13
Volunteer soldiers,
   camps, 129-31
   recruitment drive in north
     Wales, 132

Wales, nationalism, 72, 74-5, 109,
   128, 216
Walker, Driver J. A., 101
Walker, James, 101
Water troughs, 51-2, 128 **[Photo 14]**
Watkin, Sir Edward, 68, 75
Weather:
   climate change, 228-29, 231
   fog, 113-119, 224
   flooding, 217-18, **222**, 225-29

snow and ice, 219, 227-28,
   wind, 45, 222, 227
Wellington, Duke of, 30, 50, 60, 231
Welsh language, 75, 105, 111, 150,
   185, 208, 213
Westminster, Marquis of, 24-5
Wig crossing, 61-2 [Photo 19]
Williams,
   John, 93
   Catherine, 61-2
Women, 57, 138, 182
Wood, Ephraim, 183-84
   Resident at Pabo Hall, 128
Wrexham, Mold and Connah's Quay
   Railway, 57
Wright, George, 98